D1487548

THE
LEMON
BOOK

BOOKS BY THE CENTER FOR AUTO SAFETY
Mobile Homes: The Low-Cost Housing Hoax
Small On Safety: The Designed-In Dangers of the VW
The Yellow Book Road: The Failure of America's Roadside Safety Program
Unsafe At Any Speed: The Designed-In Dangers of the American Automobile,
by Ralph Nader

THE LEMON BOOK

BY RALPH NADER
CLARENCE DITLOW AND JOYCE KINNARD

A CAROLINE HOUSE CONSUMERBOOK™

CAROLINE HOUSE PUBLISHERS, INC.

OTTAWA, IL & OSSINING, NY

10 9 8 7 6 5 4 3 2 1

Copyright © 1980 by Ralph Nader, Clarence Ditlow & Joyce Kinnard

Copies of this book may be purchased from the publisher for $7.95. All inquiries and catalog requests should be addressed to Caroline House Publishers, Inc., Post Office Box 738, Ottawa, Illinois 61350. (815) 434-7905.

ISBN: 0-89803-039-0

Library of Congress Cataloging in Publication Data

Nader, Ralph.
    The lemon book.

    1. Automobile purchasing. 2. Consumer protection—Law and legislation—United States. I. Ditlow, Clarence, joint author. II. Kinnard, Joyce, joint author. III. Title.
TL162.N28   629.2′222   80-22293

ACKNOWLEDGMENT

It is difficult in a brief acknowledgment to express the kind of appreciation we owe to the many people who contributed long hours collecting and organizing the information included in this manual.

For undertaking the initial work in writing a book to help lemon owners, we thank Lowell Dodge and Ralf Hotchkiss, co-authors of *What To Do With Your Bad Car* (Grossman Publishers: 1971; Bantam Books: 1971).

For their many useful contributions, including research on auto safety features, we thank John Hubbard and Russell Shew of the Center for Auto Safety.

For reading drafts and offering valuable suggestions, we thank Larry Kanter, Katherine Meyer and Arthur Glickman.

For their helpful research on the legal rights of lemon owners, we thank Judith Axe, Matthew Finucane, Diane Botwick and Paul Bullis.

For their good-spirited, tireless contributions to typing and retyping the manuscript, we thank Jean (Froggie) Fallow and Faith Little.

For their enthusiastic support and encouragement, we thank the entire staff of the Center for Auto Safety.

Finally, thanks to the countless frustrated consumers who took the trouble to share their problems with us, and to those in the industry and elsewhere who put their loyalty to the public good above the more parochial duty to their employer to provide the information used in this manual.

To all the embittered lemon owners who shared their frustrations with us, we dedicate this book.

CONTENTS

PREFACE

If the dictionary wished to illustrate the word *frustration*, it could not do better than describe the feelings of a new-car owner who has landed a lemon. After shelling out thousands of dollars for a new car, the consumer reasonably expects to own a vehicle that meets certain standards of quality, performance, and reliability.

At the time our first lemon owner's manual was published in 1971, the consumer was effectively shut out of the legal system—most lawyers wouldn't touch a lemon case because of the relatively small amount of money involved when compared with legal fees. The individual who fought a giant auto company in court made the headlines because it was so rare.

Today, the lemon owner still has to fight for his or her rights, but the chances of winning have increased. Many consumers have followed the advice in the first guide and have obtained refunds for their lemons; others have created new strategies in seeking redress that are reported in this book. Victorious consumers such as Toby Cagan, who took Chrysler Corporation to court and won—without a lawyer—and Vikki Huff, who organized a successful lemoncade protest, are described in the following chapters.

What has changed since the first lemon book? There is still generally no consistent law for dealers and manufacturers who refuse to back up their products. The manufacturers' incentive to improve quality control and reduce the frequency with which lemons are made is still insufficient. The Center for Auto Safety and I are still receiving thousands of letters every year from angry motorists who were sold lemons. In reading through the torrent of lemon letters, it is obvious that the letter writers are saying something greater than, and beyond, their individual problems. They are saying that even though the law has been improved, it is still inaccessible to their pleas for receiving the automotive value for which they paid. They are marketplace victims with neither effective rights nor practical remedies.

Many of these letters contain details of the defects and the twisted unresponsive route that the buyer pursued to the dealer and then up the hierarchy of the auto company's bureaucracy. Only a very few received justice. The rest were given the corporate straight-arm. Anarchy, carefully contrived by the auto industry, still prevails. And the auto industry still dominates the decision-making in Washington, D.C. Too often, the federal agencies responsible for protecting the auto owner and user have failed in their tasks. Industry abuses such as cheating on mileage standards, switching Chevrolet engines for Oldsmobiles, and manufacturing small cars without adequate protection all go unchecked.

It takes no special insight to observe that these failures are correctable with different leadership. Indeed, Congress has given the Department of Transportation, Environmental Protection Agency, and Federal Trade Commission additional and strengthened authority in the last decade to perform their task. What is still needed is the passage of a government officials' accountability law and an affirmative program of citizen access, with federal funds for needy petitioners. This change would provide avenues of direct

9

public discipline and direction for agencies who now surrender to inappropriate, excessive, or unlawful industry and White House pressures.

What has changed in the past decade is the consumer's willingness to fight back. In the last few years, more and more consumers have become less and less willing to tolerate the failure of the auto industry to provide the public with reliable vehicles meeting industry standards of quality, durability, and performance. When the consumer receives a lemon, or an otherwise unsafe and unreliable car, topped off with poor warranty performance by manufacturer and dealer, he or she wants to do something about it; and this greater degree of consumer awareness is reflected in the more recent outpouring of consumer complaints on automobiles.

This increase in consumer resistance and awareness has funneled into a significant consumer strength. Determined consumers are banding together to protect their rights, putting pressure on their lawmakers to provide consumers with a more responsive complaint handling system—slowly improving the lemon owners' chances of obtaining refunds for their lemons. Many of their success stories are described throughout the book to illustrate the usefulness of the strategies we suggest.

In response to this consumer outcry for greater protection, more consumer complaint centers have been established to provide individual assistance at the state and local level. Many states now have special offices under the attorney general which deal specifically with consumer protection. The attorney general's office of your state may file a class action lawsuit on behalf of you and other similarly situated consumers. For example, after receiving thousands of consumer complaints on the General Motors Engine Switch of 1977, the state attorneys general all around the country banded together and filed class action lawsuits against GM. Some states, such as California, have set up consumer protection bureaus just to deal with auto problems. The California Bureau of Automotive Repair takes an aggressive stand to protect consumers from automotive repair abuses and can take away the registration of a dealer who continually violates state law.

With the aid of thousands of personal letters from lemon owners, Clarence M. Ditlow, Joyce K. Kinnard, and I have prepared a set of materials that describes, first, how best to get your defective vehicle fixed or replaced, and next, how to avoid the lemon experience the next time you buy a car. There are no easy ways to achieve these objectives, and this book does not pretend otherwise. What it does strive to do is offer some hope to the embattled car buyer, to challenge the legal profession to take a greater interest in these cases, and to push for more basic reforms of the laws and remedies to protect the new-car buyer.

Consumers are the key to all of these objectives. Their detailed complaints provide documented examples and reflect the urgent need for reform movements that reach back into the plants and onto the design boards where the defects are born and raised. Their often creative response to manufacturer-dealer obstinacy suggests ways to break the log jams and win.

Consumer complaints often have led to recalls of defective cars. General Motors' reluctant recall of 6.7 million 1965-1969 Chevrolet V-8 cars and

10

trucks with defective engine mounts is an example of the importance of citizen pressure and widespread publicity about safety hazards. This matter came to my attention in the summer of 1971 when I received several consumer complaints describing the nightmarish failure of their cars' engine mounts—a jammed accelerator and gear shift, loss of power braking and power steering assist resulting in loss of vehicle control. On investigating the defect, I found that GM had successfully stalled a government investigation by arrogantly claiming that there was no safety defect in the engine mounts of any Chevrolets. More and more complaints were received as news stories were generated about people who had experienced this defective behavior in Chevrolets and other GM cars. Under intense public pressure, the long-dormant investigation of this defect finally was pulled from the back files of the Department of Transportation where it had been buried by corporate deceit and bureaucratic indifference. Without the tenacity of the media and concerned owners who complained loudly and persistently about the potentially catastrophic consequences of engine mount breakage, this defect might have remained uncorrected.

Just as important are contributions by enlightened dealers and concerned assembly-line and engineering employees in the auto plants. Letters from these citizens have often led to corrections of major vehicle defects in large model runs and have undoubtedly saved lives and avoided injuries.

More suggestions and more information and more successes are needed from readers, as future editions of this manual will depend heavily on and grow from readers' response. In effect, the readers have helped to build, piece by piece, an ever more effective handbook of action, which in turn should stimulate the emergence of a just system to resolve complaints quickly and cheaply for all car buyers, new and used. Finally, the more basic objective—better-quality automobiles—is more fully attained when the consumer obtains justice in the marketplace.

The immense impact of the auto industry on the economy, the environment, and automobile casualties, requires an equally immense consumer alert. Last year more than 50,000 lives were lost on the highways and over two million more suffered disabling injuries. Safer motor vehicles, utilizing practical and inexpensive safety features, could have prevented well over half of these fatalities and injuries. Likewise, the contamination of the air by automobiles could have been stopped years ago if known and knowable technology had been applied to auto engines. Additionally, billions of consumer dollars are wasted yearly because of ridiculously fragile bumpers and many designs and frauds that jack up repair costs. Doing something about all these outrages is what the consumer movement is all about. And the consumer movement is no stronger than consumers, for whom this manual is written.

Your decision to act, along with other buyers, depends on your determination. If you would prefer to suffer silently rather than develop the know-how to fight and win, this book is not for you. If you crave for justice and see yourself as a sparkplug to help achieve it, then read on, my friend, read on.

RALPH NADER

11

CHAPTER 1 *The Lemon*

Des Plaines, Ill. 60016
September 13, 1976

Chrysler Corp.
Customer Relations
2200 S. Busse Rd.
Elk Grove, Ill. 60007

Gentlemen:

I really hesitated to write to you because of the probable futility of it all but last night was "the last straw that broke the camel's back."

My husband has a 1975 Chrysler Imperial. We have had cars for more than thirty years and never had such a "lemon" as this. The motor was replaced because it was cracked; there is a burning of rubber smell that has never been corrected even though the car was into several Chrysler dealers for repair; the engine constantly smokes; the automatic windows are broken; the car has stalled at least ten times and needed repair and towing and costly rental fees.

Last night, the back part of the driver's seat broke off and my husband lost control of the car. Luckily, there was no other car close to us as there certainly could have been a serious accident.

I could go on and on about the defects in this auto. It has caused us untold aggravation and expense. In fact, the Imperial is the joke of the neighborhood. Some joke!!! $12,000.00 worth. Well, maybe in the long run, the joke will be on you. After seeing the performance and quality of your automobile, I doubt very much if you get any business from any of our friends and associates and certainly none from us. Word does get around.

We cannot wait to get rid of the car. Heaven help anyone who buys it used from the dealer. When this car is turned in, it should be destroyed. It is a menace. It is the most expensive piece of junk we ever had.

Sincerely yours,
/s/
Mrs. R. Z. Pierce

It's like being rudely awakened from a good dream. You've had your new car for only a day or two, and you've already begun to notice the defects.

But it's nothing to worry about, you hope. The manufacturer will stand behind its product, and the promise is right there in the new-car warranty. So, before your first trip back to the dealer, you make a list of the things wrong with your car—nothing too serious, just little things. You assure yourself they will be fixed without charge under the warranty. True, when you pick up your car, there is little or no charge for the warranty items you listed. But then you discover that most of the defects haven't been touched.

13

Some of them may never be fixed no matter how many times you ask the dealer to fix them.

The defects you found may not have been especially hazardous. However, some common defects are very dangerous, since they are hidden and often undetectable even by a good mechanic. These defects can gradually become worse until they suddenly take all control of the car from the driver. After the accident the driver may be cited for reckless driving.

Carbon-monoxide leaks are a good example. People often feel a little tired after driving a fair distance and the fatigue is usually attributed to strain and monotony. Herbert Herring of Old Saybrook, Connecticut, wrote: "My wife and I have a 1967 Biscayne . . . and we have always felt tired in the car and didn't know why. They [the service department] 'pooh-poohed' the idea of carbon monoxide." Then "on June 30 [1969] we had three valuable dogs pass away in our car in a sleeping position with windows open about six to eight inches as usual." When the Herrings had their car examined by blowing an air hose up the exhaust pipe, the airstream threw a cloud of dust up into the trunk on the right side near the back seat. Had they been in an accident during the two years in which they had always felt tired in the car, chances are the reason for their dulled reflexes would never have been discovered.

Like many owners, you are probably led to believe there is not much chance that your own car has defects that might cause an accident. You should look behind the assuring advertisements. And even if you are fortunate enough to get a car with only minor defects, you can plan on a good bit of work and frustration putting that new car into shape and keeping it that way. Consumers Union, publisher of *Consumer Reports*, bought dozens of new cars in 1978, as it does each year. In the 1978 domestic cars, Consumers Union testers found an average of twenty-six defects *in each car*, ranging from minor to serious. Foreign cars fared a little better, but still had an average of seventeen defects each.

What is it that makes a car a lemon? To most, a lemon is a rare occurrence, an infrequent or even a freakish assembly-line product that just won't run at all. While it is true that most new cars will run, the number of new cars that limp along and haunt their owners with fears of unreliability and danger is alarming.

DEFINITION

Lemons come in two basic varieties. The first type is a car with known defects, defects which develop into a perpetual source of frustration for the owner. This type seems to generate a continuing stream of problems, some minor and others more serious, some of which can be fixed and others which can never be satisfactorily repaired.

The second, and more pernicious, type of lemon has defects that, like Mr. Herring's exhaust leak, are relatively undetectable. This variety of lemon has been called a "risk waiting for an accident to happen." It occurs with a frequency which, unfortunately, is not well known. Rarely are the causes

14

of accidents thoroughly investigated on the scene. Accidents are usually viewed as driver failures rather than as vehicle failures because, with rare exceptions, police and insurance investigators are not equipped to detect and evaluate vehicle failures, or because damage to the car makes the analysis of defects difficult. Most important, the laws and courts have long avoided bringing the vehicle to account, because it is easier to blame the driver.

HOW LEMONS ARE PRODUCED

All lemons, whatever the variety, grow from a common source—sloppy design and assembly by the auto manufacturers or manufacturers of component parts. A defect caused by an erroneous design of the car or its component parts is called a *design* defect. Potential defects are occasionally left in the design in order to save the manufacturer money. A defect in production caused by an assembly-line error is called a *manufacturing* defect. Often defects caused by poor quality control on the assembly line go undetected because of faulty inspection and testing performed by the manufacturer and dealer.

Whether because of poor design on the drawing board or poor quality control on the assembly line, either defect can produce a lemon. If the defect is traced to an assembly-line error, many cars may be defective or only yours, depending upon how many cars were misassembled. If the defect is in the design, all cars of that make and model will be defective. Although most cars become more complex every year, there is no excuse for delivering dangerously designed, poorly inspected, wholly untested cars to the public—cars which are unrepairable when they prove defective and cause needless injury when an accident occurs. Lemons serve as tangible evidence that vehicle safety depends as much on the quality of the car's basic design and assembly as on the presence of certain government-required features called safety devices.

In this book, we will make obvious the manufacturer's capability to improve the situation markedly. We will also suggest ways consumers can help convince the manufacturers of the wisdom of altering their current patterns of irresponsible behavior.

HOW MANY LEMONS ARE SOLD?

There is no way of arriving at an exact figure. The manufacturers do not publicize this information. But we do know that thousands of letters come into the National Highway Traffic Safety Administration (NHTSA) of the U.S. Department of Transportation every year. Ralph Nader and the Center for Auto Safety receive at least 20,000 consumer automotive complaints a year. Many more complaints pour into other consumer offices around the country.

Almost every national poll taken within the past three years has found that automobile problems were the largest source of consumer complaints. According to the following sources, problems with the purchase and repair

15

of automobiles represent the number one complaint across the country: the White House Office of Consumer Affairs, a Louis Harris national opinion research survey, Federal Trade Commission chairman Michael Pertschuk, Council of Better Business Bureaus, a congressional survey by the U.S. Senate Consumer Subcommittee, and many state consumer protection agencies and consumer groups around the country.

It is clear that there are thousands of consumers who are very upset about the quality of their new cars. We can estimate that the automobile manufacturers produce thousands of lemons every year. If only one out of every thousand cars sold is a lemon, then *10,000 lemons* would be sold each year (based on ten million new cars being sold annually).

CHAPTER 2 *The Basic Procedures: An Overview*

Madison, Indiana 47250
January 18, 1977

Dear Mr. Nader:

Around December 19, 1975, I received my factory-ordered 1976 Ford Granada. From the beginning it's had problems. No passing gear; used 1½ quarts of oil every 600 miles; got 10–11 mpg (it's a 6 cylinder); has no power and all of a sudden won't even run properly. The dealer has worked repeatedly on it and still can't get it to run properly. Mr. Charles Craig, service manager at Croxton Motors, can verify all this. He has now been working on it for two weeks and can't find the problem.

It's definite that this car was not assembled correctly. What recourse does a person have who pays $6,000 for such a headache?

/s/
B. Fensel

Many lemon owners are under the false impression that defects in their cars can be fixed for free only during the original warranty period and that once their written warranty expires they must pay for everything that goes wrong with the car. Actually, car buyers have many rights, including other warranties that are created by law at the time of the sale—they simply have to exercise them. Nonetheless, manufacturers and dealers often tell lemon owners that they have no obligations to the owner outside of the written warranty. If the manufacturer and dealer refuse to repair defects in your car voluntarily, outside agencies or organizations or individual self-help tactics may force the manufacturer or dealer to fix the car.

Besides persistence, the foremost key to success in getting a defective car fixed or replaced is documenting everything that goes wrong with the car. Keep a list of the car's problems along with a record of all attempts in getting the car repaired. Whenever you send a letter, always make a copy for your files. Whenever you visit the dealer, always obtain and keep a copy of the repair order (be sure it is legible). By keeping written records of all defects that plague your car and the many attempts to have them repaired (dates and receipts of service), you will have an easier time proving your car is a lemon. Well-kept records documenting that a car is a lemon are invaluable if a lawsuit is necessary.

Resolving an automobile complaint is often tedious and frustrating. If it is a lemon case, the dealer or manufacturer invariably stalls, rejects, or otherwise arbitrarily wards off attempts to get the car fixed or replaced. The

17

reason is pure economics. If car manufacturers replaced defective cars like appliance manufacturers replaced defective toasters, it would cost car makers at least $50 million per year. So be prepared for frustration and the stonewall. No one gets a lemon replaced on his first, second, or third trip to the dealer or the manufacturer; but unless those trips are made, the lemon will never be replaced, nor a total refund given.

WITHIN THE SYSTEM

Every manufacturer has a system to handle consumer complaints, which should be followed even though it may not work in most cases. The reason to use the system is twofold: (1) sometimes it works, and (2) complaint-handling mechanisms outside the system require exhaustion of all reasonable remedies that the manufacturer provides; that is, you must have done everything within reason to get the car properly repaired by the dealer and manufacturer.

Safety Problems. The first thing to do if your car has a safety problem like stalling or faulty brakes is to call the National Highway Traffic Safety Administration (NHTSA), of the U.S. Department of Transportation, auto safety hotline, toll-free, at 800-424-9393. In Washington, D.C., call 426-0123. Although NHTSA cannot take direct action in resolving individual complaints, your call may generate a recall where the manufacturer has to repair your car and others like it without charge. By reporting your problem to NHTSA, you may be helping other consumers whose cars have not yet experienced that problem. Occasionally, consumers have received favorable treatment from the manufacturer after NHTSA sent a copy of the consumer's complaint to the auto maker.

The Dealer. If your new car does not work properly while under warranty, the dealer or manufacturer should repair the car without charge. Just exert your rights a step at a time, keeping records all the way. First, give the dealer a chance to fix the car. Go back to the dealership at which you purchased the car, if possible. Ask to see the service manager. If no results, see the owner of the dealership or the general manager. The higher-ups can always overrule a stubborn or unknowledgeable subordinate and can authorize a free repair to "retain the goodwill of a customer." A dealer who did not sell you the car is less likely to authorize goodwill repairs.

If the dealership refuses or cannot repair the car satisfactorily, pursue the claim through the rest of the manufacturer's system. If you immediately go through legal channels and have not given the dealer and manufacturer a reasonable opportunity to repair the car, you will probably lose. So do not stop if the dealer refuses to repair the car; go on to the manufacturer.

The Manufacturer. Sometimes the reason for the dealership's failure to fix the car is the dealer's service department may not have been able to diagnose the problem. Other times, dealers simply refuse to fix cars for fear that they will not get reimbursed by the manufacturer. Since the manufacturer not only

18

has superior expertise in finding and repairing malfunctions in the car but also has greater authority to order defective cars to be repaired, call in the manufacturer's representative to look at a defective car the dealer cannot or will not repair. Once again, the manufacturer's representative has a "goodwill" budget to repair cars even where they determine the manufacturer is not at fault.

Most automobile manufacturers have several different divisions within the corporation, such as the Chevrolet Division of General Motors or the Plymouth Division of Chrysler Corporation. Contact the divisional (also called regional, district, or zone) office in your area. The locations and correct names of district offices and the complaint procedures are often spelled out in the owner's manual, which normally accompanies each vehicle when purchased from the dealership. You can insist on arranging an appointment with the manufacturer's district representative through the dealer. If the dealer refuses to cooperate, call the representative yourself. If the manufacturer's representative refuses to see you, contact the regional office or the manufacturer's owner relations office, often located in Detroit.

After the Warranty Expires. If the car is no longer under the manufacturer's warranty but it fails to operate properly because of a defect that was not corrected during the warranty or that appeared after the warranty expired, follow the same procedures with the dealer and manufacturer outlined above for a warranty complaint. You may have a tougher time getting the dealer or manufacturer to cooperate after the car's warranty has expired, but there is a reasonable chance of success if you are persistent.

Sometimes the manufacturer will repair a defect common to many cars of the same model because the manufacturer recognizes its liability and is willing to remedy the defect. Normally this is done through a warranty extension, policy adjustment, or secret warranty offered by various manufacturers over the past few years. So frequently does this happen that at any one time there may be hundreds of these warranty programs going on throughout the auto industry. For example, Ford claims to have fixed without charge about 69,000 of its 1969 to 1973 cars and light trucks for premature rusting, even though the normal twelve-month, 12,000-mile warranty on the cars had expired. But there were about twelve million cars on the road which suffered from this premature rusting. That means less than one out of every 100 prematurely rust-damaged cars was fixed by Ford. Consumers who complained loudly and persistently were told of this otherwise "secret" warranty extension, while the millions of others who did not complain enough had to absorb the loss themselves.

Other times, if enough complaints are registered with the NHTSA auto safety hotline on safety defects, the manufacturer is required to repair the defect because of an NHTSA-ordered "recall." The Environmental Protection Agency (EPA) can order similar recalls for emission-control-system defects. Such emission defects frequently go beyond what is commonly thought of as emission control, to components such as costly-to-repair engine valves.

19

OUTSIDE THE SYSTEM

Springfield, Illinois 62704
February 1, 1978

Eugene A. Cafiero, President
Chrysler Corporation
Detroit, Michigan 48231

Subject: 1976 Volare Demo
S/N HP41C6F179327

Dear Sir:

My dealer has reached the end of his capability. The service manager advises he has done all he knows how to do. A "factory man" has made one visit; he did sound like he knew what he was talking about. Innumerable "kits" have been installed; infinite adjustments have been made. I have now made 19 (yes 19) trips to your dealer; for a large number of these I was without my car for one or two days.

My warranty is about to run out as far as the calendar is concerned; it would appear a warranty shouldn't run out if the item it covers *never* ran (right). I have called your Service Office in St. Louis, Mo.; I have written and called your Man-in-Detroit office; except for Detroit calling me once, neither has apparently been able to do anything. I called your Mr. S. L. Terry, listed as V.P. of Consumer Affairs, to find he was "not available."

I hope you agree I have exhausted all apparent recourse below you—and my engine still hesitates, backfires, dies, and otherwise doesn't want to run.

What I want is someone who can help. I hope it's you.

/s/

J. A. Baska

cc: Capital Chrysler-Plymouth
Center for Auto Safety

If the system does not work, the next step is to make enough noise outside the manufacturer's complaint-handling system to get results. A strong commitment is necessary to successfully use this procedure, because you will not get results unless you are willing to persistently follow up letters and phone calls. Having followed the procedures "inside the system" outlined above, you should have a thorough documentation of the refusal of the dealer and manufacturer to remedy your defective car. This documentation will make the steps outside the system easy to follow and results more likely to happen.

Letter Writing. The first letter can be used as a "basic instrument" in an expanded complaint campaign. Send this basic letter to the manufacturer's chairman of the board or president with copies of that letter to others. Type your letter if possible. A surprising number of complaints are ignored at this stage simply because they cannot be read, take too long to read, or are misread. If you cannot type the basic letter, print or write very legibly. Set forth the car's problems clearly and precisely within that letter and refer to the collected documentation of the car's troubles and your attempts to have the car repaired "within the system." There is no need to send every repair order or other piece of documentation with the letter. Instead, list the history of the lemon troubles, giving the nature of the problem, when it first occurred, what was done about it and when, and the results. Include that list as part of the letter. If there are key documents in the car's history such as major repair bills or admissions by the dealer, include copies of those also. Never send out the original of any document.

Send copies to various organizations such as local and national consumer groups, local and state consumer protection agencies, state attorneys general, federal agencies and members of Congress. Some groups which are able to take on individual cases may give direct assistance while others may be able to give advice on how to proceed further. Some organizations use complaint letters in conjunction with other complaints they receive to generate broad relief—such as recalls—which benefits not only the complainant but all others similarly affected. Even if these agencies or groups cannot act directly on your behalf, they may send complaints on to the manufacturer requesting the manufacturer to take action. When the manufacturer receives enough complaints from consumers and organizations, it may decide to repair the defective cars as the best means of quieting the uproar.

Telephone Contacts. After writing a letter and sending copies to various organizations, call local agencies or groups, especially those that do work on a case-by-case basis with consumers. A telephone call to the manufacturer's main office is recommended if it offers a hotline or you have access to a "WATS" line or do not mind spending money on what may be a longshot. Some people have succeeded in getting their cars fixed by using repeated telephone calls as a symbolic form of protest. For example, call the boss (dealer or manufacturer's representative) or the boss's secretary and say, "I am going to call four times a day every day till doomsday or until you fix my car." This procedure works best where the consumer manages to get a direct-dial number of the extension for a top executive. Main switchboards do not respond well to this technique.

TOWARD LEGAL ACTION

Even if consumers have met with utter frustration and rejection by the dealers and manufacturers to this point, they have accomplished one major feat. They have laid the groundwork for successful direct action. Every defect is documented as is every trip to the dealer, every day the car was not in working order, every item of extra expense, every contact with the manufacturer. And this is the basis for a successful resolution of the complaint in the next stage.

Picketing and Lemon Signs. When an unresolved complaint is against the dealer as well as the manufacturer, you can attach large lemon signs to the car and then park the car near the dealer's showroom (BUT NOT ON THE DEALER'S PROPERTY). It helps to list your basic complaints on some of the signs. Many consumers who have used this tactic successfully have encouraged others with similar complaints to organize a "lemoncade," driving slowly around the block where the dealer is located. A few local consumer groups specialize in picketing dealers. But picketing is a controversial tactic, and dealers have occasionally invoked the authority of the courts and the police in attempts to halt its use. The courts are divided in upholding the right of consumers to use lemon signs and picket a dealership. The cases frequently turn on a minor point such as whether the picketers were on dealer property or interfering with consumers trying to enter the dealership.

Negotiation and Arbitration. Many consumers have successfully negotiated with the dealer through the use of a local consumer group. Others have achieved results through a local AUTOCAP (Auto Consumer Action Panel), organized in some states by the local dealers' association to handle auto complaints. Occasionally, consumers have entered into arbitration with the dealer or manufacturer. Ford Motor Company is experimenting with arbitration panels in North Carolina before going nationwide. Many small-claims courts attempt to informally mediate or settle a claim before hearing the case.

Legal Action. When you have repeatedly registered your complaints strongly and do not seem to be getting anywhere, your next step may be a lawsuit. But this does not necessarily mean hiring a lawyer.

Lawsuits are like car maintenance and repairs; some are so simple and minor, you can do them yourself. For example, if your complaint involves a defect which would cost, say, $100 to repair, you can have a mechanic at an independent service facility repair the car and then you can go to small-claims court to recover the cost of repairing the car. (The jurisdictional amounts vary from state to state.) The procedure in small-claims courts is usually simple and no lawyer is needed.

Before hiring a lawyer, consult with one. He or she can point out deficiencies in your case or indicate whether small-claims court might be better. You can appraise the lawyer, whether he or she seems competent and interested in your case. Look for a lawyer who is willing to take the case on a contingency or percentage basis, where payment depends on your winning, or one who will attempt to recover attorney's fees under the Magnuson-Moss Warranty Act. Traditionally, lawyers have been reluctant to handle lawsuits against giant corporations such as the auto companies, because attorneys' costs can easily be greater than the judgments awarded to the consumers if they are billed on an hourly basis. But under a recent federal law, the Magnuson-Moss Warranty Act, the court may decide to award attorney's fees as a part of the judgment. This provision makes it economically feasible for consumers to pursue remedies against the auto manufacturers in court.

In some situations a class action may be the best approach. In essence, a group of individuals brings a lawsuit against a manufacturer, thus reducing

22

each individual's fee by sharing the costs of hiring an attorney. For instance, a class action may be filed on behalf of all purchasers of the manufacturer's product who suffered in the same way because of a defect in the product. Even if a class action is not possible, you can find other individuals with defective cars like yours and hire an attorney jointly. If one person cannot afford a lawyer, two, four, or more might be able to afford one.

THE ULTIMATE WEAPON—RETURNING THE LEMON

October 21, 1977

Center for Auto Safety:

I purchased a new Volkswagen Rabbit in November 1975 and since that time, have left this car at the dealers (Mt. Read Volkswagen) 20 times trying to correct a defect. This defect is best described as a "surging" which is evident in all four gears at all speeds in varying degrees. I have written three letters to World-Wide Volkswagen Corporation and have made two phone calls trying to resolve this problem, but I keep getting referred to the local dealer who cannot correct the problem. I have enclosed copies of my correspondence with World-Wide Volkswagen with their answers, along with dealer work orders. I feel that World-Wide Volkswagen should replace my engine with a fuel injection engine at no cost to me. Present mileage on the car is 10,100.

I have been very patient over the last 20 months trying to resolve this "surging" problem, but I feel I have exhausted all avenues. What do you suggest? Can you help me resolve my problem in any way?

Sincerely,

/s/

R. M. Stimson
Rochester, New York

Some cars, like Mr. Stimson's, simply cannot be fixed. Usually legal action is necessary to obtain a refund of the purchase price or a replacement car, since the dealer and manufacturer will almost invariably refuse to take back the car. Why are the auto manufacturers so stubborn in refusing to compensate the lemon owner? Because the automobile manufacturers produce thousands of lemons every year; and a reasonable policy of taking back lemons in exchange for a full refund or replacement (as a manufacturer of toasters may be more willing to do) would cost the auto manufacturers millions of dollars every year. If only one out of every thousand cars sold is a lemon; then, 10,000 lemons would be sold each year based on ten million new cars being sold annually. At approximately $6,000 per car, a refund policy would take $60 million from industry profits yearly. It is no wonder the manufacturers refuse to compensate the lemon owner who then must pay for the manufacturer's errors.

Several different legal theories have been successfully used in collecting

23

compensation for lemons. None of them is so simple, or the dealer and manufacturer so willing to oblige, that you can do it yourself. Thus see a lawyer before proceeding. Lemon owners wanting to get rid of their lemons can follow two general routes. One is to trade the car in and then sue the dealer and manufacturer for damages arising out of the sale of the lemon. The other general strategy is to cancel the ownership of the car, return it to the dealer or manufacturer, and sue for a refund or replacement.

Revocation of Acceptance/Cancellation of Ownership. Consult a lawyer if you have decided to return the car to the dealer. The legal procedures for revocation of acceptance must be carefully followed in order to cancel your ownership of the car.

If the dealer cannot or will not fix the one or more defects that plague your car within a reasonable time, and the defect is one that "substantially impairs" the value of the car, you have a right to demand a replacement or your money back. Some lemon owners have revoked acceptance of their new cars and have received a replacement car or most of the purchase price back from the dealer or manufacturer, without having to file a lawsuit. Others have revoked acceptance of their cars and have successfully sued in court for the return of their purchase price. Some have obtained even more than the purchase price as compensation for their troubles. To be successful at this point is rare. The reason is not that the manufacturer is always right but that most consumers give up or have not followed the steps listed above. If consumers follow those steps, dealers and manufacturers will be the ones who rarely win.

24

CHAPTER 3 *How to Follow the Manufacturer's Complaint Procedure*

May 12, 1978
Denver, Colorado 80227

CERTIFIED MAIL
Consumer Relations Representative
Chevrolet Central Office
Chevrolet Motor Division
Detroit, Michigan 48202

Attention: Mr. H. S. Bock

RE: 1978 Camaro I.D. Number 1Q87L8L562817
    Model 1FQ87, 2 door sport coupe
    Delivery Date: 3-17-78
    Mileage: 9
    Purchased from: Frontier Chevrolet
The reason I am writing this letter to you is because, as you will be able to clearly see, I have not gotten any satisfaction from Frontier Chevrolet in Denver. All I have gotten are many headaches, money and time lost from work, paying for a car I have not been able to drive, and a total *run around*. In the back of my owners manual under "Owner Assistance" Step 1, I tried many times to discuss my problem with the dealer, but as you will find out throughout my letter I tried once too many times. Step 2, I contacted the Chevrolet Zone Office and they gave me your name. And here is Step 3, my letter to you stating the nature of my problem(s). . . .

/s/
Mrs. M. Vaught

One week after mailing the above letter, Mrs. Vaught received a letter from the president of the Frontier Chevrolet dealership which stated in part:

After considerable analysis and discussion with the eleven people involved in my organization, I sincerely apologize for the problems you are experiencing with your new 1978 Camaro.
In referring to page 5 of your letter, I feel the following is due to you as a result of any or all inconvenience caused by my collective group of employees: I will refund to you the total purchase price of $6,007.66 that you paid to Frontier Chevrolet for the automobile. This figure also includes the sales tax that you paid. In fact, this figure represents all monies paid to Frontier Chevrolet.

25

I sincerely apologize for any inconvenience I and my 11 employees named in the letter have caused you and trust that General Motors and Chevrolet will be able to retain you as a satisfied customer.

/s/

R. Douglas Spedding
President, Frontier Chevrolet

INTRODUCTION

Every manufacturer has a system to handle consumer complaints, which should be followed even though it may not work in most cases. The reason to use the system is twofold: (1) sometimes it works, and (2) complaint-handling mechanisms outside the system require exhaustion of all reasonable remedies that the manufacturer provides; that is, you must have done everything within reason to get the car properly repaired by the dealer and manufacturer.

Besides persistence, the foremost key to success in getting a defective car fixed or replaced is documenting everything that goes wrong with the car. There is nothing hard about this; in fact, it is done for you. The dealer, independent garages, and service stations provide the basic documents to make any consumer successful in getting his or her defective car repaired, replaced, or the vehicle's sales price returned. Basically, these documents are the repair orders (ROs) or other service receipts one gets every time a car is taken in for service. Keeping these documents in an organized manner improves a consumer's chance for effective car relief at least threefold.

For example, A. Ybarra of Palo Alto, California, saved her receipts and correspondence with Ford, successfully using them against the manufacturer in small-claims court. In her March 1976 letter to Ralph Nader she wrote:

We bought a Ford Econoline Van, with a specified pay load. The salesman assured us it was going to take its advertised load. We even have a brochure on it. As it turns out the truck will not carry near its advertised load. [We notified the dealer and the manufacturer that] the truck was uncontrollable. We were even stopped by the Highway Patrol, because they saw our truck swerving all over the road. They checked our load, saw that the truck was properly loaded and we told them we were trying to get Ford to take care of the dangerous problem.

At the end of our warranty we received a letter from Ford Motors stating that they were sorry to hear about our problem and that if we would have notified them sooner they could have helped us, but now our warranty was up. Too bad. That was sickening, to say the least.

When we took Tuban [the dealer] to court, I showed this letter to the judge; he said he expected as much.

A. Ybarra also showed the judge the receipts and correspondence proving her case—that the manufacturer was notified immediately when she first bought the truck in 1974. She took the truck back to the dealer and met with

26

Ford representatives. But neither the dealer nor the manufacturer would help her during the time the truck was under warranty. Ford was beaten in small-claims court by the consumer whose records helped prove her case.

One very helpful document is a written checklist of the work to be done on the car every time it is taken in for service. Not only does this cut down the number of trips made to the dealership when they "forget" to correct a problem, but also this documents the appearance and symptoms of the various defects in the vehicle. Place a copy of this list requesting repairs and pointing out problems to the dealer in your recordkeeping files. Some consumers record all periodic maintenance such as gas consumption and oil added. This is a very organized approach but not essential. If you do not keep a continuous record of all periodic maintenance, save the receipts from each service performed (except perhaps gasoline purchases)—and *that* is essential.

A reliable service station or independent garage is usually the best place to have the car's periodic maintenance performed (such as oil change or tune-ups). Independents tend to be more competitive and charge less than an auto dealership for such service. (See chapter 13.)

> The independent specialty shop is frequently the best place to get your car fixed, particularly if the shop has been in business for a long time and the owner is one of the mechanics. If you can't find a good specialty shop, your second choice should be an independent general repair shop in which the owner is one of the mechanics.
>
> "The independent garage is . . . best . . . because they don't sell anything but service and they depend on the customer's coming back [whereas] dealers are not in business to sell service. They are in business to sell cars."*

Most surveys show greater consumer satisfaction with the performance of independent shops when compared with that of dealerships. One survey in Washington found that eighty-two percent of customers at the average independent shop were satisfied with the way the shops fixed their cars, whereas but fifty-four percent were satisfied with the average dealership. Large retail outlets such as Sears, Roebuck and Montgomery Ward received a sixty-six percent satisfactory rating. Similarly, fifty-eight percent of the independent shops had no Better Business Bureau complaints or a "very low complaint rate," compared with only thirty-two percent of the dealers with no complaints sent to Better Business Bureaus.

SAMPLE RECORDKEEPING SYSTEM

Repair and maintenance records should be kept in one place. A spiral notebook or a pad of paper makes a good recordkeeping tool. A large envelope or folder is another helpful tool in keeping all repair orders and receipts in one spot. Good organization comes easy if a recordkeeping system is used from

---

*D. A. Randall and A. P. Glickman, *The Great American Auto Repair Robbery* (New York: Charterhouse, 1972), pp. 167–68.

27

the beginning and the records are kept in a convenient place. If you usually cannot organize anything, just find an empty drawer or box and at least keep the service receipts in that one place as you get them.

Good organization makes it easy to spot and document a defect. Confronting a dealer with a receipt for a broken gear showing that it had been repaired just 2,000 miles before will often result in a free repair without further argument. But if a consumer cannot find the bill or receipt, hassles are almost guaranteed. (Good dealers and repair shops will keep an alphabetical file by owner of all repair work performed.)

RECORDKEEPING: PROBLEM ANALYSIS

If you decide to use a recordkeeping notebook, staple each service receipt to a separate page and reserve space toward the rear of the book for analysis of the car's problems. For repair records kept in a drawer or box, take and sort them at least once a year or when a defect is suspected. If there is more than one repair bill for the same or similar problem, this indicates that something is wrong. Look through the repair orders and the service requests given to the dealer or garage for all repair work that might relate to the same problem. For example, complaints of stalling on starts, excessive warm-up time required, hesitation or poor acceleration, backfiring, poor gas mileage, and frequent spark-plug replacement indicate a defective carburetor.

After gathering all the related repair orders and other service documents, write down the following information in the notebook or on separate paper:
1. The number of trips to the dealer or repair shop and the repair order or bill numbers for a particular problem.
2. Number of days without the vehicle.
3. Whether a loaner car was provided.
4. Other items, such as whether the car broke down on the road, whether a vacation was interrupted, days of work lost, and cost of alternative transportation. This not only helps identify and document defects or other problems but also arms you with the information necessary to tackle the manufacturer's complaint mechanism.

HOW TO COMPLAIN TO THE DEALER

First give the dealer a chance to fix the car. When a vehicle defect shows up, if possible, go to the dealership at which you purchased the car. There are several reasons for this. (1) Since the dealer who sold you the car views you as a customer and would like to sell you your next car, he or she is more interested in seeing that your car is fixed properly. The dealer can do this in several ways: (a) assigning the car to an experienced mechanic for repair, (b) authorizing a goodwill repair, or (c) having the car road-tested before returning it. (2) Since reimbursement to the dealer by the manufacturer for warranty repairs is usually less than that which dealers charge customers for nonwarranty repair work, dealers are more reluctant to provide warranty work for cars they did not sell. If it is not possible to return to the original dealership,

28

find a more convenient dealership with a reputable service department. Local consumer groups and government agencies may rate or recommend local dealers.

The dealership is the first resort on almost all questions and complaints. At the dealership, ask to see the service manager. If the service manager does not help you, see the person who sold you the car. Sometimes the salesperson will put pressure on the service department to repair the car in order to keep your goodwill for a future sale. If the service department does not satisfy the complaint, go to the top person at the dealership (the owner or the general manager). The top person can always overrule subordinates or grant exceptions to general policies and authorize a free repair to "retain the goodwill of the customer."

Even when the problem is one which only the manufacturer's representative can decide, you can sometimes succeed in enlisting the dealer to go to bat for you in the first contact with the manufacturer's zone office. If the dealer does not help and it becomes necessary to contact the manufacturer's representative, you can at least tell the manufacturer that you have exhausted all possibilities with the dealer. This will help avoid one of the manufacturer's favorite ploys—referring you back to the dealer.

If the dealership refuses or cannot repair the car satisfactorily, pursue the claim through the rest of the manufacturer's system. If you immediately go through legal channels and have not given the dealer and manufacturer a reasonable opportunity to repair the car, you will probably lose. So do not stop if the dealer refuses to repair the car—go on to the manufacturer.

THE MANUFACTURER

December 15, 1972

Ford Marketing Corporation
U.S. Highway 46
Teterboro, New Jersey 07608

Attention: Mr. W. Flagg

Dear Sir:
I am the owner of a 1972 Ford Thunderbird, purchased new in March 1972 from Westfield Motors, Westfield, New Jersey.
I have recently had a loud, whistling noise when operating the blower motor and heater. I took the car to Washington Motors in West Orange, N.J., where I live, and left it there for a total of six days, in order that they might locate and correct the problem. I picked up the car yesterday, December 14, 1972, and was told that the service manager was not able to locate the noise, and, if it bothers me, to turn up the radio louder so that I would not be able to hear it.
Is this one of Ford's better ideas?

/s/
H. G. Rosenstein
Cranford, New Jersey

29

Contact the manufacturer's representative. Most automobile manufacturers have several different divisions within the corporation, such as the Chevrolet Motor Division of General Motors or the Lincoln-Mercury Division of Ford Motor Company. Each division within the corporation is usually represented in various geographical locations across the country by a zone or district office. The zone office locations are often spelled out in the owner's manual which accompanies each vehicle when purchased from the dealership. The zone office acts as a liaison between the main office, the dealer and the consumer. You can insist on arranging an appointment with the manufacturer's representative through the dealer. If the dealer refuses to cooperate, call the representative yourself. Local zone offices are listed in the white pages of telephone books across the country. The manufacturer's representative will usually ask for the following "basic information":

1. Owner's name, address, and phone number
2. Make, model, and year of the car
3. Selling dealer's name and location
4. Date of purchase and odometer reading (mileage)
5. Nature of problem plus attempts dealer has made to repair it

The manufacturer's representative can arrange to inspect the car at either the dealership or another location convenient to the consumer, as the zone offices have traveling service representatives who make regular rounds to all dealers in the zone.

Contact the main office. Almost all auto manufacturers have a consumer complaint or owner relations office at their corporate headquarters or main office. The real purpose of the manufacturer's complaint-handling campaigns, such as Chrysler's "Your Man in Detroit" or Ford's "We Listen Better," is not to provide direct action upon each consumer's complaint but to channel the consumer back into the manufacturer's bureaucratic complaint-handling system.

Thus the main office probably will not resolve your complaint, but it can set up an appointment with the zone representative if you previously could not do so, or it may pressure the zone office to reconsider your complaint. It is the zone office and not the main office which actually comes out and looks at the car. Occasionally, manufacturers have a toll-free number available for what is advertised as a hotline to expedite consumer complaints. Even when the manufacturer has a toll-free number or hotline, consumers have trouble finding and using it. For example, one consumer, Harold Fairfield of Portland, Maine, complained to the Center for Auto Safety in 1978 that Ford's 800 toll-free complaint number is changed so frequently that every number he was given had recently been disconnected and he could not find the correct number.

Where it is difficult to reach the manufacturer's main office by calling an advertised hotline or where no hotline exists, call the regular telephone number and report your complaint. Later on, after trying everything in the manufacturer's complaint-handling system, the main office can be contacted by letter, rather than by telephone, to follow up the complaint. But for initial efforts to get a defect or lemon corrected when the local dealer and zone representative are irresponsive, telephone calls are the most efficient way of making contact with the manufacturer's main office.

Even though the main office usually puts consumers back in the proper channels, that is, the dealer or zone office, ask the main office to take direct action on your complaint. If it refuses, what have you lost? But at least get the main office to pressure the zone office to reevaluate your complaint. Provide the main office representative with the "basic information" given to the zone office and the objections to the way the dealer and the zone office representative handled your complaint. Be sure to take notes on all telephone conversations with the manufacturer, including the name and title of everyone to whom you talk, along with the dates of the calls.

If the main office decides to review your case or otherwise intervenes, consider yourself lucky. If the main office orders further action to be taken on your case, it will usually have the zone office contact you. Unfortunately, the manufacturer too often approves the previous handling of a complaint and sends the consumer a form letter which fails to address the real problems.

An example of this is found in the form letter sent to M. L. G. Ryan of West Hartford, Connecticut, which states in part:

> Thank you for taking the time to write us about the problem you have experienced with your Maverick. We are sorry you have found it necessary to write for assistance, yet we appreciate the opportunity to review this situation with you.
>
> I have contacted the service representative and reviewed your file with him, and I am sorry to say that we must stand behind his decision. As a result of this review, I find no reason to reverse his findings.

SUMMARY

If a consumer has done all of the above, then either his car is in good running condition or further negotiation with the dealer or any other representative of the manufacturer is likely to result only in frustration. But the consumer now has the complete documentation of a defective car that the manufacturer refuses to or cannot fix. From here on, the consumer must go outside the manufacturer's system to get the defective car fixed, replaced, or the purchase price returned.

One consumer tried for three months to get his car repaired at the dealership and through the manufacturer's representative, but without satisfaction. Iman Womack of Norman, Oklahoma, could stand no more "runaround," so he painted lemons and slogans on his new 1970 Chevrolet stationwagon. Then he drove around the Murdock Chevrolet salesrooms on December 9, 1969. Unfortunately, the owner's son, Cliff Murdock, Jr., physically attacked the dissatisfied customer, and Womack ended up in the hospital for thirty-two days. The younger Murdock was convicted of assault and battery by a jury. Womack was awarded $3,000 in actual damages and $10,000 in punitive damages in his lawsuit against the dealership.

CHAPTER 4 *How to Complain: Strategies "Outside the System"*

ANGRY CUSTOMER FACES TRIAL

Cincinnati (AP)—A Hamilton (Ohio) man accused of driving his stationwagon through an auto dealer's service door because he considered the car a lemon will go on trial March 1.

John Bottles, 26, is accused of ramming the vehicle through the service door of the Lake Sweeney Chevrolet agency in suburban Springdale Tuesday morning.

Damage was set at $1,000. The case will be heard in Hamilton County Municipal Court.*

Although some irate consumers use more radical solutions, many consumers resolve their complaints without going quite this far. When the manufacturer's complaint-handling system does not work, the consumer can often make enough noise through aggressive and innovative complaints to get results. And, of course, it is not necessary to break the law. But a strong commitment is necessary to use these strategies successfully. Having followed the procedures in Chapter 3, "inside the system," you should have a thorough documentation of the refusal of the dealer and manufacturer to remedy your defective car. This documentation will make the strategies outside the system easy to follow and results more likely to happen.

THE SIGNIFICANCE OF LETTER WRITING

As a responsible consumer you should communicate your dissatisfaction and impatience with a foreign and domestic industry that markets new cars averaging twenty-two defects on delivery, according to *Consumer Reports*. Through letter writing you should demand to participate in decisions which affect you. As it now stands, whether or not you get satisfaction when you complain is the company's decision, not yours.

At present, with but a few challenging voices, manufacturers can persist in the comfort of self-deluding circularity—"We make them that way because that's what the consumer buys"—and escape facing the customer's reality: "I have to buy a shoddy and unsafe car because that's all there is on the market." In your letter challenge the manufacturer to respond positively to your request for action or change. At the same time, request a copy of the report which the zone office sends to the corporate or division office after action is taken on your case.

American consumers deserve less defective cars and better repair service

---

*Cincinnati Evening Sun, February 9, 1973, p. A-3.

32

when defects appear. They also deserve a complaint-handling process which displays sensitivity to the substance of the customer's complaint and to the constructive aspects of his or her role as a complainer. When letters begin to accumulate from those who in the past simply tolerated the defect without thinking of writing a complaint letter, and those who meant to do it but didn't get around to it, the automobile industry, the government, and the public will be furnished with a more accurate view of the quality of the American automobile. This added disclosure will spur a variety of efforts within industry and government to eliminate excessive defects and callous complaint handling.

THE LETTER

The first letter can be used as a "basic instrument" in an expanded complaint campaign. Send this basic letter to the manufacturer's chairman of the board or president with copies of that letter to others. Type your letter if possible. An astonishing number of complaints are ignored at this stage simply because they cannot be read, take too long to read, or are misread. If you cannot type the basic letter, print or write very legibly.

SAMPLE COMPLAINT LETTER

Date

Chairman of the Board
Belchfire Industries
(*address*)

Dear (*name*):
                    (*identification of vehicle*)
    I bought my new (*year*) (*make*) (*model*) from (*dealer's name*) (*address*) on (*date*). The vehicle identification number is———.

                    (*what went wrong*)
    The (*vehicle*) had (*mechanical breakdowns on an average of every two weeks since the date of purchase*). The major problem has been (*malfunctioning brakes*). The car (*leaks oil and stalls frequently*). (*The heater has never worked.*)

                    (*personal losses*)
    I have lost at least _____ days from work in order to have the car repaired. In addition, I have spent over (*$300*) on car rentals in order to perform my job as a (*sales representative*). I have been without adequate transportation ever since (*I bought the car*).

                    (*what went wrong at the dealership*)
    I have received insufficient help from the service department at the dealership when repairs were needed. On several occasions, I had to miss a day of work only to have the dealership fail to repair the car properly.

33

(detailed records)
Following are times at which repairs were performed at the dealership:
(date) Problem #1 *(transmission)*
Repair Order(s) # ————

(date) Problem # *(engine)*
RO # ————

(documentation)
I am attaching copies of service orders, repair receipts, and car rental receipts for your convenience.

(remedy)
I expect to receive either a refund on my purchase price, a replacement car, or a personal guarantee from you that my car will be properly repaired within ten days.
Please reply within fifteen days.

Sincerely,
/s/
John Doe
(address)

cc: Dealer
Zone office
Your attorney
President's Office of Consumer Affairs
Your U.S. senators and representatives
U.S. Senate Commerce Committee
U.S. House Commerce Committee
Department of Transportation
Environmental Protection Agency
Department of Health and Human Services
Federal Trade Commission
Center for Auto Safety
Consumers Union
Consumer Federation of America
National District Attorneys Association
Action Line
National Automobile Dealers Association
State attorney general
Local district attorney
State or local Dealers Licensing Authority or Department of Motor Vehicles
State senators and representatives
Better Business Bureau

GENERAL HINTS

Regardless of the nature of your complaint the following suggestions will increase the effectiveness of your letter and thus your chances of ultimate success.

a. Set forth the car's problems clearly and precisely. Refer to the collected documentation of the car's troubles and your attempts to have the car

34

repaired "within the system." There is no need to send every repair order or other piece of documentation with the letter. Instead, list the history of the lemon troubles, giving the nature of the problem, when it first occurred, what was done about it and when, and the results. Include copies of any key documents in the car's history such as major repair bills or admissions by the dealer.

b. When your car has many defects, eliminate minor complaints when registering your major objections. Trivia tend to undermine the impact of the more serious defects and should be included only when you want to paint a picture of a complete and utter lemon. If you do include minor defects, make sure the major ones stand out by underlining, capitalization, or including them in a separate section called major defects.

c. Avoid an apologetic tone. If you have a legitimate complaint, simply demand action. In our experience, timidity implied in such statements as "You may think I am some sort of crank, but . . ." or "This is the first letter like this I have ever written" does little good. On the other extreme, making yourself particularly abrasive is not to your advantage. Let your complaint carry its own weight, and try to communicate it as clearly and forcefully as you can.

d. Your letter should be as concise as possible. It is probably more effective to relate only the principal parts of an involved story. Senators and representatives, whose offices read thousands of letters, particularly appreciate brevity. On the other hand, if your predicament is complex and involved, there may be no escape from a lengthy exposition. A few of the most helpful cases reported to us have included complete logs, with daily insertions.

Mail this basic letter to the manufacturer's chairman of the board or president, certified with return receipt requested, so that you have proof it reached its destination. This one letter, alone, may resolve your complaint as it did for the following two consumers.

In his October 19, 1976, letter to Ralph Nader, A. Dirosa of New Orleans stated:

> I received the red carpet treatment after writing to the president of American Motors Corporation in Detroit, Michigan. The Houston Office called the local dealer and instructed them to satisfy my claim. The car runs like new again.

In his May 29, 1971, letter to the chairman of the board of Chrysler Corp., J. Jacobson of Philadelphia stated:

> My letter to you produced results. A new rear housing unit was installed, the rear wheel bearings and seals replaced, which is hoped will correct the continuous rear wheel bearing failure in and out of factory warranty.
>
> This was done at no cost to me with present odometer reading over 74,000 miles. I also received full credit of $51.00 for the cost of a set of wheel bearings I paid to install.

35

I want to thank you very much for your consideration and to let you know that a copy of this letter is being mailed to those people I sent a copy of my letter of complaint to you.

Unfortunately, a single letter does not usually work this well. More often the consumer gets an unsatisfactory response or none at all. V. Silver of San Francisco stated in her December 11, 1971, letter to the Center for Auto Safety:

The lemons drawn on the envelope probably give you a good idea what this letter is about. That's right, a lemon.

On May 7, 1971, I purchased a Chevrolet Camaro. Since May 10, 1971, I have had nothing but the usual pain and aggravation that strikes all lemon owners.

After about four months of ownership, I found out about your book, *What to Do with Your Bad Car*. And you know what, everything that was in it about how the corporations handle their dissatisfied customers is absolutely true.

Getting the car repaired under the warranty involves a costly long-distance call to the local unsympathizing zone office. Getting a new replacement car or a refund is impossible, even though we sent seven registered letters simultaneously to the dealer, zone office, owner relations manager in Detroit, chairman of the board of General Motors and the president. I told them of the problems with the car and all I got was a reply from the owner relations manager that I would be hearing from the Chevrolet Division shortly. That was October 19, 1971, and I still haven't heard.

In the mean time, more defects are occurring. As you can see from the attached chronology, the car saw the service department every week, two weeks, or three weeks. And for the first time, the dealer refused outright to fix the car, you know, "all 1971 Camaros do that," on November 15.

WHERE TO SEND THE LETTER

Address your complaint letter to the president or to the chairman of the board and send copies to the dealer and the zone office if they have failed to help you. Addresses of company officials are included in Appendix B. Zone office addresses are usually included in the owner's manual which comes with a new car, and are often listed in local telephone directories.

Writing directly to the top may prevent many delays and avoid the necessity of writing a different letter to each person along the hierarchy—if the letter is not automatically routed to the customer or owner relations department below. Pressure from the top may offset the tendency of others in the hierarchy to subject you to an annoying runaround involving the dealer, and the central, division, and zone offices. It will also exert pressure upon whichever official should take action, as it is sometimes difficult to know who in the corporate hierarchy is responsible. Also people at the top are more

36

sensitive to solving the problems listed in letters that are being sent to various federal, state, and local agencies.

The point is illustrated by this interchange of letters: When a dealer did not answer to her satisfaction an inquiry regarding her car, a Washington, D.C., Volkswagen owner wrote to the distributor. After a less than helpful answer to her request he offered this stock closing:

> Thank you for providing us with this opportunity to inquire in your behalf. We sincerely appreciate your interest in Volkswagen and take this opportunity to wish you many happy miles of Volkswagen motoring in the future.

She then wrote to Volkswagen of America in Englewood Cliffs, New Jersey, and it concurred: "We agree with you that the reply you received [from the distributor] is inconclusive. . . ." A letter initially addressed to Volkswagen of America probably would have prompted a better response from the distributor level, and saved her the need to write the second letter.

SEND COPIES OF YOUR COMPLAINT TO THE WORLD

The number of people outside the automobile industry that you advise of your problem depends on the degree of your outrage, resources, and interest in more responsible consumer protection in the future. In general, notifying appropriate agencies and officials can only be to your advantage. For example, the following consumer finally got his car repaired after a successful letter-writing campaign.

December 27, 1971
Minneapolis, Minn. 55404

British Leyland Motors, Inc.
600 Willowtree Road
Leonia, New Jersey 07605

Dear Sir:
I am happy to report that I have driven over 600 miles since my MG Midget was repaired and that all systems seem to be functioning properly. The last minor adjustments are being completed at the present time.

Thank you for your attention to the problems I have been encountering and your participation in their solution. Hansord's have assured me of their cooperation in solving any future difficulties which may arise.

Sincerely,
/s/
J. M. Bowers

cc: Hansord Pontiac
President's Committee on Consumer Interests
Representative Don Fraser

37

Senator Humphrey
Federal Trade Commission
Center for Auto Safety
Consumers Union of the United States
National Automobile Dealers Association
Governor's Office, State of Minnesota
Attorney General's Office, State of Minnesota
Action Line

P.S. [to Center for Auto Safety]: Thank you for your interest, I am sure that the appeal for aid I made to organizations such as yours was the essential factor in the dealer's decision to fix the vehicle.

Another successful letter-writing campaign brought a refund of the car's total purchase price to one consumer. When M. Vaught of Denver could not get her 1978 Chevrolet Camaro repaired properly at the dealership, she followed the manufacturer's complaint-handling system through step 3—a letter to the Chevrolet Relations Representative stating the nature of her problem. She listed sixteen carbon copies at the bottom of the letter. The dealer responded with a letter of apology and an offer to refund the total purchase price of $6,007.66. At the bottom of the dealer's letter were listed the same sixteen names of individuals, organizations, and agencies as were listed in the consumer's letter. The consumer wrote about her success to the Center for Auto Safety:

I feel that the reason R. Douglas Spedding [president of the dealership] refunded the money was because of my letter being sent to as many people and places as I did. I even received a job offer from Channel 7 (CBS) to work with their "Call for HELP" program.

Send copies of the basic letter to various organizations such as local and national consumer groups, local and state consumer protection agencies, state attorneys general, federal agencies, and members of Congress. Some groups which are able to take on individual cases may give direct assistance, while others may be able to give good advice on how to proceed further. Some organizations use complaint letters in conjunction with other complaints they receive to generate broad relief such as recalls, which benefit not only the complainant but all others similarly affected. Even if these agencies or groups cannot act directly on your behalf, they may send complaints on to the manufacturer requesting the manufacturer to take action. When the manufacturer receives enough complaints from consumers and organizations, it may decide to repair the defective cars as the best means of quieting the uproar.

One example is the action taken by the Center for Auto Safety in response to a large number of consumer complaints on 1976–77 Chrysler Volares and Aspens. Hundreds of angry consumers who were experiencing many problems with these cars wrote to Ralph Nader or the Center for Auto Safety. Most

38

of the complaints concerned carburetor, brake, driveline, steering problems or poor fuel economy. The Center in August 1977 wrote Chrysler Chairman John J. Riccardo about the unusual and disproportionate number of Chrysler complaints. When Chrysler stubbornly refused to recognize the defects in these vehicles, the Center petitioned the National Highway Traffic Safety Administration (NHTSA) to investigate the defects and compel Chrysler to recall defective models. Caught between a determined NHTSA and hundreds of complaints received by the Center, Chrysler initiated a record number of vehicle recalls in late 1977 and 1978.

These defective Aspens and Volares were recalled four times within the next six months for the specific problems pointed out to Chrysler by the Center for Auto Safety. First, 1.3 million Aspens, Volares, Diplomats, and LeBarons were recalled for defective brakes. Then Chrysler recalled 1.7 million 1975–77 vehicles with 318-cubic-inch V-8 engines and 225-cubic-inch six-cylinder engines for stalling. Next, the same 1.3 million vehicles recalled earlier for brake problems were recalled for defective hood latches that let the hood fly up during driving. Finally, 1.2 million 1976–78 Aspens and Volares were recalled for the repair of a front suspension pivot bar bracket which could fail, causing loss of vehicle control. About eighty percent of all Aspen and Volare owners had their cars subject to all four recall campaigns.

INFORMING YOUR SENATORS AND REPRESENTATIVES

Together with a cover note, send a copy of your complaint to your representative and to your senators. They were elected to represent you in Congress, so advise them of problems you face which they can help solve. Keeping them informed has a twofold advantage. It may lead, with other letters, to increased concern in Congress, and eventually to action; Senator Gaylord Nelson initiated the first tire-safety legislation after being alerted by letters from citizens.

It may also bring you direct results. J. M. Bay, of Chicago wrote that he had received four replacement tires from Firestone at no charge after he had complained about defects in the tires which came with his new Thunderbird. Asked how he managed to receive such treatment, he responded:

> I initially complained in September 1968 but did not receive any satisfaction at that time. . . . I decided to write Senator Nelson, and also gave copies of that correspondence to the senators from Illinois. . . . It was after I had sent the correspondence to Washington in February of 1969 that I received a call from the district manager of Firestone Tire and Rubber Company offering to handle my complaint.

Firestone provided Mr. Bay with the new set of tires, and in a subsequent letter requested:

> Since you were kind enough to send us copies of your letters, particularly the one to Gaylord Nelson, I think it would be fitting for you

39

to send them another letter commenting on the treatment you received from Firestone. . . .

/s/
G. L. Reid
Chicago District
March 17, 1969

The tire industry has displayed a noticeable sensitivity to the name of Senator Gaylord Nelson. Here his involvement prompted satisfactory consideration of a consumer's problem.

Unless members of Congress receive consumer letters which reflect consumer needs, consumer legislation will not be enacted. The yearly battle between consumers and some business organizations over the proposed Consumer Protection Agency is a good example. Many legislators, after being heavily lobbied by business, repeatedly said there was simply "no need" for such an agency. Consumers were unable to mount an intensive and expensive lobbying campaign to offset the Chamber of Commerce, Business Roundtable, and other anticonsumer organizations. As a result, the bill was defeated again in 1978, with a record of defeats stretching over previous years. Even with the support of the President of the United States, the bill was not going to make it in Congress without more "grassroots" support from consumers. If more letters had poured into the offices of Congress in support of the bill, the lawmakers could never have been so blind to the tremendous need for such an agency.

INFORMING OTHER GOVERNMENT OFFICIALS

1. The President of the United States

Writing the President makes more sense than most realize, not to take up his time with your personal complaint, but for other reasons. First, addressing your letter to the White House will help it find its way to the most appropriate federal agency when you are not sure where to send it. Once the letter reaches its destination, the White House referral slip attached to it may mean more expeditious handling. In addition, all the officials who see it along the way become exposed to the problem. But most important, you have provided top officials, even the President, with an additional opportunity to learn what problems are affecting people. The result might well be that these top officials, even the President, *will* decide it is important for them to spend time on widespread consumer problems.

Do not fear that your letter will distract the President or presidential staff from more important concerns, because there is a part of the President's staff charged with responsibility for handling citizen complaints, to which your letter will be referred. Called the Office of Consumer Affairs, it is part of the Executive Office of the President and is headed by the President's special assistant on consumer affairs. The current assistant is Esther Peterson. She and her staff represent the consumer before the President, draft consumer legislation, and keep the federal government informed on consumer problems.

40

The office advises the President on policies with identifiable consumer components. It has a tiny office with a small staff, but you can make it grow by sending copies of complaint letters you write, whether auto-related or not, to the President, White House, Washington, D.C. 20500.

2. Specific Agencies and Congressional Committees

On the federal level, in addition to writing the President, send a copy of your complaint letter directly to a particular federal official or to a congressional committee known to be concerned with the special type of problem you are facing. In particular, congressional committees do not regularly hear from consumers and will benefit from a direct letter. There are other reasons as well.

A lawyer representing a West Coast lemon owner wrote: "When the car company found out that everyone in the country was going to hear about Mr. Hickey's problems, the dealer fixed the car." You will multiply the weight of your complaint letter to the manufacturer by including a list of five or six carefully selected names to whom copies are being directed. The manufacturer then knows its behavior may be studied by government personnel who can use its nonperformance to strengthen a record of consumer dissatisfaction.

A complaint letter may encourage a public official to go to bat for you. With each copy of your letter, include a very brief cover note requesting the person or agency to suggest what you can do to solve your problem or take whatever steps possible to solve it. Most government agencies are not empowered to act on behalf of one person. However, in a recent case detailed later in this chapter, a single complaint from a Ford van owner with an unpadded instrument panel initiated the recall of 250,000 Ford vans and wagons. Also, as exceptions to the general rule, members of Congress can and do act on individual complaints.

When agencies add your letter to those from others with similar problems, action may result. Pressure of this sort is beginning to mount for legislation to force improvement in automobile warranties.

Finally, writing decision-makers is a way of participating in decisions that affect you. Although letter writing is hardly the most ideal form of involvement, it can often turn out to be more significant than the act of casting a vote in an election. Large numbers of well-written letters will eventually force the government to create a system for making better use of citizen letters to define and eliminate injustice and abuse. Even under the current system, when a letter is left unanswered or just perfunctorily acknowledged, it nonetheless often has had a strong impact on those who read it, and helps them define problems they are trying to solve.

Regulatory Agencies. There are particular officials or agencies in Washington to contact regarding:
1. Safety-related auto defects
2. Poor service under the warranty on your car
3. Problems with auto repair service not connected with the warranty
4. Tire problems

5. Deception and fraud in the purchase of your automobile
6. Emission-control-related auto defects

a. Safety-Related Automobile Defects

In 1966 President Johnson signed a bill which created the National Highway Safety Bureau, now the National Highway Traffic Safety Administration, of the Department of Transportation. The NHTSA sets safety standards for new cars and enforces them. It is required to investigate safety-related defects in vehicles, equipment, and tires and to order recalls where defects are found. Consumer complaints frequently form the basis for an NHTSA recall order. In the case of the Chrysler recalls cited above, the agency received over one thousand consumer complaints. In some instances, a single complaint is sufficient.

One recall campaign was initiated on the basis of a single complaint from the owner of a 1977 Ford Econoline Van. Steven H. Lynn of Rockville, Maryland, complained to the NHTSA after he received severe facial lacerations from impact with the unpadded instrument panel, in his van, which shattered in an accident. On the basis of Mr. Lynn's complaint, the NHTSA opened an investigation that quickly resulted in the recall of 250,000 1975–77 Ford Econoline Vans and Club Wagons that had unpadded plastic instrument panels. The recall involved installation of an instrument panel pad to prevent injuries to passengers who might hit the panel during an accident or sudden stop.

Address copies of letters detailing safety-related defects to:

Director
Office of Defects Investigation
National Highway Traffic Safety Administration
Washington, D.C. 20590

Anyone interested in proposing a new safety feature for automobiles or in getting a vehicle recall can petition the NHTSA to establish a new safety rule or to find that a safety-related defect exists. The petition process is little more than a letter sent to:

Administrator
National Highway Traffic Safety Administration
Washington, D.C. 20590

To be considered a petition, the letter must:
1. be written in the English language
2. have a heading that includes the word *petition*; preferably the heading should be in capital letters
3. state the facts that show NHTSA that action or an order is necessary
4. give a brief description of the substance of the action or order that should be taken
5. contain your name and address

The NHTSA must then either grant your petition and initiate the appropriate

42

rulemaking or defect-determination process, or deny it. The agency has 120 days to respond to your petition.

How to Obtain Safety Information from NHTSA. The NHTSA operates an auto safety hotline, toll-free. It serves the citizens of every state except Hawaii and Alaska. The number outside the Washington, D.C., area is 800-424-9393. In Washington the number is 426-0123. The hotline serves four major purposes:

1. Purchasers or owners of vehicles may verify the safety-defect/recall history of their vehicles.
2. Owners can report vehicle defects to generate recalls.
3. Consumers can request a variety of information from the hotline staff, including consumer educational material, equipment fact-sheets, and copies of safety standards and investigatory reports.
4. For vehicle and highway safety problems outside NHTSA's jurisdiction, the hotline can refer you to the correct agency or proper source.

Consumers who call the hotline should be prepared to provide the year, make, and model of their vehicle and its vehicle identification number. If a safety problem is being reported, a brief description of the problem, mileage, and results of the problem also should be provided.

After calling the hotline, a consumer will receive a form from NHTSA to be filled out and returned. Occasionally, a manufacturer will help the consumer after receiving pressure from NHTSA. For example, R. Babitz of Hamburg, New Jersey, had a badly frayed seatbelt on his 1976 Gremlin. After the dealer refused to repair the safety harness without charge, Mr. Babitz called American Motors (AMC), which did not seem concerned.

> At this point I called the U.S. Dept. of Transportation hotline and requested a questionnaire to report my problem. On May 7 I received the form, filled it out, and sent it in.
>
> On May 16 I received acknowledgment from the Dept. of Transportation that they had received my questionnaire and were processing it. The letter stated that if I did not receive any corrective effort within thirty days to notify them and a follow-up would be made.
>
> On June 16 I was contacted by a rep. of AMC in Detroit who said he was calling in reference to the complaint I had made to the Dept. of Transportation. I spent an hour on the phone with this man who was very nice and understanding. What a change.
>
> On June 21 I heard from the AMC road man who wanted to see my car. After a short conference between the dealer and the road rep. I was told that the seatbelt would be repaired at no cost to me. Both the dealer and the rep. were extremely nice to me. What a change in attitudes.

b. Complaints on Warranty Service
   The Federal Trade Commission is interested in the quality of customer

43

service under the warranty offered by car makers. Address copies of warranty-related complaints to:

> Warranty Project
> Bureau of Consumer Protection
> Federal Trade Commission
> Washington, D.C. 20580

The FTC does not generally act on the basis of a single complaint, but your letter, together with those from other consumers, may indicate that there is a general warranty abuse requiring action by the commission.

For example, as discussed in Chapter 5, action by Consumers Organized Against Ford (COAF) alerted the FTC to a "piston-scuffing" problem experienced by many owners of 1974–77 Fords with four- and six-cylinder engines. Ford offered free repairs to affected consumers in Wisconsin, Minnesota, and Massachusetts, but failed to announce publicly its new plan, which amounted to an extended warranty on these cars nationwide. Upon the earlier request of the Center for Auto Safety, the FTC had been looking into such "secret" warranty policies where auto manufacturers authorize free repairs for certain defects beyond the warranty period for a handful of consumers who complain most persistently, leaving those consumers who do not complain paying for repairs on their own. As a result of its investigation, the FTC issued a complaint against Ford alleging violations of federal law in the cover-up of these extended warranty practices involving piston scuffing, premature camshaft and rocker arm wear, as well as cracked engine blocks in some six million 1974–78 Ford vehicles.

In a proposed settlement reached between Ford and the FTC, Ford finally agreed to tell consumers about future secret warranties and will inform all owners of any extended warranty programs, make publicly available technical service bulletins that describe many mechanical problems, and explain how defects can be repaired under the extensions. Further information on these new programs will be available from Ford dealers and a toll-free (800) number to be set up by Ford when the settlement is finalized. For more information on secret warranties, contact the FTC Cleveland Regional Office, 118 St. Clair Avenue, Cleveland, Ohio 44114, (216) 522-4207.

c. Auto Repair Problems Not Connected with the Warranty

Auto repair industry abuses can be found along with warranty problems or entirely separate therefrom. Repair abuses can range from the incompetent mechanic to the downright fraudulent repair shop. Normally repair abuses are better handled on the state and local level but a number of federal agencies and committees are actively investigating the matter. The Senate and House Commerce Committees recently concluded hearings on abuses within the auto repair industry. Legislation on problems consumers face with auto repairs is presently being considered. Letters providing additional insight into these problems, particularly those concerning the need for federal regulation, should be directed to:

44

Consumer Subcommittee
Committee on Commerce, Science, and Transportation
U.S. Senate
Washington, D.C. 20510

Subcommittee on Consumer Protection and Finance
Committee on Interstate and Foreign Commerce
U.S. House of Representatives
Washington, D.C. 20515

Director
Division of Consumer Affairs
Department of Transportation
Washington, D.C. 20590

Director
Office of Consumer Affairs
Department of Health and Human Services
Washington, D.C. 20201

Director
Economic Crime Project
National District Attorneys Association
1900 L Street, N.W.
Washington, D.C. 20036

Bureau of Consumer Protection
Federal Trade Commission
Washington, D.C. 20580

Also contact your regional FTC office.

d. Tires

Legislation to improve tire safety still leaves many serious tire imperfections unchecked. Tire complaints of all varieties should be sent to both Senate and House Commerce Committees as well as the office of:

Senator Gaylord Nelson
U.S. Senate
Washington, D.C. 20510

Your letters will help keep Senator Nelson informed of the negligence of federal agencies charged with handling the problems.

If the problem relates specifically to tire safety, direct a copy of your letter to:

Office of Defects Investigation
National Highway Traffic Safety Administration
Washington, D.C. 20590

The NHTSA investigates safety defects in tires just as in cars. Include the ten-digit DOT number found on the sidewall. Some tire companies have been putting this number on the inside wall, that is, the side without the white wall. The number tells in which plant the tire was made and when. The number usually looks like: DOT # VDV4YEL288.

e. Deception and Fraud

The Federal Trade Commission is empowered to issue cease-and-desist orders to those individual businesses that are engaged in interstate commerce and found to be practicing deception or fraud on consumers. The FTC issued such an order to an auto dealer in northern Virginia to prevent him from selling used Volkswagens as new and from falsely advertising himself as an authorized Volkswagen dealer.

If you have been the victim of any sort of deception or fraud in purchasing a new car, a copy of your complaint letter should be sent to:

Chairman
Federal Trade Commission
Washington, D.C. 20580

f. Emission-Control-Related Defects

In 1970 the Environmental Protection Agency (EPA) was created and Congress passed the Clean Air Amendments. The EPA sets emission standards for new cars and enforces them. It is required to investigate emission-related defects in vehicles and equipment and to order recalls where defects are found. Consumer complaints frequently form the basis for an EPA recall order just as they do for an NHTSA recall order. To complain about defects in the vehicle emission-control system, write to:

Director
Mobile Source Enforcement Division
Environmental Protection Agency
Washington, D.C. 20460

3. State and Local Agencies

While you may succeed in getting help on your complaint from officials at the federal level, it is also possible to obtain individual assistance at the state and local level.

a. The State Attorney General and Your Local District Attorney

If you have been a victim of deceptive practices or fraud, send a copy of your letter to your state attorney general and to your local district attorney. Many states now have special offices under the attorney general which deal specifically with consumer protection. The attorney general in some states has the power to initiate hearings. For instance, in 1966 the attorney general of Iowa held hearings on poor design for safety in automobiles. Include a copy of your letter of complaint to the manufacturer.

The attorney general's office of your state may file a class action lawsuit

46

on behalf of you and other similarly situated consumers. For example, a surprised Joseph Siwek found that his new 1977 Oldsmobile Delta 88 had a *Chevrolet* 350-cubic-inch V-8 engine instead of an *Oldsmobile* engine when he took his car to the dealer for routine service. He was told that the Oldsmobile parts would not fit his Chevrolet engine. Humiliated and deceived by General Motors' sneaky operations, Siwek complained to the Illinois attorney general's office. His complaint and the following investigation received national news coverage. Other owners of 1977 Oldsmobiles began checking their own cars for evidence of the Great Engine Switch. After receiving thousands of consumer complaints on the switch, the state attorneys general around the country banded together through the National Association of Attorneys General and filed class action lawsuits against General Motors. In December 1977, about a year after Joseph Siwek first complained, GM and forty-five state attorneys general settled. GM agreed to reimburse owners of 1977 Oldsmobiles, Buicks, and Pontiacs with the switched Chevrolet engines with $200 and a transferable three-year or 36,000-mile warranty on the engine and drive train.

State and local officials can take action only if specific laws have been broken. The district attorney and the attorney general are both public prosecutors. It is up to them to decide whether to prosecute after they receive a complaint. If they do take your case to court, charges will be pressed by the state; any conviction will usually result in a fine or imprisonment for the guilty company or company official. In Montgomery County, Maryland, the former owners of a transmission repair garage were convicted of fraud and sentenced to jail terms of six years.

In San Francisco the city's district attorney's office joined the state's Department of Consumer Affairs in filing a lawsuit aimed at reducing the cost of auto repairs. Filed early in 1978, the lawsuit successfully attacked the auto repair industry's practice of using the so-called flat-rate system of charging for repairs, which system leads to overcharges for most auto repairs. According to San Francisco District Attorney Joseph Freitas, Jr., mechanics can beat the flat-rate time on seventy-five percent of all jobs as shown by a National Automobile Dealers Association study.

In a June 1978 decision, Superior Court Judge Ira Brown issued a preliminary injunction against the use of the flat-rate manual system of determining vehicle repair charges unless the consumer were told of its use and the actual hourly charge. Previously, consumers would unknowingly pay $30 an hour for repairs instead of the posted $15 an hour where the mechanic could do the repair in half the time listed in the flat-rate manual.

b. Dealer-Licensing Agency/State Department of Motor Vehicles

Most states and some cities license automobile dealers. Licensing agencies have the power to initiate proceedings to terminate the license of a dealer. Dealers are generally anxious to settle any complaints brought to the attention of the local licensing authority as quickly as possible. Rarely are licenses revoked, but a rash of complaints against any one dealer may cause that dealer serious trouble.

The Department of Motor Vehicles (DMV) of your state may have the

47

authority to cancel a dealer's or repair shop's registration or even file suit against a business after an investigation. For example, the California Department of Motor Vehicles recently filed suit against the owner of Bargain Barney's Sunnyvale Dodge based on its investigation and numerous consumer complaints. Although Sunnyvale Dodge had advertised rebates of $100 and $300 to customers who purchased new cars, the DMV found only one customer ever received a rebate and then only after persistent efforts. The owner of Sunnyvale Dodge was ordered by the judge to stop the false advertising and other deceptive business practices and to pay a $75,000 fine.

The California Bureau of Automotive Repair also takes an aggressive stand to protect consumers from automotive repair abuses. The Bureau of Automotive Repair, established by the California Automotive Repair Act, began operating in 1972. It was the first state agency of its kind to file court or administrative actions against hundreds of repairmen and dealers. The major enforcement tool of the bureau is its power to take away the registration of a dealer, thus prohibiting him from doing business in California. Besides licensing and regulating auto repair shops, the bureau administers the official lamp, brake, and smog device programs for the state.

The bureau accepts and processes complaints at various offices throughout the state. An attempt is made by consumer representatives to resolve the complaint by contacting the dealer. If no agreement is reached, the complaint is referred to a field investigator who meets with the consumer and dealer. In some cases, the investigator examines the repair work in question and makes sure that the provisions of the state law have been followed. In cases where no illegal activity has occurred, the bureau may act as a moderator between the consumer and the repair shop. When the bureau determines that state law has been violated, it may take administrative or criminal action against the violator. In the bureau's first year, it processed over 30,000 complaints, about sixty percent of which were settled. At that time, the bureau had successfully prosecuted about ten repair dealers, and had about eighty cases pending in the courts and nearly 800 under active investigation for fraud.

Another aggressive state agency is the New York DMV. During 1977 the New York DMV arranged for the return of $45,823 to 390 dissatisfied customers of New York State repair shops. The department also arranged for the free repair of 382 vehicles that had been repaired unsatisfactorily the first time. The department gave warnings to 554 other shops that had evoked complaints from customers. As a result of hearings conducted, fifty-six shops were suspended and thirty-one had their registration revoked during the year.

c. State Senators and Representatives

With some notable exceptions, elected officials at the state level have lagged behind in matters of consumer protection. One exception is the former New York State senator Edward Speno. In 1964 a half dozen letters from motorists who experienced new-tire blowouts prompted him to launch tire hearings in New York State. The investigation alerted officials in Washington, D.C., to the problem of poor tire quality.

On the theory that your state representatives must be kept informed,

48

send them copies of complaint letters you have written to automobile manufacturers. If you do not know the name of your state representative, check at your local library for a copy of your state's current legislative handbook, which lists the names of all representatives. If your state does not have a good auto consumer agency like that of California, your letters can help create one.

d. Local Consumer Protection Agencies

New York City can claim what is one of the most effective Departments of Consumer Affairs. In operation since 1968, the department has resolved an average of 40,000 complaints a year. Its powers and activism include wide-ranging investigative, licensing, and regulatory authority. The department actively intervenes in behalf of consumers. Cities establishing such agencies, or citizens seeking ways to strengthen their local consumer protection agencies, may benefit from writing:

Commissioner
Department of Consumer Affairs
80 Lafayette Street
New York, New York 10013

Ask specifically for copies of the legislation under which the department operates.

Another city cracking down on motor vehicle repair fraud is Dallas, Texas. The Dallas Motor Vehicle Repair Ordinance is enforced by an investigative staff of the Dallas Department of Consumer Affairs, which recovers almost $3,000 for consumers every month. The Dallas ordinance took effect in 1974, and the department's supervisor, Edward B. Meeks, has observed that the department now handles a type of complaint different from those in the beginning. He explained in a letter to the Center for Auto Safety:

In 1974 we had people in Dallas that were not actually in the auto repair business, but were acting as brokers for auto repair. All their business was conducted by telephone, and they used independent wreckers. They would not give an address, and they would change their telephone numbers and business names in the classified ads regularly. I do not know of any broker operations in Dallas at this time. We still get complaints about low-balling and charging for services not performed. However, the number of these complaints are much smaller compared to our first year of operation.

During the 1976–77 fiscal year, the department investigated 1,223 complaints, issued 225 violation notices, assessed $3,800 in fines, and recovered $30,667 for consumers.

Dade County in Florida also has an active consumer fraud unit, which frequently files criminal complaints against offending automobile dealers. Dade County consumer advocate Walter Dartland recently filed a $700 million class action lawsuit against Ford Motor Co., charging that the company's 1969–74 vehicles are prematurely rusting and corroding.

OTHER PLACES TO SEEK HELP

Action Line. In most large cities, newspapers and radio and television stations operate quick-action citizen complaint services, sometimes referred to as "Action Line," "Hotline," etc. If your problem is (a) simple, (b) susceptible of brief description, and (c) loaded with a relatively high level of injustice, your chances of interesting a reporter or investigator in your problem are good. Using the thinly veiled promise of negative publicity, they can often negotiate a victory for you. Clearly, action lines are more effective against local operators than against corporate giants like the auto makers.

The Better Business Bureau. The BBBs in most communities are financed by member businesses and exist to serve the interests of the business community. Their main task is to keep fly-by-nights out of town. Few are any use to individual consumers, and little effort should be expended trying to get them to act in your behalf. Some BBBs may write a letter of inquiry if your complaint is against a local dealer; others may give you access to a tally kept on the number of complaints against various dealers and repair establishments. One value of complaining to a BBB is that consumer groups frequently use BBB complaint totals in evaluating the quality of auto dealers and repair shops. Unless consumers complain to BBBs, a dishonest dealer or shop may get a good rating and continue to victimize consumers.

Informing Industry Public Relations Groups. The automobile and tire industries are well organized into trade associations, foundations, and councils to advance the interests of member companies through joint lobbying and public relations efforts. These groups are insulated from company-consumer relations and often profess ignorance of serious consumer dissatisfaction. To enlighten them we suggest you direct any surplus copies of your complaint letters their way.

The major trade groups for the tire and auto industries are:

> Motor Vehicle Manufacturers Association (MVMA)
> 300 New Center Building
> Detroit, Michigan 48202

As the domestic automobile industry's trade association, the MVMA looks after the interests of the "Big Four." Before 1972, it was known as the Automobile Manufacturers Association (AMA). The MVMA fosters industry unanimity on many consumer issues, feeding the press with calculated answers to soften the effect of the Big Four's anticonsumer positions. The MVMA publishes "Motor Vehicle Facts and Figures" annually.

> Automobile Importers of America, Inc. (AIA)
> 900 17th Street, N.W., Suite 1100
> Washington, D.C. 20006

The AIA represents the major automobile importing companies, including certain parts suppliers and overseas associations. The association keeps its members up to date on federal, state, and local laws and regulations that affect the manufacture and sale of imported automobiles and parts.

Tire Industry Safety Council
766 National Press Building
Washington, D.C. 20045

This organization was formed effectively to serve as a lobby against new-tire safety standards and legislation. It protects the tire industry's slipping image by heading off disclosures in Washington that are unfavorable to tire companies. Despite its title, it has little to do with advancing improvements in tire safety. It describes its purpose as providing "a medium through which constructive suggestions and information can be fed back to the tire industry."

Rubber Manufacturers' Association (RMA)
1901 Pennsylvania Avenue, N.W.
Washington, D.C. 20006

The RMA represents 170 member companies that manufacture tires, tubes, mechanical and industry products, sporting goods, and other rubber products. The association provides monthly and annual statistics on consumption, production, and inventory of rubber products.

National Automobile Dealers Association (NADA)
1640 Westpark Drive
McLean, Virginia 22101

The automobile dealers are organized nationally into NADA. If your complaint is primarily against a dealer, send NADA a copy. NADA can also state whether there is an AUTOCAP (Automotive Consumer Action Program) organized in your area by the local auto dealers association to handle auto complaints. (AUTOCAPs are explained later in this chapter.)

Insurance Research Group

Insurance Institute for Highway Safety (IIHS)
600 Watergate, Suite 300
Washington, D.C. 20037

The IIHS is not a trade association, although it is funded by major insurance companies. It is a nonprofit organization, active in the fields of auto safety and damage reduction. The IIHS is a scientific and educational organization, dedicated to reducing the losses that result from crashes on the nation's highways. The IIHS has been a leader in advocating measures in U.S. laws and regulations to prevent auto-related deaths, injuries, and property damage.

National and Local Consumer Groups. Send copies of your original letter

51

of complaint to national and local consumer groups, which may use your complaint to help you directly or indirectly. See Chapter 5 for more information on consumer groups. The following are national consumer organizations that should be alerted to any complaints that affect large groups of consumers:

Consumers Union
256 Washington Street
Mount Vernon, New York 10550

Consumers Union is a nonprofit organization, nationally recognized for its magazine, *Consumer Reports*. *Consumer Reports* is unique in that it accepts no advertising. Its product reports and ratings are thus protected from possible commercial incentives and advertiser interference. The April issue is its annual report on automobiles.

Center for Auto Safety
1223 Dupont Circle Building
Washington, D.C. 20036

The Center for Auto Safety is a nonprofit public-interest advocacy group organized in 1970 by Ralph Nader and Consumers Union but now independent of both. The Center bases much of its research priorities on consumer complaints. Each letter is most useful in determining patterns of defects or other problems to be investigated. The Center seeks general remedies, such as vehicle recalls, that will aid large numbers of similarly situated consumers. This is the primary way that the Center is able to help the tens of thousands of individuals who directly seek its assistance each year or who are referred to it by Ralph Nader.

Consumer Federation of America (CFA)
1012 14th Street, N.W.
Washington, D.C. 20005

See Chapter 5 for information on the CFA.

SUMMARY

Send copies of your original letter of complaint to those who may be able to assist. For different types of complaints, the list of persons receiving copies will vary somewhat.

See earlier in this chapter the "cc" list in the "Sample Complaint Letter" to the manufacturer complaining about the refusal of a dealer to make repairs under the warranty.

WHAT THE MANUFACTURERS DO WITH COMPLAINT LETTERS

When they choose, the manufacturers can turn the complaint-handling process

52

into an exercise in consumer futility or, in some cases, even an engine of consumer harassment. Their tactics range from complete silence to evading your complaint by means of a time-consuming runaround between the central office, zone representative, and the dealer. In most cases you are at the complete mercy of these devices, but by understanding them you can avoid delay, prevent additional losses, score a point or two, or even win a just settlement.

A survey of automobile company complaint-handling procedures conducted by Congressman Benjamin Rosenthal disclosed the system by which the manufacturers protect themselves and their dealers at the expense of the complaining consumer. Note, for example, these excerpts from General Motors' response to Congressman Rosenthal's questions.

At the General Motors central office the owner relations department, under the direction of the owner relations manager, receives and acknowledges all owner complaints addressed to our corporate headquarters. . . . Each car and truck division has an owner relations department. . . . In turn, each of the 166 divisional field zone offices has people assigned to [handle complaint letters]. . . .

If the subject of [a customer's complaint] cannot be completely resolved in the acknowledgment, an explanation is given him of the manner in which the complaint will be investigated.

The nearest zone office brings the matter to the attention of the dealer [under the terms of his selling agreement, each dealer agrees to assume responsibility for the investigation and handling of any complaint received directly by him or referred to him by General Motors in connection with a General Motors product which he is authorized to sell and service] and requests that proper steps be taken to investigate the complaint, to clarify any questions the owner may have raised, to make certain that any obligation under the terms of the warranty is fulfilled, and to make any necessary corrections. Where circumstances indicate a personal contact is desirable [as where a dealer's assessment of the problem would not satisfy the customer, or major warranty repairs are in question] a representative from the zone office is assigned to inspect the car. . . . A written report is prepared and returned to the office of the corporation or division to which the complaint was addressed. The report must describe the action which was taken and whether or not a satisfactory conclusion was reached with the owner. . . . [If] the owner is still dissatisfied . . . the corporation procedure makes it the responsibility of the zone manager to personally review the details to make certain that every reasonable effort was made to satisfy the owner.

. . . Owners sometimes remain dissatisfied even after all reasonable efforts have been made to satisfy them. . . .

Our records indicate that of all the complaints received [more than 143,000 in 1968] approximately eighty-five percent were reported concluded to the customer's satisfaction.

. . . Records further indicate that complaints are handled to a con-

53

clusion in approximately eight days on the average.

Other manufacturers have systems similar to GM's.
It is clear that your letter is digested by a system with glaring deficiencies:

1. Low-Level Concern
Complaint letters, even when addressed to chief executives, are often routed to customer or owner relations departments, staffed by persons whose prime qualification, judging from their pronouncements, is that they go by the book; that is, they are proficient at form letters.

The ritual of the system bothered Mrs. J. L. Outten of Wilmington, Delaware, who wrote:

March 30, 1970

Dear Mr. Nader:
If you read through this correspondence you will note letters from GM which are actually nothing but form letters, one of which expresses a negative opinion before anyone from GM had actually seen the car. All the letters refer to a concern with customer satisfaction, but there appears no real interest in accepting an obvious manufacturer's responsibility.

/s/
Mrs. J. L. Outten

Henry Ford II's signature appears on an occasional form acknowledgment letter to a complaining owner, selected for personal response when he has time and when serious problems are raised in letters addressed to him. But this touch of personal concern does not seem to improve the handling of the complaint; after his blessing, it is referred to the standard complaint-handling channels. Mr. Ford stated: "We do not do as good a job of handling customer complaints as we should. But we are improving and will continue to improve."

One consumer, tired of Ford's empty promises, wrote:

May 11, 1971

Ford Motor Company
Dearborn, Michigan 48121

RE: Your Advertisement *Newsweek*, 5/10/71
"We would like to hear from you."
"Do write us. We listen. And we listen better."

Gentlemen:
Your current "Customer Relations" messages, so far as I am concerned, are sickening—so listen to this:
I have a ream of correspondence, covering several months, most of it one way—me to you—about the unsatisfactory performance of a 1968 Mercury Montclair concerning faulty power steering, improper

54

front-end suspension, and absolute disinterest in solving same.

If you're "still listening"—and I doubt it—don't bother replying with one of your usual form-type letters—I received too many of them when trying to obtain proper attention from March to September 1968.

/s/

H. E. Jordan
Niantic, Connecticut

2. No Consumer Participation

Once the investigation of the zone office is initiated there is little or no opportunity for the customer to participate. Decisions costing consumers hundreds of dollars are made sometimes without consulting the owner, sometimes without even inspecting the vehicle in question. D. Short of Alexandria, Virginia, whose new Chevrolet engine failed, specifically requested to be present at the dealer's when the zone service representative came to inspect his engine. When he called a week later to check, he was told the zone representative had completed his visit. He was, therefore, deprived of an opportunity to present his case.

A. R. Bauersfeld of Brooklyn, New York, wrote Ford of fourteen complaints about her 1968 Ford Galaxie. A few weeks later she found herself writing a second letter:

February 25, 1969

Ford Motor Company
Dearborn, Michigan 48121

Attn: R. J. Northway, Customer Relations

My telegram to you and letters to Mr. Knudsen did not even warrant the common courtesy of a reply, only another questionnaire. You mention in your letter dated 2/18/69, "our New York office informed us that your car is now running satisfactorily." How would they know? Have they ever seen or driven the car in question? Have your local automotive engineers seen or driven the car? Have I, the poor sap owner, been consulted? NO. Yet you base your conclusion on the operating condition of the car on this opinion of your New York office. . . .

Perhaps your completely detached, farcical method of handling customer complaints is specifically designed by your experts to wear down the buying public. It is a pity that the effort expended in avoiding responsibility for inferior products is not applied to turning out products in which you could take pride.

/s/

A. R. Bauersfeld

3. Inaccurate Reporting

General Motors states that eighty-five percent of the complaints were resolved to the satisfaction of the owner. It does not say, however, whether this figure is based on zone representative reports or on checks with com-

55

plaining owners. The owner has no way of knowing whether the zone representative has accurately reported the outcome of the matter. Particularly in cases where the decision is against the consumer, as for instance where warranty coverage is denied, the owner should be informed in detail of the reasons for rejecting his request. Providing owners as a matter of course with a copy of the zone representative's reports to the central office (excluding, of course, comments on dealer performance intended for internal consumption) would add immeasurable legitimacy to the system.

4. No Appeal Procedures

By General Motors' figures, 21,000 persons in 1968 were left unsatisfied. To this number must be added the thousands with complaints who never voiced them to GM (perhaps on the presumption that the effort would be futile), and another large number whose complaints GM presumes are remedied on the basis of reports from zone representatives, but which in fact are not solved or only partly solved in the view of the owner. These persons are left totally at the mercy of a decision concerning which they have no appeal or recourse within the company.

As Mr. and Mrs. C. P. Gaudreau of Weirton, West Virginia, stated in their letter:

February 8, 1978

Ford Motor Company
Dearborn, Michigan 48121
Attn: R. J. Northway, Customer Relations

The message of this letter is to let you know that we appreciate your effort to satisfy the complaints that were registered with Mr. Walla's office in the last three letters we mailed.

My feelings from the beginning were and are that our complaint was considered less than casually by Mr. Dorsey and Cattrell Motor Co. and that we were heretofore penalized by their "kangaroo court."

It is especially disturbing to realize that a company as big as Ford Motor Co., particularly the Lincoln-Continental Division, carries a complaint as adamant as ours no further than one local representative whose word appears to be final—to us and to Mr. Barringer.

/s/

S. Gaudreau
C. P. Gaudreau

Other problems with the complaint-handling system, not touched on by the General Motors letter, have aroused owner reaction. The following specific devices used by zone representatives have aroused particularly strong reactions from lemon owners.

5. Wearing You Down to the Point of Exhaustion

The engine of a 1967 Pontiac owned by J. W. Myers of Indianapolis broke down in April 1969 before his warranty expired. Under protest Mr. Myers paid $350 for a replacement engine. He wrote three letters to General

56

Motors' Pontiac division, on May 22, July 7, and July 23, 1969, demanding warranty coverage, carefully supporting his claim. His request was denied. In his July 7 letter he wrote:

> It is evident that your [zone representative's] decision is based entirely on the opinion of Wells Pontiac, Inc., who stands to profit from the unfortunate incident.
> . . . Considering the information given you in my earlier letter, I am appalled by your handling of this matter. Your replies to my pleas are completely uninformative. Your letters make factually unfounded allegations and seek only to pacify me with flimsy excuses. . . . You do not appear sufficiently interested in my problem to contact me locally or to request additional information from me. Your attitude seems to be one of "put him off until he tires of writing"; an attitude which speaks very poorly of Pontiac Motor Division and of General Motors.
> /s/
> J. W. Myers
> Indianapolis, Ind.

Some owners write considerably more letters than the three Mr. Myers wrote, and get no further. One irate Chevrolet victim from Coopersburg, Pennsylvania, sent off over forty letters and still had only frustration to show for it.

Sometimes manufacturers add insult to injury in their form responses, as did General Motors in the following response to J. J. Mautner, Jr., of Mamaroneck, New York:

> December 8, 1977
> Dear Mr. Mautner:
> This is with reference to your letter directed to our Detroit office concerning your Chevrolet.
> Certain high standards have been developed over the period of years of manufacturing automobiles, and such standards are the basis of any decision made pertaining to a purchase of a product by a consumer or the judging of it by the purchaser.
> As explained to you, your Chevrolet can be considered normal and falling within the established standards for it.
> /s/
> M. L. Valerio
> Consumer Relations

Mr. Mautner wrote to Ralph Nader that "I cannot imagine getting such a letter, but seeing is believing. I guess they just don't care about us little guys." He enclosed this response to General Motors.

> December 12, 1977
> General Motors Corp.
> Chevrolet Motor Division

Detroit, Mich. 48202

Attn: Mr. R. D. Lund, General Manager
I have just about run the gamut with Chevrolet. I have been treated poorly by the dealer and by Tarrytown, and what I think the December 8th letter says is S——W me. I am not only very upset, but stunned by the fact that your Tarrytown office seems to be indifferent to valid customer complaints.
Unfortunately, I have a lemon. Also unfortunately, I purchased the vehicle from a dealer who does not watch over his people, and who evidently does not care about repeat customers. Perhaps they think I am a nut, but really, all I want is my $9,300.00 worth of car.
At the present time, I feel the vehicle is unsafe. It doesn't handle properly, and it bounces in a funny way—diagonally—rear left to front right. My last Suburban, which is the "standard" which I based this purchase on, handled beautifully, and while it bounced over certain kinds of bumps, it bounced front to rear in the conventional bouncing manner.
Since I started this letter-writing campaign, there have been other problems with the vehicle. All I am asking you for is some prompt action.

Very truly yours,
/s/
J. J. Mautner, Jr.

6. Passing the Buck to the Dealer
Attorney Daniel R. Kirshbaum of Fort Worth, Texas, complained to the Pontiac Motor Division about a defect in the windshield-washing system of his car which caused it to clog repeatedly. He wrote letters on June 9, July 4, August 6, and October 13, 1969, to various General Motors personnel. A letter to him from J. B. Milligan of the Dallas zone office contained the well-worn Pontiac line of evasion:

August 5, 1969
We feel particularly handicapped in situations such as this, because a manufacturer does not have the authority to dictate courses of action to a dealer. . . . Any decision reached is that of the dealer, and must be negotiated between the dealer and his customer. . . . All dealers are independent merchants.

/s/
J. B. Milligan

Amazed that Pontiac should attempt to avoid responsibility in this way, Attorney Kirshbaum replied:

. . . most of my complaints with my car have stemmed originally from manufacturing defects. . . . Your comments about the limitations on your obligation as a manufacturer are . . . I think . . . incorrect, due

58

to the fact that you do franchise and certify certain dealers as "authorized . . ." and prescribe the rates they charge and the training mechanics must undergo. . . .

Mr. Kirshbaum supplied us with copies of his correspondence together with the note: "They illustrate the wall of inconsistency and double talk with which the consumer is confronted on even the most minor problems."

M. Donnelly of Elizabeth, New Jersey, was told by Chrysler representative M. D. Zielke of Chrysler's Valley Forge, Pennsylvania, office, after four months of correspondence, that "Chrysler is not a third party to a retail transaction involving Chrysler cars purchased from a Chrysler dealer and that Chrysler is in no way at all responsible for the business ethics of their dealers, that they are independent businessmen," and so on. As Mr. Donnelly explained his reaction in a January 1, 1972, letter to Ralph Nader:

> I have not even gotten a dirty Kleenex from Vittori [Chrysler-Plymouth dealer, Salem, N.J.] and nothing from Detroit . . . After all my correspondence, this entire spectrum of so-called customer relations is like the false fronts of buildings in old western movies. You think it's there, but in reality it amounts to nothing. Zielke, using usual Chrysler techniques, states in his only letter that both N.Y. and Valley Forge offices have made countless tries to contact me, etc. This is an absolute lie.

What these consumers realize well is that manufacturers describe dealers as "independent" only when dealers are needed to insulate the manufacturers from their own mistakes.

7. Telling a Simple Lie

When John Donovan of Washington, D.C., whose school buses carried the children of prominent Republicans to and from private schools each day, complained about gas leaks from three of his 1969 school buses, the General Motors representative checked them, but blamed the error on the builder of the school bus body in North Carolina. When Mr. Donovan called the body builder, he was told that the gas tanks were installed by GMC in Pontiac, Michigan. Informed of this, the GMC representative admitted he had made a "mistake" about the gas tank. GMC, he said, did make and install them.

The gas leak problem rose again. General Motors attributed it this time to a faulty tank neck extension which, GM told Mr. Donovan, was made in North Carolina and not by GM. This time the *Washington Post*, which was investigating Mr. Donovan's problems, called North Carolina, and again it turned out General Motors had to admit a "mistake."

S. Breitkopf of North Brunswick, New Jersey, could not get his 1976 Dodge Aspen lemon fixed. He expressed his ire at Chrysler's tactics in a November 22, 1976, letter to E. Landvay, Chrysler customer relations coordinator:

> I do not for one minute believe one word of your initial correspondence

59

since everything in it has turned out to prove totally untrue. This car was so full of defects that my wife still asks me who is getting the car this week, she or the dealer.

I can only hope that the last line of your letter contains some element of truth and that you are always glad to hear from owners of Chrysler products. You just heard from me.

8. Promises and Silence

Many owners indicate that even if they receive an initial acknowledgment letter, usually from Detroit, the promise of a follow-up from a local zone representative is never kept.

Mrs. G. Kaffeman had a frightening experience when the hood of her Ford car snapped open. Her husband wrote to Ford Motor Company on July 16, 1971, after seeing "their full-page ad 'We Listen Better' and hearing all the commercials about that on TV." Eleven days later the Kaffemans received a Mailgram from Detroit "advising us that we will be contacted soon." On August 9, they received a call from the district office which "promised to look into the matter and contact us within a week or so." After waiting over a week, they contacted the district office and got the same reply. The Kaffemans wrote on August 30. They heard nothing until September 19, when "we received a query as to whether our complaint had been taken care of. . . . Since then nothing. They may listen better but then they evidently don't have to do anything—even give you a civil explanation."

J. C. Richter of Sudbury, Massachusetts, also experienced broken promises and silence. In his May 3, 1976, letter to Ralph Nader, he wrote:

Attached is a package of correspondence I have had with Chrysler Corporation on this subject. My last two letters have not been answered despite the acknowledgment and promise of prompt response from the Chrysler customer relations department. Sufficient time has elapsed such that I conclude Chrysler Corporation does not intend to answer these letters. As I told Mr. Nichols, Chrysler vice president of public responsibility and consumer affairs, this leaves me with the conclusion that Chrysler Corporation:

- Does not stand behind its Owner's Manual information.
- Is unable/unwilling to advise me on how to service my car when the Owner's Manual has been challenged by the dealer.
- Does not follow up to assure that its customer policy of "Your Chrysler Man in Detroit" really works.

9. Cost

The absurdity of corporate complaint-handling procedures is not at all diminished by the fact that the costs of customer relations are passed on to the car buyer, who is, therefore, made to pay for his own harassment. A less callous approach would lead the manufacturers to decide marginal and minor cases on the side of the consumer, save the time and expense of runaround letters, and recoup the cost of fixing the cars in future repeat sales.

60

AND STILL NO SATISFACTION

Retaliation through further communication with the manufacturer through normal channels, as suggested in this chapter, is of limited value. It relies on the presumption that a reasonable request, reframed and repeated, will appeal to the corporate conscience. Now and then it may work. But to overcome the monumental indifference of the complaint-handling system in the larger number of cases, devices are required which creatively seek out points of vulnerability in corporate defenses, or which mount a more credible challenge than can be posed by an isolated consumer.

Ways of seeking weak points in corporate armor and organizing with other consumers are discussed in Chapter 5. Ways of mounting a credible challenge through a lawsuit follow in Chapter 6.

INDUSTRY COMPLAINT BUREAUS

Finally, awakened by the mounting consumer complaints on automobiles, the auto industry is taking a few initial steps in setting up complaint-resolution mechanisms. It is too early to tell whether the industry is committed to making these systems work for consumers or whether they are just another public relations gimmick like "Your Man in Detroit." The following are some of these efforts.

AUTOCAP. In 1974 the U.S. Office of Consumer Affairs encouraged the Automotive Trade Association Managers (ATAM) and the National Automobile Dealers Association (NADA) to set up the Automotive Consumer Action Program (AUTOCAP). AUTOCAPs exist in thirty-two states and are expected to spread eventually to most states. (See Appendix A for a list of participating states.) Where one exists, the local AUTOCAP may help you and the dealer settle the complaint. As a result of this first step, only twenty percent of all cases go to a panel. If the parties cannot agree, the case goes before the panel—usually without your having to appear in person. Decisions by the panel are not legally binding for either the dealer or the consumer.

The average panel has six members: three "consumer representatives" and three dealers. As of 1978, approximately 9,000 dealers had given their support to AUTOCAP. This method of resolving auto complaints will resolve some complaints. But the panels will not resolve the worst cases or the genuine lemon. In addition, the panels are still too few to have any immediate effect on the overall problem. Whether they are reliable and operate fairly remains to be seen.

Detroit Auto Dealers Association. A program begun in 1974 to handle consumer complaints against Detroit area new-car dealers has resolved almost 2,000 complaints in its first three years of operation. The Detroit Auto Dealers Association (DADA) organized and operates the following complaint-handling program. According to DADA, when complaints are made to local consumer groups or the news media, the letters are often passed on to the

61

association. DADA officials mail the complaint to the dealership owner who contacts the consumer. If the problem is resolved, the dealership makes a written report within thirty days to DADA, describing action taken to solve the consumer's complaint. If the dealer does not respond within thirty days, DADA sends a second letter asking for the report. If another thirty days pass without a response, DADA sends a registered letter informing the dealer that the complaint will be sent to the state attorney general's office. Copies of the consumer's letter and the dealer's letter, if written, are sent to the newspaper or agency that was first contacted.

Ford Consumer Appeals Board. In September 1977 Ford Motor Company began a test program to help resolve its consumer service complaints. A five-member consumer complaint panel, called the Consumer Appeals Board, was set up in North Carolina for a two-year period. In 1978 and 1979 Ford expanded the program with boards in New Jersey, the Washington-Oregon area, Washington, D.C., Maryland, and Virginia. Unlike the AUTOCAP program, any decision by the Ford board will be binding on the company and the dealer. But decisions of the board are not binding on the consumer, who is free to take further action if he or she desires. The boards are usually made up of two dealers, a state official, a vocational educator, and a "consumer advocate."

General Motors Arbitration Program. In June 1978 General Motors began a test program of binding arbitration of consumer service complaints in the Minneapolis–St. Paul area. The experiment differs from the Ford program in that both the manufacturer and the consumer must agree to accept the arbitrator's decision. Then GM expanded the arbitration program, with some revisions, to the Buffalo area. In GM's Buffalo program, arbitration decisions are binding on GM but not on the consumer, like the Ford program. Both GM programs are administered by the local Better Business Bureaus.

As with the Ford programs, the GM programs may or may not benefit consumers. It is too early to tell whether the programs are simply another public relations' stunt like "Your Man in Detroit" and "Ford Motor Company Listens," or a sincere attempt at resolving consumer complaints.

APPENDIX A—Chapter 4

AUTOCAPs in These States (as of July 1, 1978)

Arizona	Nevada
California	New Hampshire
Connecticut	New Mexico
Delaware	New York
Florida	North Dakota
Georgia	Ohio
Illinois	Oklahoma
Indiana	Oregon
Iowa	Pennsylvania
Kentucky	Rhode Island
Louisiana	South Dakota
Maryland	Texas
Massachusetts	Utah
Michigan	Virginia
Mississippi	Washington
Montana	Wisconsin

APPENDIX B—Chapter 4

Addresses of Major Auto Companies and Names of Top Officials

AMERICAN MOTORS CORP., 27777 Franklin Rd., Southfield, Mich. 48034.
Phone: (313) 827-1000.
 Chairman—Gerald C. Meyers.   President—W. Paul Tippett.
BMW OF NORTH AMERICA, INC., Montvale, N.J. 07645.
Phone: (201) 573-2000.
 President—John A. Cook.
CHRYSLER CORP., P.O. Box 1919, Detroit, Mich. 48288.
Phone: (313) 956-5741.
 Chairman—L. A. Iacocca.   President—J. P. Bergmoser.
FORD MOTOR CO., The American Road, Dearborn, Mich. 48121.
Phone: (313) 337-6950.
 Chairman—Philip Caldwell.   President—Donald E. Peterson.
GENERAL MOTORS CORP., General Motors Building, Detroit, Mich. 48202.
Phone: (313) 556-2030.
 Chairman—Thomas A. Murphy.   President—Elliott M. Estes.
INTERNATIONAL HARVESTER CO., 401 N. Michigan Ave., Chicago, Ill. 60611.
Phone: (312) 836-2000.
 Chairman—Brooks McCormick.

MAZDA MOTORS OF AMERICA, INC., 3040 E. Ana St., Compton, Calif. 90221.
Phone: (213) 537-2332.
President—Toru Ogawa.
MERCEDES-BENZ OF NORTH AMERICA, INC., One Mercedes Dr., Montvale, N.J. 07645.
Chairman—Dr. Gerhard Prinz.   President—Karlfried Nordmann.
NISSAN MOTOR CORP., 18501 Figueroa St., Carson, Calif. 90248.
President—Tetsuo Arakawa.
PEUGEOT MOTORS OF AMERICA, INC., One Peugeot Plaza, Lyndhurst, N.J. 07071.
Phone: (201) 935-8400.
Chairman—Pierre Peugeot.   President—Pierre Lemaire.
SAAB-SCANIA OF AMERICA, INC., Saab Dr., Orange, Conn. 06477.
Chairman—G. A. Douglas.   President—Robert J. Sinclair.
SUBARU OF AMERICA, INC., 7040 Central Hwy., Pennsauken, N.J. 08109.
Chairman—Sherman Rose.   President—Harvey Lamm.
TOYOTA MOTOR SALES, U.S.A., INC., 2055 W. 190th St., Torrance, Calif. 90504.
President—Isao Makino.
VOLKSWAGEN OF AMERICA, INC., 27621 Parkview Blvd., Warren, Mich. 48092.
Phone: (313) 574-3300.
Chairman—Toni Schmuecker.   President—James W. McLernon.
VOLVO OF AMERICA, CORP., Rockleigh, N.J. 07647.
Phone: (201) 768-7300.
President—Bjorn Ahlstrom.

64

CHAPTER 5 *The Leverage of Group Organization*

When Consumer Federation of America talks, congressmen listen. . . . Consumers are a powerful constituency.*

CEPA WINS NEW CAR

The Baltimore Branch of CEPA [Consumers Education and Protective Association] settled a complaint by acquiring a new car for Shelley Miller, of Baltimore, from Larry's Mazda, Randallstown, Md.

On April 1, 1973, the Miller's Mazda was involved in a head-on collision and suffered extensive damage. The vehicle was towed to the dealership from which it was bought and after approximately six weeks Mr. and Mrs. Miller picked up their car.

The original estimate for repairs was $339. However, additional charges were added on until the final bill came to $812.90!

Furthermore, a thorough investigation of the car after completion of the work exposed poor workmanship. The hood was improperly aligned, the paint job was poor and the radiator was misaligned.

The Millers contacted the Baltimore branch of CEPA. Once the dealership was notified that CEPA had entered the case, they offered to pay off the lien on the car and return all money that had been paid on the automobile. In return, the dealership asked for return of the Mazda and the money paid to the Millers by the insurance company.

After further negotiation it was agreed that the Millers would be given a new Mazda, and the damaged car would be returned to the dealer.

In a letter of appreciation to CEPA, Mrs. Miller wrote, "My husband and I thank you most sincerely for your support. If CEPA had not become involved on our behalf . . . we may never have received a just settlement. . . . The reputation of CEPA alone seemed to be the pivotal factor.**

EXPANDING YOUR ARSENAL

No matter how dedicated, intelligent, clever, or persistent you may be, it is difficult to have a lasting impact on the auto industry by yourself or even with an attorney. With organization behind you, a wide range of additional strategies can be invoked, many of them aimed at changing the system which generates these abuses, as well as solving your own lemon problem. So seek out consumer groups in your area (or if no suitable groups exist, start one

---

*Wall Street Journal.
**Consumers Voice 8, no. 11 (1973)

65

along the lines suggested later in this chapter), and consider the group-action devices that follow.

Contact the State Attorney General. In the spring of 1977 more than ninety Wisconsin Ford owners experienced similar problems with their four- and six-cylinder engine 1974–77 models. They banded together and formed a group called Consumers Organized Against Ford (COAF). COAF filed its complaints with the Wisconsin attorney general's office in an action which eventually led to nationwide relief.

Before contacting the Wisconsin attorney general's office to intervene on their behalf, the irate Ford and Mercury owners had complained to Ford that a cost-cutting step taken by the manufacturer (elimination of the oil-feed holes that lubricate cylinder walls) had caused serious scuffing of the cylinder walls, leaving car owners with costly engine repairs. COAF wanted Ford Motor Company to install new engines in their cars or to compensate owners for costs already incurred. The group also tried to find out if the problem with Ford's four- and six-cylinder engines was nationwide. COAF contacted newspapers throughout the country in search of Ford and Mercury owners who were having the same problem. They received about 200 responses.

Based on its complaints and research, COAF petitioned the Wisconsin attorney general's office for assistance. The Wisconsin Department of Justice investigated these "piston-scuffing" complaints and reached an agreement with the manufacturer. Ford offered free repairs for four- and six-cylinder engines which experienced piston scuffing within thirty-six months or 36,000 miles, whichever came first. The manufacturer also agreed to reimburse consumers for repairs already performed that were caused by the defect. Ford reached similar agreements with Minnesota and Massachusetts. Then Ford quietly notified its dealers nationwide of a policy-adjustment plan to pay for correcting engine damage caused by piston scuffing. However, Ford failed to announce publicly its new plan to offer what amounted to an extended warranty on these cars nationwide.

This action alerted other consumer groups and the Federal Trade Commission (FTC), which had been looking into such unpublicized "goodwill" or secret warranty policies established by auto manufacturers. Under secret warranties, auto makers repair certain defects for consumers who complain, even though the normal warranty has expired. But the manufacturers fail to disclose the extended warranty to all owners. Thus many consumers end up paying for repairs on their own. As a result of its investigation, the FTC issued a complaint against Ford for violating the law by failing to inform all 2.7 million car owners of the design flaw. Shortly thereafter, Ford capitulated and agreed to tell all affected owners about the secret warranty. All this happened because one group of consumers decided to stand up to a giant auto maker.

Inform the Auto Makers That Your Group Is a Watchdog. Consumer Action (CA) of San Francisco is a nonprofit, voluntary organization that handles local consumer auto complaints. CA is too understaffed to answer

66

all complaints personally; thus, the complaints are handled through Complaint Resolution Committees. These committees are based on the consumer's personal attendance and participation. All its members help each other by working on the cases of other members. Through these committees, CA has returned over $300,000 in goods and services to committee members. As a result of its activities, CA has earned the respect of the community as well as a reputation with the auto manufacturers. A letter sent by Ford management to all Ford dealers in the San Francisco area included this message:

> As you undoubtedly realize, the San Francisco Consumer Action group obtains high visibility and exerts great influence in its field. Therefore, please handle all contacts or referrals from this group in the following manner:
> 1. Accept collect phone calls.
> 2. Treat the contact as a Priority Case.
> 3. Consider the contact of the utmost importance and pursue the case to its ultimate conclusion as completely and quickly as possible.*

Picket Dealers or Repair Shops. Picketing by groups of consumers has proved to be a very successful tactic. See Chapter 9 for a more complete description of this strategy and examples of its use in auto cases. The device is so successful, that sometimes just the threat of picketing is enough to resolve a complaint. For example, in 1972 Estelle Spears of Philadelphia bought a 1969 Mercury stationwagon from Kardon Motors, Mt. Holly, New Jersey. A few months after purchase, the consumer found that the whole floor of the car was covered with rust and holes. The dealer had attempted to conceal the rust with newspaper and carpeting. Mrs. Spears contacted the Philadelphia branch of CEPA. The dealer would not negotiate. As soon as a picket was scheduled, the dealer decided it was time to reach some kind of agreement. The picket was called off, and a delegation was set up. After negotiation Kardon agreed to take the car back and give the consumer a $791 refund.**

Group Efforts Improve Chance of Successful Legal Action. Groups of individuals who band together can usually invoke certain legel strategies better than if each individual had acted alone. For example, thirty-nine owners of prematurely rusting Fords obtained a $27,500 out-of-court settlement in a joint suit against Ford Motor Company. The thirty-nine plaintiffs had contended that their Fords were rusting prematurely and that it cost about $700 a car for rust repair or loss of market value. The case eventually was settled for over $700 each. An individual alone frequently cannot afford to sue a manufacturer. But a group of individuals can share the costs of filing suit as did these thirty-nine people.

Another legal strategy successfully used by groups is the delicensing

---

*Automotive News, August 6, 1973, p. 15.
**Consumers Voice 8, no. 11 (1973): 3.

67

approach. For example, if many consumers were misled by a dealer's or manufacturer's deceptive advertising, they can persuade state licensing authorities to open delicensing proceedings against the offending dealer or manufacturer. It is unlikely that a state licensing authority would suspend or revoke a dealer's or manufacturer's privilege to sell cars in the entire state on the strength of a single consumer complaint. A consumer group might lend enough weight by complaining on behalf of all consumers misled.

In one case, though, an organized group was not necessary, because consumer complaints filed by many individuals set the stage for one particularly grievous individual complaint. The subsequent license revocation and closing of Joe May Chevrolet in Detroit were described in the *Detroit News*, on March 3, 1970:

> Leading to license revocation were complaints against the dealer from dissatisfied customers. Eventually, one prospective buyer complained that he had signed a blank contract which was later filled in with a price $500 higher than he and the salesman had agreed to.

When enough complaints had reached the Michigan secretary of state, the dealership was closed down. Although a single complaint can arouse the attention of a state authority, it will generally take many complaints from other consumers with the same or different problems to bring the authority to take action against the dealer. Here consumer organization is invaluable.

Bring a Class Action Suit Against the Manufacturer. Having an organized auto consumer group will facilitate the identification of abuses and problems that are widespread and affect enough consumers to make a class action suit appropriate. See Chapter 6 for a more complete description of this device.

Other Efforts. One value of organizing consumer discontent into a cohesive force is the added muscle it can bring to bear on resolving the complaints of member consumers. Other efforts, possible only through organization, may also help you and others:

1. Investigations and reports, with press coverage of exposures
2. Boycotts of offending dealers or even certain makes found to be unsafe or unreliable
3. Lemoncades (as well as picketing) against dealers, repair shops, or finance companies that have victimized consumers (see Chapter 9)
4. Lobbying for changes in laws affecting consumer rights and for programs to reduce the enormous dependence of urban and suburban residents on the automobile
5. Enlisting attorneys to develop test cases and auto mechanics to assist in diagnosis and negotiation
6. Contacts with industry insiders to help place the responsibility where it belongs

These are some of the levers of lasting change.

A consumer group can function also as a clearinghouse on a particular

68

topic. For example, when the Center for Auto Safety received numerous consumer letters complaining of automatic-transmission problems in General Motors' automobiles caused by faulty transmission fluid, the group mailed out a form-letter response containing information on how to proceed to the frustrated consumers. One consumer, F. A. Rosscoe of Richmondville, New York, wrote back to the Center asking for a copy of the GM service bulletin referred to in the form letter. Although GM had announced that it would pay for a transmission overhaul regardless of mileage, GM had not been honoring its promise in many cases, including Rosscoe's. After sending GM a copy of the information on GM's own service bulletin along with the repair bill, Rosscoe received a refund for the cost of repairs with GM's full apology. In his most recent letter to the Center, Rosscoe stated, "Once again I thank you for all your help in supplying the needed information that had to be used, even though it took almost two years to culminate in success."

Occasionally, just the threat of an investigation by a consumer group will bring success. For example, in 1977 the Center for Auto Safety received a disturbing complaint from J. Kaufmann, Jr., of Richfield, Minnesota. His 1976 Kawasaki motorcycle had a severe shaking of the front fork and wheel upon deceleration or when one hand was removed from the handlebars. Kaufmann could not obtain proper service on his motorcycle, which was purchased new from Bloomington Kawasaki, Bloomington, Minnesota. Kaufmann described his attempt to get his bike repaired as follows:

> The service manager at Bloomington Kawasaki where I purchased the bike told me that this problem was due to a factory design defect and it could not be cleared up. [H]e said to me, "You've got a lemon and you'll have to live with it."

Kaufmann wrote Kawasaki for an explanation of the service manager's comment. After four letters to Kawasaki over a ten-month period, he still had no reply. Being a persistent consumer, Kaufmann called ten different Kawasaki offices or agents. A Lincoln, Nebraska, Kawasaki agent told him that the problem with his bike was very common for that model (model no. KZ400D3) and year (1976). Undoubtedly, as a result of his efforts to shake up the Kawasaki bureaucracy, the consumer received a telephone call from Kawasaki of California the day after speaking with Lincoln Kawasaki and learning about the high frequency of this safety problem in 1976 Kawasaki motorcycles. The California office told Kaufmann that the Lincoln office had given him incorrect information and that there was no basis for his claim about a safety hazard in this particular bike.

At that point, Kaufmann wrote the Center, which in turn wrote a letter to the manufacturer. The Center explained the situation to Kawasaki Motors Corp., stating that it was thinking of beginning an investigation into Kawasaki's complaint-handling procedures and possible safety hazards in models like Kaufmann's.

Shortly thereafter, the Center received a letter from Kawasaki Motors Corp. executive Sid Saito. He denied the existence of any safety-related

69

defect on Kaufmann's bike. But, he wrote, because "the product does not meet his [Kaufmann's] general expectations" and "our failure to adequately control the handling of some customer contacts," Kawasaki will agree to repurchase the motorcycle at no cost to him.

Kaufmann responded to the Center:

Regardless of what Kawasaki said wasn't wrong with the bike, there was a very serious problem with that particular vehicle.

In regard to your very kind assistance with my motorcycle problem, I could not be happier about the way it was resolved. Kawasaki did buy back my motorcycle with no questions asked. I would like to say that your strategy in this situation worked just perfectly.

CONSUMER GROUPS

The advantages of having an organized consumer group, as shown above, are many. Of course, a large degree of effort and skill is needed to launch a hard-hitting consumer action group. But examples of successful organizations are numerous, and information on them is available to those who wish to start groups where none exists. Six organizations, described here, illustrate varying approaches to organizing around consumer issues. Further information on these organizations is available in most cases from the organization itself or from the

Center for Auto Safety
1223 Dupont Circle Building
Washington, D.C. 20036

The Center will also consult directly with new and developing consumer groups.

1. The Consumer Federation of America (CFA)
1012 14th Street, N.W.
Washington, D.C. 20005

CFA is a federation of over 200 national, state, and local organizations that have joined together. CFA helps influence public policy as that policy is formulated by Congress, the President, regulatory agencies, the courts, and industry. Established in 1968, "CFA is organized for and dedicated to advancing the consumer viewpoint through its lobbying efforts and its informational and educational services."

CFA is governed by a board of directors elected at its annual meeting. CFA also has thirteen committees, which meet regularly, analyze developments in their areas, and make appropriate recommendations. Each CFA member organization selects one or more delegates to cast its votes at the annual meeting.

Although CFA does not take direct action on auto complaints, the organization is instrumental in supporting the laws and policies that protect the

70

rights of auto consumers, and the efforts by other similar groups. CFA publishes an annual "Directory of State and Local Organizations" (nongovernmental), available for $2.00 from CFA. If you would like information on creating a consumer group, contact CFA's State and Local Organizing Project.

2. Automobile Protection Association (APA)
   292 O. Boul. St. Joseph
   Montreal, Quebec
   Canada H2V 2N7

An imaginative and resourceful group of automobile owners banded together in Quebec to form the Automobile Protection Association, also known as Association pour la Protection des Automobilistes. It is an ombudsmanlike organization handling "everyday grassroots complaints of motorists, while at the same time rewarding industry personnel who are competent and honest." APA takes complaints on auto insurance, auto dealer–consumer problems, gas stations, and auto repair gripes. It develops dossiers to back up charges and confronts industry spokespersons. If complaints or abuses remain unsettled, the offending organization may find itself exposed on the media and picketed at its main office. Says APA President Louis-Phillipe Edmonston: "Without breaking the law, we conduct our own consumer-corporate guerrilla warfare."

One of APA's most notable efforts to date has been the production of a report on abuses in Esso Auto diagnostic clinics, based on requests for diagnosis of the unmarked private cars of prominent public officials. Each clinic tested arrived at a startlingly different list of defects. In one case, a car was diagnosed twice at the same clinic on consecutive days, resulting in dissimilar lists of defects. The report's findings won wide coverage in newspapers and on radio and television. APA issued a press release announcing the election in February 1970 of Canadian Esso (Imperial Oil) as the "most deserving industry" to receive APA's monthly Certificate of Consumer Negligence award.

APA was instrumental in getting the Ford Motor Company of Canada to reopen its rust compensation program for the owners of 1970 to 1973 model cars afflicted with premature rust damage. Ford vehicles manufactured between 1969 and 1973 were rusting one to two years earlier than cars made by Ford's competitors. The rusting was severe and usually resulted in large perforations along the doors, front fenders, hood and rear end. In 1974 a rust compensation program for owners of 1969–73 Ford vehicles was publicized by consumer groups led by the Center for Auto Safety; however, less than 100,000 owners out of twelve million were able to receive compensation as Ford ended the program not long after it was made public.

APA then led a yearlong consumer protest campaign involving boycotts, demonstrations, letters of protest, class action suits, and lengthy direct negotiations, which continued until Ford gave in on September 24, 1976, and reopened the extended warranty program. Until then, Ford owners in Canada (as well as in the U.S.) found the auto company "stonewalling" their rust

71

complaints. Ford had previously refused to admit it had a rusting problem and denied the existence of its secret J-67 warranty extension program for rust repairs. Ford USA has refused to reopen this rust compensation program to benefit its customers in the U.S., where premature corrosion is also a problem.

APA's most recent effort has been the publication of a book titled *Lemon-Aid*. The book provides car ratings for 1971–79 foreign and domestic cars, gives list prices, lists secret warranty extensions for VW, GM, Ford, Chrysler, and Toyota, explains depreciation rates, and lists frequency of repairs and premature rusting for major models.

> 3. Consumers Education and Protective Association (CEPA)
> 6048 Ogontz Avenue
> Philadelphia, Pennsylvania 19141

CEPA is an organization of consumers, started in 1965 by Max Weiner, who is the education director. Through ingenious organizational devices and its achievement of an almost unbroken string of victories over those who would defraud local consumers, CEPA remains a strong and growing organization.

CEPA's strength comes from its organizing philosophy. It will not lend its organizational backing to aid a single victimized consumer until the consumer first joins CEPA or a CEPA branch and participates in the solution of the problems of other members whose problems have come up for action. The CEPA branches in Philadelphia are autonomous strike forces, each covering a separate geographical area.

CEPA has considerable organizational weight to offer. When a branch decides to take action, the plan moves through several stages. CEPA first sends a letter outlining the complaint to the offending auto dealer. (A copy of CEPA's form complaint letter is found in Appendix A.) If the letter does not lead to a solution, the branch organizes a delegation to visit the dealer to propose a solution directly. Failing that, the branch throws an "informational" picketline in front of the dealership premises. A negotiating team accompanies the pickets and if progress is not made in the initial negotiations, the team joins the picketline. The picket continues until an agreement acceptable to CEPA is reached, often within an hour.

The central office of CEPA stores picketing placards on racks for easy access. The office coordinates the picketing schedule of the branches, assists on strategy when a new type of abuse is encountered, and is on hand to take photographs. CEPA pickets focus on educating passersby rather than disrupting business. The central office informs the local police department in advance of each picket. CEPA's wise policy is to obey court injunctions obtained by local merchants in state court against their picketing. CEPA has been very successful, however, in winning in federal court the dissolution of the state court injunctions.

CEPA's successes are innumerable, many of them against auto repair shops, used-car lots, and established automobile dealers. For example, a

72

salesman at Crisconi Oldsmobile in Philadelphia was fired when CEPA pointed out to the owner that the salesman had induced a CEPA member to sign a contract in blank and then had proceeded to add $1,200 in fictitious charges. CEPA also secured a revised contract for the member.

Reports of CEPA's activities, pictures of pickets displaying signs, photocopies of refund checks, and fraudulent or misleading contracts are published regularly in CEPA's monthly newspaper, *Consumers Voice*.

CEPA is now forming a national organization and invites local affiliates.

4. Consumer Action
   26 Seventh Avenue
   San Francisco, California 94103

Consumer Action (CA), described earlier in this chapter, gives this self-portrait:

> At Consumer Action we believe that *every* consumer should stand up for his or her rights whenever the victim of shoddy products or unfair business practices. Yet we understand all too well that a consumer alone can be nearly helpless: consumer laws are poorly enforced; individual consumer losses are often too small to justify the hiring of a lawyer (at $50 an hour); and a complaining consumer must be prepared to outwait a runaround from the merchant that may last one year or more.
>
> Consumer Action exists to even up the odds in the battle for consumer justice in the marketplace. We are a nonprofit, community organization. Formed in 1971, our goal is to help consumers achieve greater control over their lives and a stronger voice in the decisions of government and business that affect us all. We are part of a growing, nationwide movement of consumers who believe that by working together we can correct many of our nation's problems. Consumer Action works through research and publication, and through the Complaint Resolution Committee method of grievance handling.
>
> We are totally dependent for survival on the support of our members, book sales, and foundation grants. Membership in Consumer Action is $10 per year, and includes a subscription to our newsletter, a 20 percent discount on publications, a discount on legal services through a group legal services program, and participation in our Complaint Resolution Committees.

5. Automobile Owners Action Council (AOAC)
   1025 Vermont Ave., N.W.
   Washington, D.C. 20005

AOAC is a nonprofit membership organization which acts on individual members' complaints against auto makers, dealers, repair shops, and insurance companies. The AOAC staff investigates and attempts to resolve each complaint through informal resolution methods, including Dealer Recourse

73

Agreements with local dealers and repair shops. AOAC has conducted seminars to educate consumers on auto consumer protection, mechanics, sales, service, insurance, and safety. This group works closely with local consumer offices and enforcement officials. AOAC was instrumental, along with the Center for Auto Safety, in getting the Chevrolet Motor Division of General Motors to expand its warranty coverage from twelve months or 12,000 miles to five years or 50,000 miles for 1974–75 Vega engines that failed because of overheating caused by defects.

AOAC was founded by Archie G. Richardson, Jr., who is now president of the group. During its first three years, AOAC successfully resolved 3,000 complaints and saved metropolitan Washington, D.C., residents about $185,000.

> 6. CAR Club, Inc.
> 2033 Eastern Avenue
> Baltimore, Maryland 21231

CAR Club (the Coeducational Auto Repair Club) is a membership organization that provides its members with a facility to perform their own mechanical work. Members pay a $10.00 membership fee which entitles them to use the club's facilities for $3.50 an hour. At their disposal are tools, hydraulic lifts, and technical assistance. CAR Club estimates that its 700 members spend fifty percent less to repair and maintain their cars at the club than if they paid professional mechanics to do the work.

> Automobile Club of Missouri
> 201 Progress Parkway
> Maryland Heights, Missouri 63043

While the Automobile Club of Missouri, a chapter of the American Automobile Association (AAA), is not itself a consumer group, this auto club is one of the most innovative auto clubs in the country. The club was one of the first to set up an auto diagnostic inspection center for the use of its members. Now the club has a computerized data bank on defects in various makes and models, plus extensive files on repair practices.

ORGANIZING DIRECT-ACTION CONSUMER GROUPS

If there is no consumer group in your community, organize your own. Consumer groups are valuable tools in resolving car complaints and saving you money. The group can be organized around only one issue, such as Wisconsin's Consumers Organized Against Ford, aimed at resolving piston-scuffing complaints. It can concentrate on many types of auto ripoffs, as AOAC does. Or it can handle everything from auto complaints to problems with furniture, televisions, or health care, as CEPA does. Depending on the purposes of the group, you may or may not need letterhead stationery, legal advice, or a charter. Many helpful guidebooks and organizing manuals exist,

74

including *A Nader Guide for Establishing Local Consumer Auto Complaint Organizations*, to help you work out these details. (See Appendix B for a list of titles and where they can be obtained.)

Consumer action will have more lasting impact and benefit a wider number of consumers if a major share of the effort is put into organizing action groups. Imaginative efforts on your part may solve your own problem, but will do nothing to ensure that you will not run into the same set of problems with your next car.

As mentioned earlier in the chapter, the Consumer Federation of America encourages the creation of local, regional, and state consumer organizations and the continuing success of existing groups. Its State and Local Organizing Project provides background information and support for new and established groups, and acts as a resource clearinghouse on a variety of consumer issues. Contact the Project for more information at:

Consumer Federation of America
1012 14th Street, N.W.
Washington, D.C. 20005

The Center for Auto Safety serves as a clearinghouse for persons and groups developing new consumer tactics and forming new organizations particularly in the areas of highway and mobile-home safety and any aspect of the automobile. Send questions and success stories to us:

Center for Auto Safety
1223 Dupont Circle Building
Washington, D.C. 20036

75

APPENDIX A—Chapter 5

A Model Consumer Organization Complaint Letter

This is the form letter that the CEPA uses to initiate its highly successful campaigns on behalf of consumers. A businessman who does not respond constructively to this letter is likely to find himself picketed. The letter-and-picket program may be used successfully by other consumer groups.

CONSUMERS EDUCATION AND PROTECTIVE ASSOCIATION

_____BRANCH

Date_____

To: Concerning: (Consumers Name)

_____   _____

_____   _____

To Whom It May Concern:

We have been authorized by the above-named member(s) of the Consumers Education and Protective Association (CEPA) to investigate a complaint against your company. The complaint is as follows:

_____

_____

_____

_____

The consumers request is_____

_____

We would appreciate hearing from your company within (3) days regarding your intentions in adjusting this complaint.

Please send reply to: And please send copy to:
                                            CEPA

Name_____   Grievance Department
Address_____   6048 Ogontz Avenue
City_____   Phila., Pa. 19141
Telephone #_____   Tel: 215-424-1441

76

APPENDIX B—CHAPTER 5

Guidebooks and Manuals for Organizing Direct-Action Consumer Groups

Action for a Change: A Student's Manual for Public Interest Organizing by Ralph Nader and Donald Ross (New York: Grossman Publishers, 1971). Available for $1.75 from:

National PIRG Clearinghouse
1129 21st St., N.W.
Washington, D.C. 20036

"A Directory of State and Local Organizations (Nongovernment)" by the State and Local Organizing Project. Available for $2.00 from:

Consumer Federation of America
1012 14th Street, N.W.
Washington, D.C. 20005

For the People: A Consumer Action Handbook by Joanne Manning Anderson, introduction by Ralph Nader (1977). Available for $5.95 from:

Addison-Wesley Publishing Company, Inc.
Reading, Massachusetts 01867

"Forming Consumer Organizations" by the Office of Consumer Affairs of the Executive Office of the President. Available for 35 cents from:

Superintendent of Documents
U.S. Government Printing Office
Washington, D.C. 20402

Fundraising in the Public Interest by David L. Grubb and David R. Zwick (1977). Available for $4.50 from:

Public Citizen, Inc.
Box 19404
Washington, D.C. 20036

"A Guide to Consumer Action" by Helen E. Nelson, Univ. of Wisconsin, HEW Pub. No. (OE) 77-15800. Single copies available free from:

Consumer Information Center
Pueblo, Colorado 81009

"How to Form a Consumer Complaint Group" by the Cleveland Consumer Action Movement. Available for 75 cents from:

Consumer Federation of America
(See above address)

A Nader Guide for Establishing Local Consumer Auto Complaint Organizations, available from:

Center for Auto Safety
1223 Dupont Circle Building
Washington, D.C. 20036

Also reprinted in the *Congressional Record*, Dec. 1, 1971, p. E 12794.

Public Citizen's Action Manual by Donald K. Ross, introduction by Ralph Nader (1973). Available for $1.75 from:

Grossman Publishers
625 Madison Avenue
New York, New York 10022

CHAPTER 6 *Your Legal Rights*

Spartanburg, S.C. 29302
February 20, 1978

Sitton Buick Co., Inc.
Greenville, S.C. 29606
ATTENTION: General Manager

Dear Sir:

I have waited patiently for an extended period of time for repairs to be performed on a new '78 Buick, which I purchased on October 28, 1977. This vehicle has been in your shop for a total of seven weeks—November 21 and 22, '77; December 15, '77 to January 5, '78, and was left again on January 25 and, as of this date, is still there waiting repairs.

It is felt that you have had sufficient time to perform repairs to this new vehicle. Since it has required such a long time to repair this car, it is felt that there must be too many serious problems within the vehicle to correct.

After waiting such a lengthy period of time, my patience has worn thin; therefore, I am requesting at this time that you provide me with a refund for $7,478.00, as outlined in the attached car invoice. If this amount is not refunded to me, legal action will be taken.

Respectfully yours,
/s/
W. S. Anderson

When the manufacturer's complaint-handling procedure does not work, the consumer can often turn to a lawyer for help. As discussed in Chapter 8, it is not always necessary to hire a lawyer to enforce one's legal rights. But, in any event, the consumer would be wise to investigate his or her legal rights. Consumers who know their legal rights are almost always more successful with their complaints than those who do not know their rights. Some legal rights arise from the manufacturer's written warranty. Other rights arise from applicable laws, both federal and state. One important right, freedom of speech, is guaranteed in the U.S. Constitution. This chapter is a primer for consumers on their legal rights.

THE MANUFACTURER'S WARRANTY: OVERVIEW

The written warranty that comes with a new car is a sales tool. The new car warranty "reassures" the buyer that the car is guaranteed against defects within a given time period, usually twelve months or 12,000 miles, whichever comes first.

79

In reality the new-car warranty is designed not so much to protect your interests as to limit the manufacturer's liability. The written warranty does not promise you a working car, does not promise to replace the car if there are serious defects, and does not accept liability for any loss or damage as a result of defects. But the law favors you, and you may be able to get these!

The essential consumer right under the written warranty is that the dealer must replace or repair parts that to the dealer's "reasonable satisfaction" are defective in workmanship or materials. The buyer has certain obligations under the warranty. The principal one is following specified service or maintenance schedules, which can be performed by the dealer or an independent garage or service station. Keep the invoices for such service in order to show that the manufacturer's required maintenance was done.

Beyond this central right, the language of the warranty makes it clear that the manufacturer is limiting its liability. An example is the Chevrolet Motor Division Limited Warranty on new 1980 Chevrolets. The warranty says: "Chevrolet does not authorize any person to create for it any other obligation or liability in connection with these cars." This means that advertising claims or promises which are not in the written warranty made by the dealer's salespeople will not be upheld by the manufacturer.

Beware of spoken explanations of the warranty by the salesperson. What the dealership *says* about the warranty may not count when it comes time for warranty service. Check what is *written* in the manufacturer's warranty. These are your undisputed rights. If the dealership makes claims in an advertisement or gives you a *written* explanation or addition to the manufacturer's warranty, then it is the dealership and not the manufacturer who may be obligated to those additional promises.

The warranty makes clear that "loss of time, inconvenience, loss of use of the vehicle or other matters not specifically included are not covered." If a consumer's car is tied up for three weeks at the dealership for repairs and a rental car costs $300, the manufacturer will not voluntarily pay you back. As we will see later, this and other attempts to limit the manufacturer's warranty liability may be voided or modified by state law.

YOUR WARRANTY RIGHTS

There are other warranties, besides the manufacturers' skimpy written ones, that protect the new-car buyer. The most important of these are *express* warranties and *implied* warranties that arise under state law. These apply to your car both during and after the manufacturer's written warranty period. In addition, certain vehicle components such as parts of the emission-control system may have federal- or state-mandated warranties. Beyond the federal-mandated emission-control warranty, federal and state law may set requirements on how the manufacturers limit or honor their warranties.

In sum, your car may have a total of four warranties: *written* warranties, other *express* warranties, *implied* warranties and *federal-* or *state-mandated* warranties. Warranty problems are often the first and most frustrating problems faced by new-car owners. Knowing that you are protected in the following ways will encourage you, the owner, to enforce your warranty rights.

80

WRITTEN WARRANTIES

All automobile manufacturers provide written warranties with the cars they sell. Most of these warranties are limited to specific parts and expire after a certain period of time and mileage. The average warranty covers major components such as steering, transmission, drive train, and brakes. Some companies limit the warranty on paint defects to the first few days, claiming that such defects in paint, trim, or other appearance items are normally noted and corrected during new-vehicle inspection. The manufacturer suggests that any paint or appearance defects be called to the attention of the dealer without delay, since normal deterioration from use and exposure is not covered by the warranty. (See Appendix for "Warranty Information on 1980 Chevrolet Citation New Cars.") Manufacturers often offer longer warranties on some components, such as the drive train, than on the rest of the car. Tires are frequently warranted by the tire manufacturer under a separate warranty included with the owner information brochures supplied with the vehicle. Many new-car dealers have service agreements with tire manufacturers to handle warranty problems with tires.

In order to regulate written warranties on consumer products, Congress passed the Magnuson-Moss Warranty Act of 1975. The act covers all 1976 and later model year vehicles. The purpose of the act was to make it easier for consumers to get defective cars repaired and total lemons replaced, and to sue successfully the auto companies. According to Federal Trade Commission Chairman Michael Pertschuk, "The act established a rational scheme for warranty disclosures in advertising and marketing, and prevented the use of warranties as a means of decreasing consumers' rights." For detailed information from the Federal Trade Commission on this law, read "Warranties: There Ought to Be a Law . . . There Is," which can be obtained by writing: Consumer Information Center, Pueblo, Colorado 81009.

THE MAGNUSON-MOSS WARRANTY ACT

Although the act has many deficiencies, it does provide new remedies for consumers whose car warranties are not honored and should make it easier for lemon owners to find attorneys to represent them in breach-of-warranty lawsuits. The act includes a "lemon" provision, which in some situations discussed below entitles a lemon owner to his or her choice of a full refund or a new replacement car if the manufacturer or dealer fails to remedy defects after a "reasonable number of attempts" to repair the car.

Under the Magnuson-Moss Act, all *written* warranties must be easy to read and understand. They must be written in ordinary language, not "legalese." Fine print is not allowed. The warranty must disclose the following in simple and readily understood language:

1. *Who* is covered by the written warranty. May only the first buyer enforce it or a subsequent buyer as well?

2. *Which parts* of the car the warranty does and does not cover.

3. *What* the seller or manufacturer will and will not do in the case of a defect or breakdown. At whose expense?

81

Table 1
Sample 1977–78 Warranties

Sample Coverage	General Motors	Ford	Chrysler	AMC*	Volkswagen	Toyota
1. Duration— months/miles, whichever occurs first	12 mos. or 12,000 miles	12 mos. or 12,000 miles	12 mos. or 12,000 miles	12 mos. or 12,000 miles; 24 mos. or 24,000 miles on engine and drive train	12 mos. or 20,000 miles	12 mos. or 12,500 miles
2. Manufacturer will repair, replace, or adjust to correct defects in materials or workmanship	Yes	Yes	Yes	Yes	Yes	Yes
3. Carburetor adjustments	Not for maintenance— only for defects	Original adjustment on a onetime basis; then only for defects	During the first 90 days, without charge, to correct deficiencies	During the first 4 mos. or 4,000 mi. for normal service adjustments	Not for service adjustments —only for defects	Service adjustments required in normal use for 90 days

82

	Warranted by the *tire* manufacturer	Warranted by the *tire* manufacturer	Warranted by the *tire* manufacturer	Warranted by the *tire* manufacturer	Credit will be allowed against the purchase of a new tire	Auto manufacturer will replace defective tire for first 12 mos. or 12,500 miles. Later, prorata basis
4. Tires						
5. Battery— auto or battery manufacturer will repair, replace or adjust through first 12 mos./ 12,000 mi.; then will replace on a prorata basis, through 36 mos.	Yes	Yes	Yes	Auto manufacturer will repair or replace through first 24 mos./24,000 miles	Auto manufacturer will repair or replace through first 12 mos./20,000 miles	Auto manufacturer will repair or replace through first 12 mos./12,500 miles

*AMC gives Full warranty: Includes right to refund or replacement if defects not repaired after "reasonable number of attempts." Also gives you incidental expenses (substitute transportation) if you are without car while waiting for repairs more than a "reasonable time."

83

4. *When* the warranty period begins and ends. How long will the car be covered? Although the written warranty on a new car will invariably read that any implied warranty is good only for the length of the written warranty, this clause is invalid in some states and should be invalid in all. See following section on *disclaimer of warranties* for further information on this.

5. What you must do in order to get the manufacturer to meet its obligations. A *step-by-step* explanation of the procedure which the consumer should follow in order to obtain performance of any warranty obligation. What are your responsibilities under the warranty? Who is authorized to perform warranty work? The selling dealer or any franchised dealer? This information must include the name of the manufacturer and an address or title of a representative responsible for the warranty performance. A toll-free number to use to contact the manufacturer or service person may take the place of an address.

6. If any informal dispute settlement procedures are available through the manufacturer, information about them must be provided.

7. Any limitations or disclaimers on your right to recover consequential or incidental damages—such as the cost of rental cars when your car breaks down. Once again, such conditions are invalid in some states so that you may have a right to collect these damages despite the limitation to the contrary in your car's written warranty. See in this chapter the section "Limitations on Remedies" for the states.

8. The manufacturer's warranty must contain the following statements telling consumers of additional rights beyond what is in the written warranty:

> This warranty gives you specific legal rights, and you may also have other rights which vary from state to state. Some states do not allow limitations on how long an implied warranty will last or the exclusion or limitation of incidental or consequential damages, so the above limitations or exclusions may not apply to you.

If the warranty does not include all of the above information, complain to the dealer and manufacturer. Write to the Federal Trade Commission, Bureau of Consumer Protection, 6th & Pennsylvania Avenue, N.W., Washington, D.C. 20580. Send a copy to the Center for Auto Safety.

"FULL" WARRANTIES

The Magnuson-Moss Act requires all written warranties to be labeled either *full* or *limited* warranties. A full warranty is far better than a limited warranty in imposing specific obligations on the manufacturer and dealer as well as giving consumers specific rights against them.

The label "full" on a warranty means:

1. A defective car or part must be fixed or replaced for free.

2. A defective car or part must be fixed within a reasonable period of time after you complain.

3. A consumer cannot be required to do anything unreasonable to get

84

warranty service, such as taking the car to a dealer 150 miles away.

4. The warranty must cover anyone who owns the car during the warranty period.

5. If the car cannot be or has not been fixed after a reasonable number of attempts, you get a choice of a new replacement car or your money back. This is the so-called lemon provision.

One thing the word *full* does not promise. A full warranty does not have to cover the whole car. It may cover only selected components or systems such as the engine or drive train.

"LIMITED" WARRANTIES

The loophole in the Magnuson-Moss Act is that auto companies are not required to give a full warranty. All other written warranties are limited and do not have to meet the federal standards included in the all-important lemon provision. A warranty must be labeled "limited" if it gives you anything less than what a full warranty gives. A car may have both a full and limited warranty. For example, it can have a full warranty on the engine and a limited warranty on the tires.

Because of this loophole, many consumer groups, members of Congress, and government agencies advocate amending the Magnuson-Moss Act to require all written warranties for new motor vehicles to meet the federal minimum standards for warranty; that is, be full warranties. To avoid a new loophole, the manufacturers should be required to give a written warranty on all new vehicles sold. Otherwise, they may opt out of warranties entirely.

But even the limited warranty gives consumers certain rights. For example, General Motors' 1980 Chevrolet Citation limited warranty gives the new car owner the following rights:

(1) DEFECTS This warranty covers any repairs and needed adjustments to correct defects in material or workmanship.

(2) REPAIRS Your Chevrolet dealer will make the repairs or adjustments, using new or remanufactured parts.

(3) WHICHEVER COMES FIRST This warranty is for 12 months or 12,000 miles, whichever comes first. [The warranty applies to all owners of the car during the warranty period.]

(4) WARRANTY BEGINS The warranty period begins on the date the car is first delivered or put in use.

(5) NO CHARGE Warranty repairs (parts and labor) will be made at no charge. A reasonable time must be allowed after taking the car to the dealer. [This also means that the dealer must make warranty repairs within a reasonable time.]

(6) WARRANTY REPAIR ORDER For your records, the servicing dealer will provide a copy of the Warranty Repair Order listing all warranty repairs performed. [Insist on obtaining a warranty repair order—it is essential for documentation purposes discussed in Chapters 2 and 3.]

(7) WARRANTY SERVICE—U.S. AND CANADA While any Chevrolet

dealer will perform warranty service, we recommend that you return to the [selling] dealer [if possible]. If you are touring or move, visit any Chevrolet dealer in the United States or Canada for warranty service. In the event your car breaks down due to the failure of a warranted part, contact the *nearest* Chevrolet dealer.

Although other sections of this written warranty do limit the extent of the manufacturer's liability to the owner, the owner still gets at least the legal rights outlined above. Everything that the manufacturer promises in its written warranty is *your legal right*; i.e., the manufacturer is legally obligated to carry out the promises it makes.

IMPLIED WARRANTIES

Implied warranties are legal rights created by state law, not by the seller. To the extent they exist, implied warranties create legal rights above and beyond what is in the written warranty. Implied warranties can give consumers the right to get free repair, a replacement, or a refund if the car is defective and does not work in the ordinary way a car is expected, provided the consumer takes the right steps. Thus, state law gives consumers rights which are similar to the rights given to car owners with a full warranty under federal law.

There are two kinds of implied warranties: an implied warranty of *merchantability* and an implied warranty of *fitness for a particular purpose*.

The most common implied warranty is the warranty of merchantability. This means that the car must be fit for the reasonable and ordinary uses of the car, which include safe, efficient, and comfortable transportation from one place to another. If it does not, you have a legal right to get a refund or a replacement.

For example, after having driven seven tenths of a mile from the dealer's showroom, Mrs. Alfred J. Smith's new Chevrolet stalled at a traffic light. It stalled again within another 15 feet and again thereafter each time the vehicle was required to stop. When halfway home, about two and a half miles from the showroom, the car could not be driven in drive gear at all. Mrs. Smith had to drive in low gear at a rate of about five to ten miles per hour. After Mrs. Smith finally arrived home, her husband immediately called the bank to stop payment on his check, and telephoned the dealer to inform him that the sale was canceled. The dealer sent a wrecker to the consumer's home, brought the vehicle in, and replaced the transmission. But Mr. Smith continued to refuse acceptance of the new car. Then the dealer sued Mr. Smith for the purchase price. The court in *Zabriskie Chevrolet* v. *Smith* (240 A.2d 195, 99 N.J. Super. Ct. 441 [1968]) agreed with the consumer that the vehicle was substantially defective; that there was a breach of the implied warranty of merchantability; and upheld the Smiths' refusal to take and pay for the car. Despite this victory, an attorney should always be consulted before stopping a check. As happened in this case, the dealer may sue you for payment on the check.

The other implied warranty, less common, is the warranty of fitness for a particular purpose. This occurs when a consumer buys a vehicle for a

86

particular purpose such as hauling a large trailer. This warranty requires the consumer to inform the salesperson of the special use and the salesperson to state that the particular model car will be good for that kind of use. When the consumer buys that model in reliance on the salesperson's advice, an implied warranty of fitness for a particular purpose is created. If the vehicle cannot then perform the job for which it was bought, the consumer is entitled to refund or replacement.

Implied warranties come automatically with every sale even though they are not in writing or the dealer says nothing about them. For further information on implied warranties, see "Down Easter's Lemon Guide," available from the Bureau of Consumer Protection, Augusta, Maine 04333, for $1.00.

EXPRESS WARRANTIES

The manufacturer's written warranty that comes with a new vehicle is one form of an express warranty. However, there may be other express warranties which are not in writing that can apply to the sale of both a new or a used car by a dealer. Like implied warranties, express warranties are also created by state law and the representations of the manufacturer or dealer about the car.

Under state law, express warranties may be created by the seller (manufacturer or dealer) through oral promises, advertisements, brochures, or other media. Any (1) *affirmation* of fact or (2) *promise* made by the seller, (3) *description*, (4) *sample*, or (5) *model* that becomes part of the "basis of the bargain" creates an *express* warranty that the vehicle will conform to the affirmation, promise, description, sample, or model. No specific intention to make a warranty is necessary if *any* of these factors is made part of the basis of the bargain. Thus, even where the seller does not use a formal word like *warrant* or *guarantee*, an express warranty may still be given. But the seller's statements in which he is "puffing his wares" are not sufficient; that is, an affirmation merely of the *value* of the vehicle (and not of *fact*) or a statement purporting to be merely the seller's opinion or commendation of the vehicle does not create a warranty. For example, the dealer who states that you are getting "a great little car" has not created an express warranty as to the condition of the car. But the dealer who tells you "this car should run without any problems for at least 20,000 miles" has created an express warranty. To best preserve your ability to enforce such an express oral warranty, always ask the dealer to put the warranty in writing.

LIMITATIONS AND DISCLAIMERS OF WARRANTIES

Manufacturers and dealers have always tried to limit their warranty liabilities as much as they can. In the past, manufacturers commonly attempted to disclaim both implied and express warranties. With a disclaimer, the manufacturer would assert that although the law may recognize an implied or an express warranty, the manufacturer would not. Today, the manufacturers can validly limit their warranty obligations, but only if certain requirements are met.

Disclaimer of *Express* Warranties. Despite what the manufacturer's written warranty may say about "other" warranties, state law gives you *express* warranty rights under certain circumstances, as discussed above. If the car does not live up to the claims made by the manufacturer, the consumer can sue for breach of warranty. For example, Steve Lastovich of Hibbing, Minnesota, saw a Ford Motor Company television commercial showing pickup trucks dashing over rough terrain and sailing through the air. He based his purchase of a Ford four-wheel-drive truck on claims made in that commercial. After his truck was badly dented during a rough trip through mud and sand, he sued Ford for the $500 cost of repairs. Lastovich argued that Ford's ads constituted an express warranty on his pickup. Even though Ford stated in its written warranty that "there is no other express warranty on this vehicle," a jury agreed with Lastovich and ordered Ford to pay the $500 in actual damages plus $175 in costs.

Steve Lastovich described the trial in an April 10, 1978, letter to the Center for Auto Safety:

> Mr. [Ken] Peterson [his attorney] gave a very brilliant summation and the judge instructed the jury. The point of law on which their discussion rested was one of "express warranties" as outlined on page 79 of your first "Lemon Book" [Grossman Publishers edition]. Indeed, the jury ruled in effect that brochures I had read, TV ads I had seen, promises made to me by the salesman and impressions I received from demonstrations of similar trucks as mine (on TV) influenced me to purchase the vehicle. By allowing such an excessive amount of flex in their four-wheel-drive truck frames so as to cause damage from box/cab contact, Ford was held liable to make repairs for this damage.

Some cases have held that advertisements may create express warranties even where there was no reliance by the buyer; that is, the consumer did not have to prove he or she actually saw the ad in question, just that it was made in an effort to induce purchases of the car.

Limitations on *Implied* Warranties. Under the Magnuson-Moss Act, if a written warranty is given, then the implied warranties may not be disclaimed. The only limitation of an implied warranty allowed (only in *limited* but not *full* warranties) is a limit on its duration (how long it lasts). The *implied* warranty can be limited in duration only to the duration of the *written* warranty; for example, if you have a one-year written warranty, the implied warranties cannot be limited in duration to less than one year. Such limitation must be "conscionable," which means that it cannot be extremely unfair or harsh. Federal law also requires such limitation to be "set forth in clear and unmistakable language and prominently displayed on the face of the warranty."

Most manufacturers do limit the duration of the *implied* warranties to the duration of the *written* warranty. That means that when the written war-

88

ranty expires after, say, 12,000 miles or twelve months, the implied warranties expire along with it. Since most auto warranties are, in fact, "limited," most consumers will find themselves in this situation.

There is one important requirement on limitations of implied warranties under the Magnuson-Moss Act that may help a consumer who takes his or her lemon case to court: the "unconscionability" argument. Usually an "unconscionable" act is one that is totally unfair or harsh to one party or is done in bad faith. If the court agrees that the consumer, as a new-car buyer, has been "unconscionably" treated by the manufacturer's warranty provisions, it may declare the warranty limitations "unconscionable" and therefore of no validity. Thus, if the dealer refuses to repair a substantial defect that exists after the written warranty has expired, the consumer should claim in court that the manufacturer has breached the implied warranty and any limitation of the implied warranty was "unconscionable."

State law under the Uniform Commercial Code (UCC), which has been adopted by all states except Louisiana, requires that a valid disclaimer of an implied warranty of merchantability must actually mention the word *merchantability*. If the merchantability disclaimer is in writing, which it usually is in the case of auto warranties, it must be conspicuous or visible to the average reader. A valid disclaimer of an implied warranty of *fitness* must be in writing and must be conspicuous. A disclaimer of all implied warranties of fitness is valid if it states, for example, that "there are no warranties which extend beyond the description on the face hereof." But this alone could not validly disclaim the implied warranty of merchantability because it does not mention the word *merchantability*.

A seller can also disclaim the implied warranty of merchantability by simply adding the words "as is" or "with all faults" to the sales contract. Watch out for this tactic when buying a used car (see Chapter 11).

Even where a manufacturer has attempted to limit the duration of an implied warranty, implied warranty rights are still good if you bought the car in a state that does not allow *any* limitations on the duration of implied warranties. These states include Kansas, Maine, Maryland, Massachusetts, Vermont, and West Virginia, which have specifically modified their state statutes or laws so that implied warranties cannot be limited to a specific time period. More states are modifying their laws in this manner, so check with your state attorney general and local consumer group or agency to see whether your state has joined the above list.

LIMITATIONS ON REMEDIES

The manufacturers and dealers try to limit not only their warranty liabilities and obligations, but the consumer's rights to a remedy as well. A remedy is a legal tool a consumer can use for the redress of a complaint. One remedy usually limited by auto manufacturers is the right to incidental or consequential damages—such as hotel bills when your car breaks down.

State law (the Uniform Commercial Code) protects the consumer from "unconscionable" limitations or exclusions on consequential damages. The UCC, sec. 2-719, provides that a "limitation of consequential damages for injury to the person in the case of consumer goods is prima facie unconscionable, but limitation of damages where the loss is commercial is not." Thus, if a consumer loses a week's pay because the defective car is being repaired, the manufacturer may be able to avoid liability if consequential damages had been excluded.

Where the manufacturer has attempted to limit unreasonably a consumer's legal remedies, the Uniform Commercial Code again comes in to aid the consumer: "Where circumstances cause an exclusive or limited remedy to fail of its essential purpose, remedy may be had as provided in this act" (sec. 2-719).

For example, one consumer revoked acceptance of his new Saab after the car kept stalling and was plagued by a series of annoying minor defects. He had been properly following the manufacturer's remedy, which provided that the dealer would repair the car under warranty for such defects. But the repeated stalling, which began five months after purchase, was never remedied, despite several attempted repairs by the dealer. Also, a defective muffler, a recurrent rattle under the dashboard, and the repeated malfunctioning of the seatbelt warning buzzer were never repaired properly. When the consumer revoked acceptance, the manufacturer argued in part that the warranty limits a purchaser's remedies to repair or replacement of defective parts, and nothing more.

When the consumer sued in this case, the Supreme Court of Minnesota, in *Durfee* v. *Rod Baxter Imports* (262 N.W.2d 349 [1977]), held that revocation of acceptance and cancellation of the contract were a remedy available to the purchaser. The lower court had found that the Saab "apparently could not, or would not, be placed in reasonably good operating condition" by the distributor or its agents or dealers. The Minnesota Supreme Court stated:

> An exclusive remedy fails of its essential purpose if circumstances arise to deprive the limiting clause of its meaning or one party of the substantial value of its bargain. So long as the seller repairs the goods each time a defect arises, a repair-and-replacement clause does not fail of its essential purpose. If repairs are not successfully undertaken within a reasonable time, the buyer may be deprived of the benefits of the exclusive remedy. Commendable efforts and considerable expense alone do not relieve a seller of his obligation to repair.

The right to incidental or consequential damages cannot be limited in those states that have all modified their laws to invalidate any limitation on a consumer's legal remedies. The laws of Kansas, Maine, Maryland, Massachusetts, Vermont, and West Virginia thus make it easier for consumers to exercise this right. Consumers from the remaining states should use other legal arguments, such as those used in the *Durfee* case, to exert their rights.

90

FEDERAL- OR STATE-MANDATED WARRANTIES

Certain components of the car such as parts of the emission-control system may have federal- or state-mandated warranties. For example, section 207(a) of the Clean Air Act requires the auto manufacturers to warrant for the first five years or 50,000 miles that vehicle emission-control systems be free from defects in materials and workmanship which cause the vehicle to exceed the emissions standards. Section 207(b) requires the manufacturer to warrant any component that causes the vehicle to fail an emission test during the first 24,000 miles and any major component such as the catalyst for 50,000 miles. This warranty helps attain clean air while it protects the consumer's pocketbook.

This emissions warranty appears on the manufacturer's written warranty because of Clean Air Act requirements. For example, General Motors' 1980 limited warranty gives the Chevrolet car owner the following rights: the Chevrolet Division warrants that the vehicle (1) was designed, built, and equipped so as to meet the U.S. Environmental Protection Agency's regulations at the time of sale, and (2) is not defective so as to meet the EPA's regulations during the first 50,000 miles or five years of use, whichever occurs first.

Although the warranty is federally created, the manufacturer is responsible for repairing cars that violate the warranty, not the federal government. A recent case illustrates how the emissions-control warranty can work for the consumer. The EPA investigated certain 1972–73 models of Toyota vehicles when it suspected that those models had a valve-burning problem. EPA was concerned that such valve burning would lead to excessive emissions in those vehicles. EPA found that the problem did exist in certain models containing valves built with material which could not withstand the heat produced by the engine. Toyota then agreed not only to repair the affected vehicles without charge to owners for five years or 50,000 miles, whichever occurs first, but also to reimburse consumers who had already paid to have the valves repaired.

The Clean Air Act makes it a crime for any manufacturer or dealer to refuse to honor a valid emission-control warranty claim. So if either the dealer or the manufacturer refuses to make a warranty repair on the emission-control system, remind him that there is a potential fine of $10,000 and then inform the Environmental Protection Agency, Mobile Source Enforcement Division, Washington, D.C. 20460, of the violation.

HOW TO ENFORCE YOUR WARRANTY RIGHTS

When a car is defective and needs repair, begin with the manufacturer's complaint-handling procedures, described in Chapter 3. If something goes wrong with the car, you usually must give the dealer a "reasonable" number of chances to repair it.

In most cases, where the defect has not caused major damage, the dealer

91

will be allowed to repair or replace the defective part. This is where the written service records discussed in Chapter 3 prove invaluable. They will show that the dealer had many opportunities to "cure" (repair) the defect. After the dealer does not or cannot repair the car and the manufacturer refuses to make good on the warranty, you have a right to demand a replacement or your money back if the defect is one that "substantially impairs" the value of the car. In some cases, especially where the defect has damaged the car or where the car is nearly new, the buyer may be able to return the car without giving the dealer a chance to fix the defect.

For example, in *Zabriskie Chevrolet* v. *Smith*, discussed above, the court permitted return of the car and refund of the purchaser's payment without allowing the dealer and manufacturer an opportunity to repair the defects. The court rejected offers made by the dealer to cure the defect under the manufacturer's warranty. The court stated that the attempted cure, a substituted transmission, was "ineffective," because it would not conform to what Mr. Smith had ordered. The court said:

> For a majority of people, the purchase of a new car is a major investment, rationalized by the peace of mind that flows from its dependability and safety. *Once their faith is shaken*, the vehicle loses not only real value in their eyes, but becomes an instrument whose integrity is substantially impaired and whose operation is fraught with apprehension. The attempted cure in the present case was ineffective. [Emphasis added]

"TOTAL LEMON" STRATEGIES

If you are stuck with a lemon, a lawyer may help. Usually legal action is necessary to obtain a refund of the purchase price or a replacement car, since the dealer and manufacturer will almost invariably refuse to take back the car.

Lemon owners who want to get rid of their lemons can follow two general routes. One is to trade the car in and then sue the dealer and manufacturer for damages arising out of the resale of the lemon. The other strategy is to revoke acceptance of the car, return it to the dealer or manufacturer, and sue for a refund or a replacement. A related strategy, "rejection," applies to cases where something major goes wrong during the first few miles, and is sometimes called the "shaken-faith" doctrine. As in *Zabriskie*, where the car broke down only a few minutes after leaving the dealership, the consumer should "reject" the car immediately. (See Chapter 11 for more on "rejection.")

REVOCATION OF ACCEPTANCE

Revocation of acceptance is usually the key to getting a refund or replacement of a lemon. The legal procedures for revocation of acceptance must be carefully followed. Acceptance must be revoked within a reasonable time after

92

the defect is discovered and usually after the dealer has had reasonable opportunity to fix the car. Of course, there are exceptions (see *Tiger Motor* below, where the consumer revoked acceptance on a one-year-old lemon). A "reasonable time" is usually within ninety days after delivery. After returning the car, confirm with the dealer *in writing* that you are revoking acceptance of the car. Certified mail with return receipt requested helps prove that you gave such notice.

To revoke acceptance, deliver the car and the keys to the dealer. Take off the license plates. Do not remove original equipment (factory- or dealer-installed) from the car, like the radio. The car must be returned without "substantial change." Normal wear and tear is no problem. Give the dealer something *in writing* at that time notifying him of your intention to revoke acceptance, listing the specific reasons you are returning the car and stating that you are also canceling your insurance and registration. Note the odometer reading at this time. A substantial increase in mileage on the odometer is evidence that the dealer accepted your revocation of acceptance—that he no longer deemed you the owner of the car.

Some consumers have used revocation of acceptance successfully, without hiring an attorney. If the dealer or manufacturer is close to taking the lemon back, this device may help. However, if the dealer does not respond favorably, tell him that you will be retaining a lawyer to pursue your complaint. Often hiring an attorney and filing a lawsuit are necessary in order to revoke acceptance successfully; that is, receiving the return of the purchase price or a new car.

In *Tiger Motor Co.* v. *McMurtry* (224 So. 2d 638 [Ala. 1969]), Thomas McMurtry had returned his new Ford stationwagon to the dealer for repairs on at least thirty occasions. The Ford remained in the custody of Tiger for repairs during a one-year period for about fifty days. Yet Tiger failed to remedy all the defects. The new car was using so much oil that McMurtry was forced to purchase it by the case. The car got approximately eight miles per gallon, and required a new fuel pump, new carburetor, new piston rings, and a new engine block. Thereafter, the auto continued to skip or misfire and to use oil by the case.

After McMurtry had enough of this lemon, he decided to revoke acceptance. He returned the one-year-old stationwagon to the dealer, removed the plates, and canceled his insurance. Then he sued the dealer for a refund of the down payment, the value of his trade-in, and all of his monthly payments. He won. The Alabama court ruled in the consumer's favor, finding a "substantial impairment of value" to McMurtry of the lemon car. Even though McMurtry waited a year before revoking acceptance, the court held that revocation was made within a "reasonable time":

> We think the evidence supports the conclusion that Tiger Motor Company warranted that it would remedy all defects for the first 24,000 miles, or 24 months after purchase, whichever comes first. In the instant case, the buyer was in almost constant touch with seller concerning the condition of the vehicle. Repeated attempts at adjustment having failed,

93

we hold the buyer revoked his acceptance of the auto within a reasonable time.

For further information and examples on revocation of acceptance, see the "Down Easter's Lemon Guide."

Consult a lawyer if you have decided to return the car to the dealer. Revocation of acceptance is to be used as a last resort—only when you never want to see your car again. This procedure is often the first step in a lawsuit, since you may have to sue to get your money back, as in *Tiger* v. *McMurtry.* Many consumers have been successful in using this strategy.

Another consumer who revoked acceptance was Angelo Asciolla of Tilton, New Hampshire, whose new 1973 Oldsmobile Delta 88 was a lemon. The day after he picked up his car, Asciolla and his wife drove to Wisconsin to visit their daughter. With only 1,390 miles on the odometer, the car broke down. The car had rust in the brakes, drive shaft, exhaust pipe, and underbody, ice in the transmission, and water in the trunk within one month of purchase. Asciolla was told that the car appeared to have been flooded or submerged. Upon finding this out, the lemon owner immediately informed the dealer that he was not satisfied with the car and wanted it exchanged for a new one. The dealer refused to supply a new vehicle, but offered either to install a new transmission with a twelve-month warranty or to extend the present warranties twelve months from the date of repairs. The dealer maintained that the car had never been flooded.

Asciolla's attorney, Willard G. Martin, Jr., filed suit against the dealer and General Motors Corporation. Martin contended that Asciolla's immediate notification of his dissatisfaction to the dealer upon discovery of defects constituted a "revocation of his acceptance" of the automobile under applicable state law. The New Hampshire Supreme Court, in a unanimous decision, overturned a lower-court ruling. The supreme court found that the buyer was entitled to revoke hs acceptance and receive a new car. The court ordered GM to pay Asciolla $6,148 in legal and storage costs and $100 for every day's delay in delivering a new 1978 Oldsmobile Delta 88.

In *Asciolla* v. *Manter Oldsmobile-Pontiac* (370 A. 2d 270 [N.H. 1977]), Justice Charles Douglas cited the *Zabriskie Chevrolet* case:

> The purchaser of a major consumer item such as an automobile may revoke his acceptance of a product when it possesses a defect which, in view of the particular needs and circumstances of the buyer, substantially impairs the value of the item to him. . . . The buyer assumed what every new-car buyer has a right to assume and, indeed, has been led to assume by the high-powered advertising techniques of the auto industry—that his new car, with the exception of very minor adjustments, would be mechanically new and factory-furnished, operate perfectly, and be free of substantial defects.

This case also illustrates an exception, adopted by a growing number of jurisdictions, to the general rule that a car buyer must return the car to the

94

dealership in order to revoke acceptance. Here, Asciolla kept the car in his garage after informing the dealer that he was not satisfied with the car and wanted it exchanged for a new one. The consumer's notification of his dissatisfaction to the dealer immediately upon discovery of the defects coupled with placing the car in the garage (that is, not driving the car) was enough.

WITHHOLDING PAYMENTS

In some cases, it may be easier to withhold payments on the car, rather than to revoke acceptance. For example, the car is not a total lemon and probably can be fixed, but the dealer has been giving you the runaround. Stopping payments may be a good incentive to get the dealer finally to repair the defects. It may help to take the car to an independent mechanic to verify that the defects can indeed be fixed and that the car is worth keeping. Show the dealer the independent mechanic's diagnosis before stopping payments to bolster your case. Consult a lawyer before withholding payments. If you do stop paying, the bank will probably *sue you* for the balance on the loan. Thus, the decision to stop paying should be made with a lawyer's advice. Stopping payments is a last resort; it is not something you do every time a small problem occurs.

Where acceptance is revoked, payments may be able to be withheld. If you financed the car through the dealer, contact the bank or finance company where you are making payments. Inform it that you have revoked ownership of the car and that you will not be making further payments. Tell it the dealer is responsible for the note since the car is back at the dealership. In some instances, the dealer will then take the loan back from the bank, leaving the dispute between you and the dealer.

You cannot withhold payments if you obtained the loan *directly* at a lending institution without the dealer's assistance. If acceptance is revoked, tell the institution what has happened, but continue to make payments on the car. In the first instance, where you financed the car through the dealer, you are legally protected if the dealer or bank sues you for the balance. In the second case, where you got your loan *directly* from a bank or a credit union, you are not legally protected if the bank or credit union sues for the balance.

HOLDER-IN-DUE-COURSE RULE

Car loans have traditionally been governed by the "holder-in-due-course" legal doctrine, which effectively required consumers to continue car payments on even the world's worst lemon. A new rule issued by the Federal Trade Commission (FTC) substantially improves the consumer's position by permitting the consumer who stops making payments to prove that the car is a lemon. The original rule allowed a bank that had repossessed a car to collect on the balance of the loan after deducting the value of the car when a buyer stopped making payments because the car was defective. If the bank sues to collect on the loan balance, the car buyer now has a "lemon" defense in court.

This new legal protection began on May 14, 1976, the effective date of the FTC regulation on the Preservation of Consumers' Claims and Defenses. The FTC rule is commonly called the holder-in-due-course rule. Where the dealer arranges the loan for the consumer on a car that is a lemon, the FTC rule protects the consumer who stops making payments.

The FTC rule protecting the withholding of payments does not protect the consumer who got a loan *directly* from a bank or a credit union. It applies only to loans that fall into certain categories. These include where the dealer "refers" buyers to a lender *or* the dealer is "affiliated" with the lender, or creditor. "Affiliation" may be created by "contract" or "business arrangement." The arrangement need not be formal in any legal sense, but it must be ongoing and clearly related to the dealer's sales and sales financing. "Referral" means that the dealer cooperates with a lender to channel consumers to that credit source on a continuing basis. Unlike an "affiliation," a referral relationship arises from a pattern of cooperative activity between the dealer and the lender, directly relating to the arranging of credit. The fact that a dealer suggests credit sources or offers information to his customers does not alone invoke the FTC rule.

The FTC rule requires dealers, among other sellers, to include this notice in all installment-sales contracts and loans they handle for consumers:

NOTICE

ANY HOLDER OF THIS CONSUMER CREDIT CONTRACT IS SUBJECT TO ALL CLAIMS AND DEFENSES WHICH THE DEBTOR COULD ASSERT AGAINST THE SELLER OF GOODS OR SERVICES OBTAINED [PURSUANT HERETO OR] WITH THE PROCEEDS HEREOF. RECOVERY HEREUNDER BY THE DEBTOR SHALL BE LIMITED TO AMOUNTS PAID BY THE DEBTOR HEREUNDER.

This means that consumers can legally invoke the lemon defense against the bank as if the bank had been the selling dealer. Where the rule applies, the buyer's right to stop making payments on defective goods is protected. (For more information on the holder-in-due-course rule, see "New Rights When You 'Buy on Time,'" *Consumer Reports*, May 1976.)

PURSUING A STATE BOND

Some states require automobile dealers to post bonds to make sure they keep the promises made to new-car buyers in guarantees and warranties. Check with the state attorney general's office to determine whether your state is one. A lawyer can assist in securing your rights under the bonding arrangement. Maryland, for instance, requires under a 1970 law that dealers post a $100,000 bond to ensure that they will hold to promises made by salespeople and in warranties to new-car buyers. The law in Maryland also increased the personal bond for the dealer himself from $5,000 to $10,000 in hopes of giving motorists greater protection.

Because of the bonding requirement in Maryland, many consumers in that state have successfully collected money from dealers' bonding compa-

96

nies. These claims have involved situations where consumers had unknowingly purchased stolen vehicles from dealers, or where consumers purchased vehicles from dealers but could not obtain a good title from the dealer. Lemon owners in states with bonding laws should try to collect money from the dealers' bonding company or the manufacturers' bonding company, if one exists.

CLASS ACTIONS

In some situations a class action suit may be the best approach to solving a consumer complaint. In essence, a class action is nothing more than a group of individuals who bring a lawsuit against a manufacturer, thus reducing each individual's fee by sharing the costs of hiring an attorney. For instance, a class action may be filed on behalf of all purchasers of the manufacturer's product who suffered in the same way because of a defect in the product.

Thus, the manufacturer is faced not with a few individual claims, in small amounts, from the few persons concerned enough to see a lawyer and bring an action, but with one gigantic claim representing the total amount lost by each and every victim. The class suit or class action is potentially one of the most far-reaching devices, legal or nonlegal, available to consumers.

The advantages of the class suit are:

1. Lawyers in class suits receive a percentage of the total recovery and with the stakes so high, the most able and aggressive attorneys will be attracted to the consumer side.
2. Public notice accorded the suit will very likely bring to light injured parties who might not otherwise ever have known of the opportunity for recovery.
3. Manufacturers will be made to assume full financial responsibility for their mistakes, instead of meeting the demands of occasional single consumers pressing only their individual claims.
4. Manufacturer responsibility will place manufacturers under much needed pressure to build more safety and reliability into their products before marketing them.

When consumers win a class suit, the defendant must pay the total judgment (often a large amount) to the court; individual members of the class then file their own claims for their share of the recovery. Class suits are becoming a rallying point of the consumer movement. New York City, for instance, recently passed a law enabling the city to file class suits for defrauded groups of consumers. Its potential is suggested by the ferocity with which it is opposed by business interests.

The Magnuson-Moss Warranty Act provides for a class action where 100 or more named plaintiffs have claims totaling at least $50,000 (exclusive of interest and costs). The act also provides for awards of attorney fees from the losing manufacturer.

The class action provision makes it paramount for consumers with similar defects to band together in order to get the 100 named plaintiffs. Consumers can report their cars' defects to the Department of Transportation and the Center for Auto Safety so that common defects can be found. Consumers can ask the department to search its computerized file of defects.

JOINT SUITS

Where there are not enough consumers for a class action, individuals with similarly defective cars can hire an attorney together. Where one or two people cannot afford a lawyer, four or more might be able to afford one. See Chapter 9 for examples of consumers placing ads in newspapers to find other unhappy owners of the same make and model lemon.

Under the Magnuson-Moss Act, such groups of individuals may still get into federal court if the total damages incurred by the group because of a common injury is $50,000 or greater. This joint Magnuson-Moss action is more attractive to private attorneys because the act specifically provides that attorney fees and court costs may be awarded to successful plaintiffs.

A highly successful example of a joint suit occurred when thirty-nine owners of prematurely rusting Fords obtained a $27,500 out-of-court settlement against Ford Motor Company. Michael Berke of Oak Park, Michigan, filed suit in April 1975 when his 1971 Pinto rusted out after two years. Berke sued for $1.2 billion on behalf of himself and the owners of two million Ford cars manufactured between 1970 and 1972. The consumer contended that Fords were rusting prematurely and that it cost about $700 a car for rust repair or loss of market value. Thirty-eight other owners were named plaintiffs for the class action. When the court refused to certify the case as a class action, the thirty-nine plaintiffs converted the case to a joint suit and eventually settled for over $700 each.

LAWSUITS: WHOM TO SUE

Although new-car purchasers come into contact with only the dealer, most lemon problems involve the manufacturers, and there is no reason not to sue them. In fact, there are strong reasons to make sure the manufacturer is included in any suit. The manufacturer, obviously, would be able to pay larger damage awards than most dealers could pay. Historically, manufacturers placed dealers between themselves and their retail customers to insulate themselves from liability. Now, statutes and court decisions in many states have destroyed the vestiges of this device, and manufacturers can and should be brought to shoulder their full liability.

Moreover, it is important that owners bringing lawsuits avoid being blinded by the smokescreen often thrown up by the manufacturers that the dealer is an independent businessman instead of an agent of the manufacturer. Despite the passage by Congress in 1956 of the Dealers Day in Court Act, which helped eliminate the most flagrant practices by which manufacturers maintained an iron grip on dealers, the manufacturers still manage to exert a subtle but pervasive control over most dealership policies. This control is achieved by means of requirements for detailed financial reporting, loans and

98

subsidies to dealers in financial difficulties, and rewards (for achieving sales goals and so forth), or by reducing the dealer's quota of hot-selling car models, forcing him to achieve his agreed-upon overall sales quota by pushing the slower-moving models. If a dealer fails to meet his prescribed annual sales volume, he may face the ultimate form of control—a threat of, or an actual, cancellation of his franchise.

CHANGE THE LAW!

Unfortunately, the Magnuson-Moss Warranty Act and many state laws do not adequately cover some of the problems you may have. There are no special protections in warranty law for owners of automobiles, even though automobiles are the number one complaint on almost every list, and their problems push many consumers to the very edge of their financial resources. At present, the law treats automobiles the same way it treats most other consumer products, such as a toaster or a radio. According to FTC Chairman Michael Pertschuk:

> Warranty problems are often the first difficulty a new-car buyer experiences. Often they are the most frustrating.
>
> People buy new cars with reasonable expectations of quality and durability. Manufacturers offer warranties to assure consumers that their cars are well designed and built. They promise to remedy defects that become apparent in the first part of the car's life. But too often these assurances of quality and promises are not met, and consumers suffer the loss. Congress was aware of warranty performance and Magnuson-Moss offered two possible remedies. . . . Unfortunately, in the case of autos, it now appears that these remedies are neither solving the problems nor lessening their severity.

If you feel that this should be changed, write to your United States senators and representatives and to the following committee chairmen:

The Honorable Howard W. Cannon, Chairman
Committee on Commerce, Science, and Transportation
U.S. Senate
Washington, D.C. 20510

The Honorable Wendell H. Ford, Chairman
Consumer Subcommittee
Committee on Commerce, Science, and Transportation
U.S. Senate
Washington, D.C. 20510

The Honorable Harley O. Staggers, Chairman
Committee on Interstate and Foreign Commerce
U.S. House of Representatives
Washington, D.C. 20515

99

The Honorable James Scheuer, Chairman
Subcommittee on Consumer Protection and Finance
Committee on Interstate and Foreign Commerce
U.S. House of Representatives
Washington, D.C. 20515

Send copies of your letters to your own representative and senators in Washington; the Federal Trade Commission, Bureau of Consumer Affairs, Washington, D.C. 20580; your representative in state government; and your state attorney general's office.

"APPENDIX —— CHAPTER 6

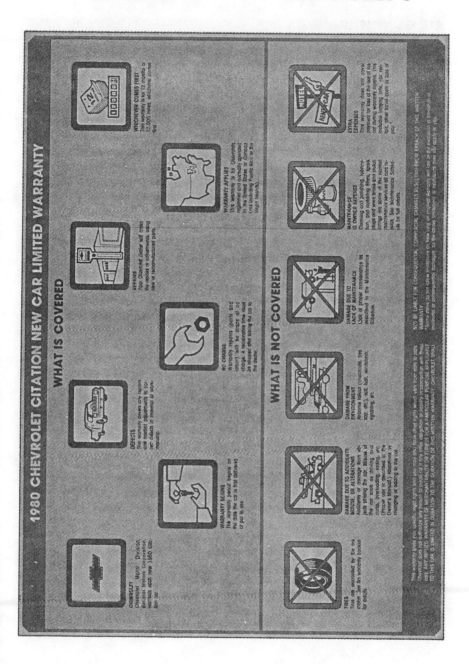

101

WHAT TO DO IF THERE IS A QUESTION REGARDING WARRANTY

The satisfaction and goodwill of owners are of primary concern to Chevrolet dealers and Chevrolet Motor Division. In the event a warranty matter is not handled to your satisfaction, the following steps are suggested:

1. Discuss the problem with your Chevrolet dealership management.

2. Contact the Chevrolet Zone Office (General Motors Zone Office in Canada) closest to you as listed in the Chevrolet Owner's Manual.

3. Contact the Consumer Relations Representative, Chevrolet Motor Division, General Motors Corporation, Detroit, Michigan 48202. (In Canada contact the Customer Service Representative at General Motors of Canada Limited, Oshawa Ontario.)

THINGS YOU SHOULD KNOW ABOUT THE CHEVROLET NEW CAR WARRANTY

General
It is our intent to repair, under the warranty, without charge, anything that goes wrong during the warranty period that is our fault. This includes replacing service supplies, such as oils, coolant and refrigerant when needed in making these repairs.

Please note the distinction between "defects" and "damage" as used in the warranty. Defects are covered because we, the manufacturer, are responsible. On the other hand, we have no control over damage caused by such things as collision, misuse and lack of maintenance which occurs after the car is delivered to you. Therefore damage for any reason which occurs after the car is delivered to you is not covered under the warranty.

Maintenance services also are excluded from the warranty because it is the owner's responsibility to maintain his/her own vehicle in accordance with the Maintenance Schedule provided.

Adjustments
The term "adjustment" as used in the warranty, refers to minor repairs not usually associated with the replacement of parts. The warranty covers adjustments necessary to correct defects. For instance, if a part should become loose or misaligned in normal service, it will be corrected without charge anytime within the full term of the warranty.

Warranty Service — U.S. and Canada
While any Chevrolet dealer will perform warranty service, we recommend that you return to the dealer who sold you your car because of that continued and personal interest in you. However, if you are on a move, visit any Chevrolet dealer in the United States or Canada for warranty service. In the event your car breaks down due to the failure of a warranted part, contact the nearest Chevrolet dealer.

Warranty Service — Foreign Countries
Where General Motors dealer service is not available in the country in which you are touring and warranty repairs are needed, obtain paid receipts covering the work form the service station that performed it. Upon your return home, a statement of the circumstances relative to the work performed along with the paid receipts, should be given to your dealer for reimbursement consideration.

Sheet Metal, Paint and Other Appearance Items
Defects or damage to sheet metal, paint, trim or other appearance items may occur at the factory during assembly or while the car is being shipped to the dealer. Normally, any factory defect or damage is detected and corrected at the factory during the inspection process. In addition, Chevrolet dealers are obligated to inspect each car for any uncorrected factory defects or damage and any transit damage which they detect before the car is delivered to you.

Sheet metal, paint or appearance defects still present at the time the car is delivered to you are covered by the warranty. For your protection we suggest that if you do find any such defects, you advise your dealer without delay, as normal deterioration due to use and exposure is not covered by the warranty.

Air Conditioning
Because of the seasonal use of air conditioning, the sealed refrigerant portion of the air conditioning system installed in your car as original equipment by Chevrolet is covered under the warranty for 12 months, regardless of mileage.

Warranty Repair Order
For your records, the servicing dealer will provide a copy of the Warranty Repair Order listing all warranty repairs performed.

Production Changes
Chevrolet and its dealers reserve the right to make changes in cars built and/or sold by them at any time without incurring any obligation to make the same or similar changes on cars previously built and/or sold by them.

DELCO BATTERY LIMITED WARRANTY

If your battery should fail under normal service due to a defect in material or workmanship after the New Car Warranty expires, but before the car has been in use 36 months, it can be replaced on a pro rata adjustment basis for a new Delco battery. The pro rata adjustment price of the new battery will be based on the number of months the original battery was in use since the start of the New Car Warranty. Contact an authorized Chevrolet or Delco Battery dealer for further details on such adjustments.

These adjustments do not apply (A) to failure in service due to abuse, accident or freezing, or (B) to recharging costs or for the use of a rental battery.

This warranty gives you specific legal rights and you may also have other rights which vary from state to state.

TIRE INFORMATION

Tires are warranted by the tire manufacturer under a separate warranty included with the owner literature supplied with your car. Any Chevrolet dealer will assist you in requesting an adjustment if this becomes necessary.

CUT ON THIS LINE

1980 DELCO BATTERY SERVICE ADJUSTMENT CERTIFICATE

Vehicle Identification No. _____
Date of Vehicle Delivery _____
(Service Date If Applicable)

Chevrolet Dealer Name and Code (5 digits) _____

Delco Dealer Name _____ or _____

Battery Catalog No. _____ Mileage _____

Replacement Date _____ No. Mos. In Service _____

Charge to Owner for New Battery _____
(No charge if replaced within the 12-month, 12,000-mile coverage of the Chevrolet New Car Warranty)

1980 DELCO BATTERY SERVICE ADJUSTMENT CERTIFICATE

WARRANTY INFORMATION ON 1980 CHEVROLET CITATION NEW CARS

CHEVROLET

Owner's Name

Street Address

City and State

Vehicle Identification No.

Date of Delivery to First Retail Purchaser (Service Date if Applicable)

Vehicle Mileage at Time of Such Delivery

IMPORTANT

This letter gives the starting date and mileage of your warranties. Keep it with your car and make it available to a Chevrolet dealer if warranty work is required. It should remain with your car when you sell it so future owners will know of any remaining warranty coverage.

Part No. 422088

1980 CHEVROLET CITATION EMISSION CONTROL SYSTEMS WARRANTY

Chevrolet (Chevrolet Division General Motors Corporation) warrants to owners of 1980 Chevrolet Citation passenger cars that the car (1) was designed, built and equipped so as to conform at the time of sale with applicable regulations of the U.S. Federal Environmental Protection Agency, and (2) is free from defects in materials and workmanship which cause the car to fail to conform with applicable Federal

Environmental Protection Agency regulations for a period of use of 50,000 miles or 5 years, whichever occurs first.

The 5-year/50,000-mile warranty period shall begin on the date the car is delivered to the first retail purchaser or, if the car is first placed in service as a demonstrator or company car prior to sale at retail, on the date the car is first placed in such service.

WHAT IS COVERED

Listed below are components affecting emissions of your Chevrolet Citation, if so equipped:

* Carburetor and Choke Controls
* C-4 Computer Controlled Catalytic Converter System
* Spark Plugs, Boots and Wires
* Distributor and Associated Controls
* Air Injection Reactor (AIR) Pump, Air Distributor and Valves
* Pulse Air System
* Exhaust Gas Recirculation (EGR) Valve and Associated Controls
* Early Fuel Evaporation (EFE) Valve and Associated Controls
* Positive Crankcase Ventilation (PCV) Valve, Filter and Hoses
* Catalytic Converter and Catalyst
* Evaporative Emission Control Carbon Canister, Filter, Hoses and Associated Controls
* Fuel Tank Filler Cap and Vapor Control Valves
* Thermostatic Air Cleaner Control Valve and Air Cleaner Element

WHAT IS NOT COVERED

THE WARRANTY OBLIGATIONS DO NOT APPLY TO:

* Conditions resulting from misuse, improper adjustment, dirty fuel, alteration, accident, failure to use recommended fuel or not performing maintenance service.

* The replacement of maintenance parts (such as spark plugs, PCV valve, filters, hoses and belts) used in required maintenance services.

* Loss of time, inconvenience, loss of use of the car or other consequential damages.

* Any car on which odometer mileage has been changed so that mileage cannot be readily determined.

Chevrolet does not authorize any person to create for it any other obligations or liability in connection with these systems. This warranty is in addition to the 1980 Chevrolet Citation New Car Warranty.

RECOMMENDATIONS FOR MAINTENANCE SERVICE REPLACEMENT PARTS

The emission control systems of your new 1980 Chevrolet Citation passenger car were designed, built and tested using genuine GM parts, and the car is certified as being in conformity with federal regulations implementing the Clean Air Act. Accordingly, it is recommended that any replacement parts used for maintenance or for the repair of emission control systems be new, genuine GM parts.

THE WARRANTY OBLIGATIONS ARE NOT DEPENDENT UPON THE USE OF ANY PARTICULAR BRAND OF REPLACEMENT PARTS. THE OWNER MAY ELECT TO USE NON-GENUINE GM PARTS FOR REPLACEMENT PURPOSES. USE OF REPLACEMENT PARTS WHICH ARE NOT OF EQUIVALENT QUALITY MAY IMPAIR THE EFFECTIVENESS OF EMISSION CONTROL SYSTEMS.

MAINTENANCE SERVICE CAN BE PERFORMED BY ANY QUALIFIED SERVICE OUTLET; HOWEVER, WARRANTY SERVICE MUST BE PERFORMED BY AN AUTHORIZED

CHEVROLET DEALER. Receipts covering the performance of regular maintenance should be retained in the event questions arise concerning maintenance. These receipts should be transferred to each subsequent owner of this car.

If other than new genuine GM parts are used for maintenance replacements or for the repair of components affecting emission control, the owner should assure himself/herself that such parts are warranted by their manufacturer to be equivalent to genuine General Motors parts in performance and durability.

*"GENUINE GM PARTS" when used in connection with Chevrolet vehicles are those parts manufactured by or for Chevrolet, designed for use in these vehicles and distributed by Chevrolet Motor Division or any division or subsidiary of General Motors Corporation.

103

CHAPTER 7 *Small-Claims Courts*

AN AUTO GIANT TAKES A FALL
By Jim Brewer

An extremely disenchanted customer took the world's largest automobile manufacturer to court and won. It happened in Marin County small-claims court where attorneys are forbidden to participate.

Judge Robert A. Smallman ordered the Chevrolet division of General Motors to reimburse a 37-year-old geologist for the cost of replacing the engine in his 1972 Vega. The car broke down last year with just over 25,000 miles on it.

It was a victory for John T. O'Rourke of San Anselmo, who said he decided "to fight it out" in small-claims court because "it was me against them—no high-powered lawyers."

Under court rules, he will only collect $500 of the $679.83 it cost him to repair the engine, but O'Rourke said it was worth it. Five hundred dollars is the maximum claim allowed in small-claims court.

"The consumer has been shafted too often," he said. "The people who buy this kind of car just can't afford to put a new engine in."

O'Rourke made his case upon a three-month-old consumer report which urged the Federal Trade Commission to require that auto makers notify car owners of any warranty extensions.

The report, by the Center for Auto Safety in Washington, D.C., said, "General Motors and other automobile manufacturers" sometimes double the life of a warranty (to two years or 24,000 miles) for "selected owners . . . without disclosing such extensions to the public or the affected owner."

It specifically cited "under-the-table extensions by General Motors on 1971 and 72 Vegas because the cooling systems in these models often break down."

The report did not say who the "selected owners" were, but O'Rourke wasn't one of them.

GM officials said the damage to the car was due to "excessive hard carbon buildup on the pistons" and not "product failure." William Perry, a Chevrolet Motors representative, told Judge Smallman that warranties were not selectively extended to some Vega owners but said his company, in some instances, "made policy adjustments to keep our customers happy."

"The way I see it, policy adjustments and warranty extensions are the same thing," Judge Smallman said. And he ordered Chevrolet to pay O'Rourke $500 plus $27 in court costs.*

Small-claims courts, designed to provide a fast, efficient, and inexpensive way to resolve claims of individuals against merchants or large corpo-

San Francisco Chronicle, April 23, 1974. Copyright Chronicle Publishing Co., 1974.

104

rations, are potentially a great resource to consumers. They exist in almost every state in one form or another. They are one of the best ways for consumers to settle disputes with a dealer, service station, repair shop, garage, or auto manufacturer.

Although court rules vary from state to state, the procedure in small-claims court is usually very simple—so simple you do not need a lawyer. In fact, some courts do not permit lawyers. You may take a complaint to the clerk of the court and file a claim; you will sign a series of papers and then pay a small charge for filing (court fees usually range from $2 to $20 and often are part of the recovery if you win). A summons is then sent to the defendant and a trial (hearing) date is set. The trial is so geared to the average consumer that the judge may help present the case by asking appropriate questions. Formal courtroom procedures and the use of legal rules are usually ignored, providing an informal atmosphere in which consumers making claims can more easily talk out their problems before the judge.

Information and other resources are available for the consumer to use in preparing to go to small-claims court. A few courts and many consumer groups and agencies publish guides or consumer manuals on using small-claims courts, with emphasis on the local procedures involved. (See Appendix C for a list of titles and where they can be obtained.) Although a lawyer is usually not necessary in a small-claims court suit, some legal assistance or advice may be helpful. Free legal help may be obtained from law students who are participating in a legal clinic, such as the Law Students in Court Program in Washington, D.C. Call the nearest law school to find out whether there is such a program in your area. Often, legal assistance is available from neighborhood legal-service organizations or legal-aid societies, which are set up to help low-income or minority groups. Where legal assistance is necessary, some courts will provide indigent consumers with a lawyer at the consumer's request.

PROCEDURES

Filing a Complaint. Small-claims courts are located in county or other local courthouses in your state. The plaintiff (person who is suing) usually must file suit in the area or district where the defendant (person being sued) lives, works, or has his or her place of business; for example, where the dealership or repair shop is located.

The small-claims court in your area will be listed in the telephone book under *courts* for either your city or county government, or there may be a general information number for courts. (See Appendix B for state small-claims court table indicating for each state the type of court, availability of appeals, maximum amount of suit, use of lawyers, and whether the procedure is informal.)

After finding the court in your area, ask to speak to the clerk of the small-claims court. Tell the clerk that you wish to file a complaint. Ask the clerk whether the court can handle your kind of case and whether it has jurisdiction over the party (or parties) you wish to sue. As a general rule, the defendant must live, work, or do business in the court's territory. Since

105

automobile manufacturers do business in all areas of the country, they can be sued in just about every small-claims court. Thus, choose the court in an area where the dealership is located when suing the dealer and manufacturer.

The clerk can assist in filling out the necessary forms. The basic and perhaps only form you need to fill out is the complaint. Many small-claims courts will have a sample filled-out complaint available. The complaint includes your name and address, the name and address of the person whom you are suing, the amount of your claim, and the reason for your suit. (See Appendix A for a sample complaint.)

The amount of your claim should include the cost of repair in the case of a defect or accident and the overcharge in the case of a fraudulent or incomplete repair, as well as any consequential damages arising out of the problem. For example, if a repair shop charged you $30 for a tune-up never performed and you paid another mechanic $25 for a tune-up—and in the meantime you had to hire a taxi costing $20—then you should sue for $50 ($30 to get back what you paid for no tune-up and $20 for the cab; do not ask for the $25 because that is what you are paying the honest mechanic for the tune-up actually performed).

Be certain the business name of the organization you are suing (which you write on the complaint) is the official *legal* title. John's GM Shop may not be enough; it may be legally registered as John Brown's General Motors Showroom, Inc. Some courts will dismiss the suit unless the company is identified in the complaint exactly as it is registered for legal purposes. Ask the court clerk whether the exact legal name is required, and, if so, how to find the correct name. This information can usually be checked with the city or county clerk, or the secretary of state. See if the dealership or the repair shop has an operating license posted on an office wall with the legal name on it.

When you fill out the complaint, be precise. State exactly what part of the engine, for example, malfunctioned or was defective. The clerk will give you a summons to be completed with the complaint. A summons is the official notification of the case delivered to the party you are suing.

After you fill out the forms, a filing fee is usually required. These vary from state to state, from a low of $2 to a high of $20. (Check Appendix B for other information on your state.) This fee usually will be returned if you win since the losing party pays it. The clerk will then give you a copy of the forms and usually a "docket number" (identifying the case) and a date for the hearing of your case. The hearing date is usually scheduled two to eight weeks from the date of filing. Some courts notify plaintiffs by mail as to whether the defendant was served with the summons. If the defendant cannot be located, you must find a better address.

Preparing Your Case. Try to attend a session of the court to learn the procedure. At least come to court early on the hearing date and observe the cases that come up before yours, in order to become more at ease with the procedure.

In small-claims court a consumer can do a good job by going before the

106

judge and telling the story of his or her complaint from the beginning. To do this easily, write down the history of your complaint. Arrange the events in the order they occurred, checking the dates. Pull together all the documents related to your claim, such as written estimates, repair orders and canceled checks. If the recordkeeping system in Chapter 3 has been followed, the important papers needed to show your side of the story will be readily available. Also bring physical evidence (broken or defective parts) if possible.

Where possible, get written statements or affidavits that support your complaint. One example is a statement in writing from a car mechanic as to what is wrong with the car and why it would be deemed a defect as opposed to normal wear and tear. If the mechanic is willing, have it notarized by a notary public. This evidence lends credibility to your case. Another helpful piece of evidence would be a report from a diagnostic inspection center in the form of a computer printout or checklist as to what is wrong with the vehicle.

The vast majority of small-claims suits are decided without witnesses. But if you want to bring witnesses, make arrangements with them prior to the hearing. It is better that a witness testify at the hearing on a voluntary basis than by court order. If the witness is not willing to come to the hearing, ask the witness to make a written statement or affidavit indicating his or her knowledge of the case.

In the rare case where success depends upon a witness actually appearing in court and the witness will not come voluntarily, check with the court clerk to see if the court has subpoena power (ability to order a witness to appear in court). For example, a mechanic at the dealership who repaired the car admitted that the failure of a part traced to a manufacturing defect. Since the dealer will not let the mechanic appear at the hearing, a subpoena is the only way to get the mechanic in court to tell the story. There is a beneficial side-effect of a subpoena issued in such a case; not only will you win if the mechanic testifies, but the dealer loses a mechanic for the day. Confronted with such a situation, the dealer will almost invariably offer to settle out of court after the subpoena arrives.

Settlement. Many small-claims suits are settled out of court before they can come to trial. Once a dealer, garage, or manufacturer sees that a consumer means business by going to small-claims court or beyond, he or she frequently agrees to meet the consumer's demands. You can even settle in the courtroom on the day of the hearing before court actually begins. Some courts have clerks or other assistants or even judges available to expedite this settlement process before trial.

If you want to settle, be prepared to bargain. Make sure you understand all the terms before you settle and get the terms of the settlement in writing. Do not settle for anything you feel is unfair. Upon settlement, file a copy signed by both parties with the court so that the settlement can be enforced by law. If the court allows, arrange to appear in court to clarify with the judge the settlement terms. Try to negotiate reimbursement of court costs as part of the settlement.

107

The Hearing. If there is no settlement, you will get your day in court. Most courts call the roll of cases and parties at the beginning before taking each case in order. If a party is late or does not appear, the case can be decided immediately in favor of the party who is present, so be on time.

When the clerk calls your case, the judge will ask each party to tell his or her side of the story. In the course of presenting your case, give the court copies of any written evidence you have. If you have any witnesses, call them before the judge and ask them to tell what they know. The judge will not expect you to have any legal knowledge; he or she will merely ask you to state the facts as clearly and concisely as you can. The judge will ask questions to clarify anything that was not clearly presented. The other party will then be given an opportunity to present his or her side. Many small-claims courts have cross-examination of witnesses only and not the parties.

The judge may give a decision at the hearing, or notify the parties of the decision by mail. If you lose, you may have the right to appeal; if you win, the defendant may be able to appeal. Check with the clerk about the appeal procedure (see Appendix B).

Arbitration. Some court systems provide for arbitration instead of or in addition to small-claims courts. Both are very similar, the main difference being that in arbitration one goes before an arbitrator instead of a judge. This method enabled a Buffalo, New York, couple to get $780 from General Motors for repairs and other expenses incurred when their 1973 Oldsmobile Cutlass broke down. The DiDomenico family was on a motor trip when the engine in their Cutlass failed and had to be completely rebuilt at a cost of $540. They had to cancel their vacation plans, rent a car, and return home. Although the car had just over 13,000 miles on it, the manufacturer's district representative refused to make any adjustment. The DiDomenicos threatened legal action and would have settled for a much smaller amount than that which they actually ended up winning in small-claims court. But General Motors remained unresponsive. A local legal-aid office suggested suing General Motors in small-claims court.

In Mrs. DiDomenico's own words:

> This entire experience was frightening, inasmuch as we had never been involved in a lawsuit; consequently we had no lawyer to ask for advice, and we felt completely helpless dealing with this giant corporation.
>
> Throughout, a pattern emerged whereby my husband would first try to reach an agreeable settlement by telephone or in person, and he would be given sympathetic understanding and be temporarily pacified—first by the dealer or repairman, then by the Olds division representative, then by the Olds division in Lansing, Michigan, and by the local dealer from whom we had purchased the car. But in each instance a point was reached where they turned off, became unavailable, unresponsive.
>
> After we had threatened legal action and they didn't offer to settle (we would have accepted just about any reasonable amount: $200 or $300), we seemed to have no alternative but to go ahead. It was as if

they were calling our bluff, daring us to take General Motors to court.

Armed with receipts to show proper maintenance, motel accommodations when they were stranded, rental-car fees, long-distance calls, and the repair bill itself, they submitted their claim to an arbitrator provided by the court.

General Motors had a lawyer present its case and even brought an expert witness to testify on its behalf. The DiDomenicos had no lawyer, but they did have good records and concrete evidence (the engine parts that had to be replaced) to give credibility to their case. They were awarded full recovery ($780) against General Motors.

Mrs. DiDomenico sent her advice to other consumers in a letter to the Center for Auto Safety:

> In retrospect I would say that it is most important to keep complete, accurate records of all work done on the car. In case of a problem, speak directly to the proper person and be persistent and don't back off.
>
> Small-claims court is the best possible place for the average consumer to take his legal matter. Every conceivable type person was among those filling the courtroom: individuals suing individuals (some still arguing), individuals having complaints against businesses, many businesses represented by lawyers.
>
> A clerk called the docket to first determine whether anyone had failed to show up, and when General Motors was called, there was such a gasp of reaction in the room that we couldn't hear the response. But of course they were present and we both agreed to an arbitrator.
>
> We did have a completely fair and thorough opportunity to have it all out.
>
> Finally, small-claims court is the place for the consumer to have his faith in equal justice restored. Every person should make it a point just to visit his local small-claims court one day and realize it is not necessary to have legal knowledge or a lawyer to have his chance to get a fair hearing.

Arbitration Panels. The concept of resolving consumer complaints outside the courtroom is being experimented with across the country. In San Jose, California, a neighborhood center began in late 1977 on an experimental basis. The plan involves mediation and arbitration, with the use of small-claims courts only as a last resort. The project was organized by a local bar association and a municipal court.

Volunteer lawyers act as mediators and arbitrators. Parties involved in the disputes are not allowed to have lawyers represent them in the proceedings. The center has evening hours to accommodate people who work during the day.

The American Arbitration Association has a similar program under way in several cities. In Philadelphia, the program was so well received that local courts adopted it into their system.

109

In Orlando, Florida, the local bar association has operated a Citizen Dispute Settlement Program since 1975. About 125 lawyers volunteer to hear the cases. The program was first aimed at helping people who were subject to criminal charges, but now is expanding into consumer problems.

Collecting the Judgment. Unfortunately, some consumers who win in small-claims court do not always collect the full amount of the award. Some defendants refuse to pay or simply do not have sufficient funds to pay. The court is not responsible for the actual collection of judgments but it can help enforce the judgment. In most automobile cases, the winning consumer has little difficulty in collecting since the losing party is frequently a multi-billion-dollar auto company or a well-to-do auto dealer that can scarcely plead the absence of funds to pay the judgment.

At the hearing, ask the judge to order the entire amount to be paid at one time in a single payment. If notification is by mail, contact the defendant and ask for the money. If the defendant does not pay within a reasonable time (two to three weeks), go back to the small-claims court clerk. Fill out the necessary forms, and the clerk will tell you how to get a sheriff or a marshal to collect the money owed by the defendant. The cost of a sheriff or a marshal can be added to your judgment. File with the clerk a list of all the costs accumulated in trying to collect the judgment.

If the sheriff or the marshal cannot collect the money owed to you, ask the court clerk for information about what to do next. If an oral examination of the defendant is possible, request a hearing before a judge to decide what action can be taken to make the defendant pay the judgment. At the hearing, you can find out whether the defendant actually has the money to pay you. If he or she does have the money, request an attachment on the defendant's wages, money in a bank account, or other property until you have collected your money. The clerk can again help you fill out the necessary forms.

And persistence does pay off, as one consumer proved when he sued the Ford Motor Company. Bob Repas of East Lansing, Michigan, had a serious rusting problem with the tailgate of his 1971 Ford Torino station-wagon. The difficulty began when the car was new and continued to worsen despite frequent trips to the shop for repairs. By 1976 the entire tailgate was rusted and required replacement at a cost of $291.90. Mr. Repas won his case and was awarded $305.30, the extra $13.40 for court costs. However, Ford stalled for several months before paying. After additional hearings he received the original judgment plus seventy-four days' interest on the sum.

Mr. Repas wrote in a letter to the Center for Auto Safety: "I am most irked about the way this company stalled on paying the judgment. . . . it is determined to give anyone a hard time who doesn't accept their verdict as final and infallible." Mr. Repas' persistence made him a winner.

WHERE NO SMALL-CLAIMS COURTS EXIST IN YOUR AREA

Some consumers have even filed suit in a higher court without a lawyer, where no small-claims court existed in their area. Often the manufacturer will offer to settle the complaint with the consumer in order to avoid going to

110

court. For example, David D. Bingham of Alexandria, Virginia, was angry and discouraged by the way General Motors and the dealer were handling his warranty complaint. When the clutch on his 1976 Chevrolet Monza wore out, he took the car back to the dealer, Mike Pallone Chevrolet. Although the new car's warranty had not yet expired, the dealer and General Motors would not authorize warranty coverage, stating that the consumer had "abused" the clutch. But Bingham refused to foot the $236.29 repair because

I felt I was right. I have driven cars for 14 years and all had stick shifts and clutches.

I then took the clutch parts to Jim McKay Chevrolet in Fairfax, the dealer from whom I bought the car and he agreed to have a different GM representative examine the parts. The service manager at McKay's said smilingly that it wasn't unusual for a person who had driven carefully 14–15 years to start driving like a teenager, a statement I found ridiculous and insulting.

I finally managed to bring suit against Mike Pallone Chevrolet, Jim McKay Chevrolet, and General Motors Corporation for—"While 1976 Chevrolet Monza was still under time and mileage warranty (1 yr. and 12,000 miles) General Motors Corporation representatives arbitrarily decided I had abused or misused the clutch and the GM representatives and dealers refused to cover parts of the clutch that were not excluded from the warranty."

I realized that my problem was much greater because it was not a small-claims court I was taking my suit to, but a civil court. For the price of the clutch it was not worth hiring an attorney, and I felt sure General Motors legal aids could easily take me apart.

However, I felt right was on my side and there was always the chance the judge had had trouble with a General Motors car. It was at least worth the nuisance value in forcing GM to pay their lawyers to spend a day in court. On this basis I went ahead and the court date was set for September 22 at 9:30. At 3:30 P.M. September 21, Mr. J. Alan Dobbs, Zone Consumer Relations Manager, Chevrolet Motors Division, called me at work and asked if I would settle out of court for the full cost of the clutch replacement. His condition was that I withdraw the suit immediately so GM would not have to appear in court and that he would immediately put a check in the mail. I agreed and called the court, who asked me to confirm the withdrawal by letter. I was still very suspicious of GM, but I got the check before I had completed my confirmation letter.

If consumers, like Mr. Bingham and Mr. Repas, would only give the courts a try, more of them would be the Davids who beat the Goliaths of the auto industry.

SUING WITHOUT A LAWYER

Even where nearby small-claims courts do exist, some consumers have chosen

111

to file suit in a higher court because the jurisdictional amount (limit on the amount you can recover in a given court) is too low in small-claims court. In order to avoid legal fees, some consumers have pursued the case on their own, without hiring a lawyer. Others did so because they couldn't find a lawyer willing to take on an auto manufacturer.

One example is Toby Cagan, who took Chrysler Corporation to court and won—without a lawyer—over her defective 1977 Dodge Aspen. She had complained over and over again about her lemon to Chrysler dealers and to the manufacturer, but Chrysler treated her complaints callously—responding with form letters and rude, reluctant service.

Before Cagan signed for her Aspen, she took a test-drive and found many problems with the car, including difficult steering, sticky windows and doors, stalling and dents. When she complained to the salesperson, he told her that, "It's a new car and these problems have to work themselves out." Trusting the salesperson at his word, Cagan drove away in her new Dodge. When the car developed more problems within a week, she took the car back to the dealer. For the next several months, Cagan tried to get six different Chrysler dealerships to repair her car, but still without satisfaction. She sent letters and made telephone calls to Chrysler. All she received was the run-around. By this time, the consumer was quite angry. "The car had been defective since the date of its purchase. After three government recalls, numerous problems and defects, I was afraid to drive the car," she said.

So Toby Cagan filed a lawsuit against Chrysler Corporation in civil court, in the city of Queens, New York. On March 9, 1979, Cagan presented her case to the court. Planning ahead, she had saved all the repair orders to document her lemon story—showing how she had brought the car into numerous Chrysler service departments again and again with no success. Chrysler simply could not fix her car. As her story unfolded in the courtroom, the shabby treatment Chrysler gave the consumer was exposed. She brought in a mechanic to verify the defects in the engine and drive train. A bodyshop owner testified that her car had formed rust.

Cagan also brought in reports from the Center for Auto Safety, describing how the Center had written to Chrysler Chairman Riccardo in August 1977 about the large number of complaints on 1976–77 Aspens and the identical Volares. Most of the complaints, which were similar to those Cagan had experienced, concerned carburetor, brake, driveline and steering problems. (Chrysler had earlier denied the Center's charges, calling the group's claims "irresponsible." But within the next six months, Chrysler had initiated a record number of recalls—with over a million 1975–77 vehicles per recall, for the very same defects experienced by consumers writing to the Center and Ralph Nader. About eighty percent of all Aspens and Volare owners had their cars subject to all four recalls.)

Although Chrysler brought in an expensive New York City lawyer, its only witness was a zone official who incredibly admitted that the car was defective, as Cagan claimed, but that given enough opportunities Chrysler could fix all the defects. After hearing Cagan's witnesses at the trial, Chrysler gave in and offered to refund the consumer's purchase price minus $500 for the eighteen months she had owned the car.

112

Cagan and other consumers who do not give up easily prove that you don't always need a lawyer to take a giant corporation to court and win. But you do need persistence and planning. Toby Cagan has plenty of both, much to Chrysler's dismay.

APPENDIX A—CHAPTER 7

SAMPLE COMPLAINT
SUPERIOR COURT OF THE DISTRICT OF COLUMBIA
CIVIL DIVISION
SMALL CLAIMS AND CONCILIATION BRANCH
613 G STREET, N.W.   THIRD FLOOR
WASHINGTON, D.C. 20001   Telephone 727-1760

(PLEASE PRINT OR TYPE)   (PLEASE PRINT OR TYPE)
YOUR FULL NAME   (1) PERSON OR FIRM YOU ARE
                          Plaintiff vs. SUING
                                          (2) (DO *NOT* PUT ADDRESS HERE)
YOUR PRESENT ADDRESS   (3)
                          (ZIP CODE)   *Defendant*
Address   *Zip Code*

HERE, YOUR TELEPHONE
NUMBER
(DURING THE DAY)

No. SC_____
STATEMENT OF CLAIM

YOUR STATEMENT OF CLAIM (BRIEFLY, AND NOT IN GREAT DETAIL),
WHAT THE CLAIM IS FOR, GIVING DATE OR DATES, AND PLACE OF
OCCURRENCE. ALSO STATE THE AMOUNT FOR WHICH YOU ARE SUING
OR FILING.

DISTRICT OF COLUMBIA, *ss:*
YOUR FULL NAME_____being first duly sworn on oath says the foregoing is a just and true
statement of the amount owing by the defendant to plaintiff, exclusive of all set-offs and just grounds of
defense.

THIS SPACE IS PROVIDED FOR   LEAVE THIS SPACE BLANK UNTIL
ATTORNEYS, IF *Attorney for Plaintiff*   YOU SWEAR BEFORE *Plaintiff (or agent)*
ONE IS USED   A CLERK OR A NOTARY PUBLIC
Address   *Zip Code*

Subscribed and sworn to before me this____day of_____, 19_____

_____
Deputy Clerk (or notary public)

114

NOTICE

To:

(1) PERSON YOU ARE SUING

Defendant

(2) IF YOU ARE SUING TWO PER-SONS

Defendant

.... ☐ CHECK ADDRESS TO BE USED FOR MAILING

Home Address　　　　　*Zip Code*

.... ☐

Home Address

.... ☐

Business Address　　　*Zip Code*

.... ☐

Business Address

You are hereby notified that _____ YOUR FULL NAME _____ _____ has made a claim and is requesting judgment against you in the sum of _____ (THE AMOUNT OF YOUR CLAIM WRITTEN OUT) _____ dollars

(AMOUNT IN), FIGURES

as shown by the foregoing statement. The court will hold a hearing upon this claim on _____ LEAVE BLANK _____ LEAVE BLANK _____

at 9:00 a.m. in the Small Claims and Conciliation Branch located at 613 G Street, N.W., third floor.

SEE REVERSE SIDE FOR COMPLETE INSTRUCTIONS

CHARLES P. HENRY, JR.
Chief Deputy Clerk
Small Claims and Conciliation Branch

(Seal)

BRING THIS NOTICE WITH YOU AT ALL TIMES

INSTRUCTIONS TO DEFENDANT(S)

IMPORTANT: IF YOU FAIL TO APPEAR AT THE TIME STATED OR AT ANY OTHER TIME THE COURT NOTIFIES YOU TO DO SO, A JUDGMENT BY DEFAULT MAY BE ENTERED AGAINST YOU FOR THE MONEY, DAMAGES OR OTHER RELIEF DEMANDED IN THE STATEMENT OF CLAIM. IF THIS OCCURS, YOUR WAGES OR BANK ACCOUNT MAY BE ATTACHED OR WITHHELD OR ANY PERSONAL PROPERTY OWNED BY YOU MAY BE TAKEN AND SOLD TO PAY THE JUDGMENT. *DO NOT FAIL TO APPEAR AT THE REQUIRED TIME.*

You may come with or without a lawyer. The Statement of Claim indicates whether the plaintiff has a lawyer. If the plaintiff does have a lawyer and you wish either to dispute the claim or attempt to work out a compromise settlement it would be in your best interest to have your own lawyer.

If you wish to have legal advice and feel that you cannot afford to pay

115

a fee to a lawyer, you may contact one of the offices of the Legal Aid Society (NA 8-1161), Neighborhood Legal Services (628-9161) OR the D. C. Law Students in Court program (638-4798) for help or come to 613 G Street, N.W., Third Floor, for more information concerning places where you may ask for such help. Act promptly.

If it is impossible for you to appear on the date of trial, notify the Clerk of the Small Claims Branch of this Court in person or by phone and the Clerk will advise and assist you in requesting a new date. In arranging this new date you may wish to consider that the court holds sessions weekdays at 9:00 A.M., Wednesday evenings at 6:30 P.M., and Saturday mornings at 9:30 A.M. If you do not appear on the new date, a judgment may be entered against you.

You are given the following additional instructions in the event that you intend to appear without a lawyer.

If you have witnesses, books, receipts, or other writings bearing on this claim, you should bring them with you at the time of the hearing.

If you wish to have witnesses summoned, see the clerk at once for assistance.

If you admit the claim but desire additional time to pay, you must come to the hearing in person and state the circumstances to the court.

A corporation may appear only through an Attorney.

APPENDIX B—CHAPTER 7

State Small-Claims Courts

State	Type of Court	Claim Limit	Informal Procedure?	Lawyers Permitted?	Appeals
Alabama	Small-Claims Division of District Court	$500	Yes	Yes	De novo to Circuit Ct. Bond or aff. of hardship.
Alaska	Small-Claims Proceeding in District Court	$1,000	Yes	Yes	Either party if over $50, on record.
Arizona	Justice Court (Arizona has no small-claims system except Boone County)	$999.99 (Boone Co. $500)	No	Yes	Plaintiff or Defendent if over $20, de novo to Sup. Ct., bond.
Arkansas	Municipal and Justice Courts	$300 ($100 if personal)	Yes	Yes	P or D to Circuit Court. Bond required.
California	Small-Claims Court, part of Municipal or Justice Court	$750	Yes	No	Only D can appeal, de novo, bond.
Colorado	Small-Claims Division of County Court	$500	Yes	No	P or D can appeal.

117

Connecticut	Small-Claims Proceeding in Court of Common Pleas	$750	Yes	Yes	None.
Delaware	Justice of Peace Courts (Delaware has no small-claims system)	$1,500	Yes	Yes	P or D can appeal.
District of Columbia	Small-Claims Division of the Superior Court	$750	Yes	Yes	P or D can appeal. No bond.
Florida	Small-Claims Division of County Court	$1,500 (County cts. generally are $2,500)	Yes	Yes	New trials and appeals.
Georgia	Justice of Peace Courts	$200	No	Yes	Both sides de novo.
	Small-Claims Division (one third of the counties)	Varies from $100–$1,000 depending on county	Yes	Yes	P or D can appeal.
Hawaii	Small-Claims Division of District Court	$300	Yes	Yes	None.
Idaho	Small-Claims Dept. of Mag. Div. of Dt. Ct.	$500	Yes	No	P or D can appeal. Bond required.

193
194

State	Type of Court	Claim Limit	Informal Procedure?	Lawyers Permitted?	Appeals
Illinois	Small-Claims Division of Circuit Court	$1,000	Yes	Yes	P or D can appeal.
	Cook County Pro Se Court	$300	Yes	No	P or D can appeal.
Indiana	Small-Claims Docket of Sup. Ct., Circuit Ct., and County Ct. Small-Claims Court in Marion County	$3,000 ($1,500 in Marion County)	Yes	Yes	P or D can appeal. Only questions of law.
Iowa	Small-Claims Procedure in District Court	$1,000	Yes	Yes	P or D can appeal. Bond.
Kansas	Small-Claims Procedure in County Courts	$300	Yes	Yes	P or D can appeal. No bond.
Kentucky	Small-Claims Division of District Court	$500	Yes	Yes	P or D can appeal. Bond. Trial de novo.
Louisiana	Small-Claims Division of City Courts	$300 ($25 for City Court)	Yes	Yes	None.

119

Maine	Small-Claims Procedure in District Courts	$800	Yes	Yes	P or D can appeal. Bond. Trial de novo.
Maryland	District Court	$500	Yes	Yes	P or D can appeal. Trial de novo.
Massachusetts	Small-Claims Procedure in District Court & Boston Mun. Court	$400 (except property damage by motor veh.)	Yes	Yes	Only D can appeal. Bond. Trial de novo.
Michigan	Small-Claims Division of District Court	$300	Yes	No	None.
Minnesota	Conciliation Court in each county	$1,000 ($500 in Mpls./St. Paul)	Yes	No	P or D can appeal. Bond. Trial de novo.
Mississippi	Justice of the Peace Courts (Mississippi has no small-claims system)	$500	Yes	Yes	P or D can appeal. Bond.
Missouri	Small-Claims Docket of Magistrate Cts.	$500	Yes	Yes	P or D can appeal. Bond.

196
197

State	Type of Court	Claim Limit	Informal Procedure?	Lawyers Permitted?	Appeals
Montana	Small Claims, part of District Court (at option of county)	$1,500	Yes	Yes, if both P and D have lawyers	P or D can appeal. No bond.
Nebraska	Small-Claims Division of Mun. or County Courts	$500	Yes	No	P or D can appeal. Bond.
Nevada	Small-Claims Proceedings in Justice Courts	$300	Yes	Yes	P or D can appeal. Bond.
New Hampshire	Small-Claims Proceedings in Municipal and District Courts	$500	Yes	Yes	P or D can appeal. No bond. Only questions of law.
New Jersey	Small-Claims Division of District Court	$500	Yes	Yes	P or D can appeal. Trial de novo.
New Mexico	Magistrate Courts	$2,000	No	Yes	P or D can appeal. Trial de novo.
	Small-Claims Court in Albuquerque	$2,000	Yes	Yes	P or D can appeal. Limited to questions of law.

121

New York	Small-Claims Court in Civil Court, District Court, and City Courts	$1,000	Yes	Yes	P or D can appeal on ground of subst. injustice.
North Carolina	Small-Claims Procedure in District Court	$500	No	Yes	P or D can appeal. Bond. Trial de novo.
North Dakota	Small-Claims Procedure in Justice Court and County Court	$200 in Justice Ct. $500 in County Ct.	Yes	Yes	None, unless case removed at beginning.
Ohio	Small-Claims Division of County and Municipal Courts	$300	Yes	Yes	P or D can appeal. Bond.
Oklahoma	Small-Claims Procedure in District Court	$600	Yes	Yes	P or D can appeal. Bond.
Oregon	Small-Claims Department in District and Justice Courts	$500	Yes	Only with consent of court	Only defendant from District Ct.
Pennsylvania	Justice of Peace	$1,000	No	Yes	P or D can appeal. Trial de novo.
	Philadelphia Small-Claims Ct.	$1,000	Yes	Yes	P or D can appeal. Trial de novo.

State	Type of Court	Claim Limit	Informal Procedure?	Lawyers Permitted?	Appeals
Rhode Island	Small-Claims Proceeding in District Ct.	$500	Yes	Yes	D only, on record.
South Carolina	Magistrate Court	$500–3,000	Yes	Yes	P or D can appeal. Trial de novo.
South Dakota	Small-Claims Procedure in Magistrate Cts.	$1,000	No	Yes	None.
Tennessee	Justice of Peace or General Sessions (No small-claims court in this state)	$3,000	No	Yes	P or D can appeal. Bond. Trial de novo.
Texas	Small-Claims Court	$150 ($200 for wages)	Yes	Yes	P or D can appeal if amount greater than $20.
Utah	Small-Claims Department of City and Justice Courts	$400	Yes	Yes	Only D can appeal. Bond. Trial de novo.
Vermont	Small-Claims Procedure in District Court	$500	Yes	Yes	P or D can appeal. No bond.

123

Virginia	General District Court (No state small-claims system)	$5,000	No	Yes	P or D can appeal if amount greater than $20. Bond.
Washington	Small-Claims Department of District and Justice Courts	$300 ($200 if not proc. under ch. 3.30-374RCW)	Yes	Only with consent of court	Defendant only, must be greater than $100.
West Virginia	Magistrate Courts	$1,500	No	Yes	P or D can appeal. Bond. Trial de novo.
Wisconsin	Small-Claims Proceedings in County Court	$1,000	Yes	Yes	P or D can appeal. Bond.
Wyoming	Small-Claims Proceedings in Justice of Peace and County Courts	$200	Yes	Yes	P or D can appeal. Bond. On the record.
Puerto Rico	Small-Claims Proceeding in District Court	$100	Yes	Yes	P or D can appeal.

APPENDIX C—CHAPTER 7

Small-Claims Courts Guides and Manuals

"The Consumer and the Small Claims Court"
State of California Department of Consumer Affairs
P.O. Box 310
Sacramento, Calif. 95802

"How to Activate Small Claims Courts"
MassPIRG, available for $1.00 from:
Consumer Federation of America
1012 14th St., N.W., Suite 901
Washington, D.C. 20005

"How to Sue in Massachusetts Small Claims Courts"
MassPIRG
233 North Pleasant St.
Amherst, Mass. 01002

"How to Sue in Small Claims Courts"
City of New York Department of Consumer Affairs
80 Lafayette St.
New York, N.Y. 10013

"How to Use Small Claims Courts"
transcript of Consumer Survival Kit show, produced by:
Maryland Center for Public Broadcasting
Owings Mills, Md. 21117

"The Role of the Small Claims Court," *Consumer Reports*, November 1979,
p. 666

"Small Claims Court"
1978 Consumer Reports Buying Guide Issue, p. 360

"Small Claims Court: Make It Work for You"
Washington Urban League
3501 14th St., N.W.
Washington, D.C. 20009

"Your Day in Court"
Montgomery Office of Consumer Affairs
24 Maryland Ave.
Rockville, Md. 20850

The above are examples—many other guides are available through local courts and agencies.

CHAPTER 8 *Working with a Lawyer*

"LEMON" OWNER WINS $5,400
By Andy Tessler

A jury has awarded $5,411 in "lemon" aid to a Midland motorist who claimed he was sold a defective car.

The jury awarded Steven H. Stube $1,600 from Sarow Chrysler Plymouth and $3,811 from Chrysler Corp. Stube sought $9,400.

He claimed they implied his 1976 Plymouth Volare was fit to drive when it was not. Stube said he paid $4,400 for the car which he drove less than 7,500 miles and which spent seven months in dealer service departments. He called the car unsafe because of vibration in the steering and misfiring, hesitation and stalling, and said the car has been garaged since March.

Sarow's lawyer claimed the dealer performed proper maintenance. Chrysler's lawyer said the auto maker provided service beyond the warranty. He said the problems were corrected except for the vibration which he said was caused by steel-belted radial tires. He said the hesitation was caused by emission-control equipment the auto maker is forced to install.

Stube testified the problems still exist and his lawyer said Stube had to buy two more vehicles because the Volare does not operate.

Stube said he bought the four-door sedan because the salesman told him it would give "many, many miles of trouble-free service" and was highly efficient and economical to operate.

His lawyer said a Chrysler representative sent Stube to Saginaw Dodge. That dealer kept the car 45 days. The major problems were not corrected, the lawyer said. Stube returned the car to Saginaw Dodge in October 1976, this time on a trailer because he did not consider it safe to drive. He picked it up March 16, drove it seldom, and it has been stored since late March.*

In a conversation with the Center for Auto Safety, Nancy Stube said, "We couldn't have done it without our lawyer. He knew that we were in the right. Our attorney knew how to zero in on the case."

INTRODUCTION

The frustrated lemon owner has a number of legal options in getting the lemon replaced or repaired. These options include many tactics less expensive than a lawsuit and sometimes just as effective and even more efficient.

Saginaw News, January 21, 1978.

127

An attorney can be helpful in finding a successful and inexpensive tactic short of actually filing suit. For instance, a simple, direct letter from an attorney is often enough to startle a stubborn dealer or manufacturer into fixing your car. Beyond this, a lawyer can call the dealer, guide you to a regulatory agency or to small-claims court, or actually file a lawsuit.

Before hiring a lawyer, consult with one. Many attorneys will give free consultations for up to a half hour to evaluate your case. He or she can point out deficiencies in the case, indicate the likelihood of success, the amount of damages and the cost. At the same time you can appraise the lawyer—whether he or she seems competent and interested in your case. At such an initial consultation, there is no requirement for the consumer to hire the lawyer.

WITHOUT A LAWSUIT

A letter or telephone call, alone, from an attorney to the dealer or manufacturer indicates that you mean business. Sometimes the dealer will offer to fix the car, settle for money damages, or otherwise resolve your complaint. For example, Laurie Davis bought a used 1971 Toyota from Seaway Motors of Detroit. The transmission needed overhauling within a few months after purchase. The purchase price of the vehicle was $1,456.00. The cost of the transmission overhaul would have been $321.00. When she could not resolve the complaint on her own, Ms. Davis consulted with her attorneys, Hurwitz and Karp of Dearborn, Michigan. As soon as the attorneys telephoned Seaway Motors, Seaway agreed to fix the transmission for one half of the usual cost, or $160.50, rather than be sued. The legal costs to Ms. Davis were a $25.00 consultation fee.

Another inexpensive use of a lawyer is a letter to the manufacturer or dealer. The following is an example:

> DIAMOND, RASH, LESLIE AND SCHWARTZ
> El Paso, Texas 79901
> October 25, 1972

Mr. John A. McKeon, President
McKeon Dodge, Inc.
El Paso, Texas 79986

Dear Mr. McKeon:

I have been retained by Mr. and Mrs. John Perry Miller to put you on official notice that, should they be involved in an accident due to the fact that their car continues to stall on busy roads and highways, they will hold you and Chrysler Motor Corporation responsible to pay for any bodily injury and property damage resulting therefrom.

The car involved is a Dodge Colt stationwagon which you sold on 8-24-71 to Mr. John Perry Miller, your account number 54615. Mr. and Mrs. Miller have brought this car to you on numerous occasions for the necessary repairs that would stop their car from stalling. Apparently you have diagnosed this problem as a fuel problem; but, to

128

date, you and your company have been unable to rectify the situation although Mr. and Mrs. Miller have been charged high sums for the repair work which you have done and which has not solved their problem.

Mr. McKeon, will you please take personal interest and charge in this situation and assign your very best mechanic to this problem and/or completely replace the Miller's fuel system at your expense or that of Chrysler Motor Corporation before a serious accident results and you get hit with a lawsuit for your failure to make repairs and/or before Chrysler Motor Corporation gets slapped with a products liability suit, if the fuel system is indeed defective and impossible to repair without replacing the entire system.

Please call me at 555-2222 as soon as you receive this letter to let me know what steps you plan on taking to rectify this situation.

Very truly yours,

/s/

Robert D. Earp

A letter like this puts the manufacturer on notice, clearly an advantage in any subsequent lawsuit, and might provoke the manufacturer to make certain that no defect exists. In the above case, Chrysler's factory representative flew into El Paso, looked at the Millers' car, and ordered the car repaired.

FILING A LAWSUIT

If the dealer and manufacturer do not respond to the attorney's first few contacts, a lawsuit may be necessary. But this does not necessarily mean a lengthy and expensive trial will result. Sometimes by filing a lawsuit an attorney can resolve your case without going to trial.

The act of initiating litigation against the dealer or manufacturer often brings about a settlement. For example, when Valerie Holmstrom bought a new Audi Fox, she was told by the selling dealer and the manufacturer (Volkswagen of America) that an authorized dealer would be available in Charleston, South Carolina, where she was moving. But when she arrived there, she found that the only authorized dealer could not repair her car. As a matter of fact, the dealer had a reputation for poor service and, soon after, went into bankruptcy. Ms. Holmstrom contacted a local attorney, Robert Rosen, who filed a lawsuit against Volkswagen of America. Mr. Rosen sought "discovery" (a legal term covering the ways parties to a lawsuit gather evidence) against VW, asking the manufacturer to produce certain documents pertaining to the Charleston dealer. Volkswagen settled out of court for $5,500 plus the car, rather than produce the possibly incriminating documents.

GOING TO TRIAL

If the parties to a lawsuit do not settle before trial, the case usually will be heard in court, where many consumers have been successful. One example

129

is Vincent J. Hamilton, Sr., of North Scituate, Rhode Island, who was awarded $12,999 in Providence Superior Court. He sued General Motors on charges that his $10,235 1977 two-door Cadillac, purchased from Lorber Cadillac-Pontiac, Inc., constantly stalled. The monetary award included the purchase price, expenses for garaging the car when it could not run, the cost of obtaining substitute transportation, and lawyer's fees.

GETTING OUT OF HOT LEGAL WATER

When a lemon owner has taken certain types of direct action, such as withholding car payments or stopping payment on a check, an attorney is usually necessary to untangle the legal tape. For example, if you have paid for a new car by check, and immediately discover it has defects so serious that the car is unfit for use, you can stop payment on the check, return the car to the dealer, and inform him by letter of your refusal to accept the car. (See Chapter 6, the *Zabriskie* case.) An attorney's help is essential here—the dealer may file suit to force you to pay for the car, or may in some places be able to obtain a warrant for your arrest.

A special need for an attorney may arise when you stop payments on a new car because the dealer is unable to repair a defect. For instance, a dispute as to whether a needed repair will be covered under the warranty may leave you without a car for weeks or months, and make continuing payments a serious problem. In this situation, a lawyer may be able to solve the problem and at the same time avoid repossession or damage to your credit rating. *Do not stop payment without consulting an attorney.*

Forest and Barbara Snyder found themselves in hot legal water when they refused to pay a $1,500 balance owed on their Cadillac lemon. The dealer, Cal Connel Cadillac, took them to court. The $1,500 judgment was granted for the dealer, and the Snyders had to pay. But the Snyders consulted with their attorneys in time to file a third-party complaint against General Motors. One of their attorneys, Warren Tipton of Louisville, Kentucky, took the case to trial.

The Snyders' major problem in going to trial was finding an expert who would testify that the car was defective when purchased. The lawyers finally convinced a Louisville service station owner, who had serviced Cadillacs for years, to testify in the Snyders' behalf. During the trial, the Snyders described the broken water hoses, unpredictable windshield wipers, collapsing front wheel, and other problems with the lemon. Mrs. Snyder told of repairs costing over $1,000 and of more than $500 in car rentals while her car was being "fixed." She explained how the car broke down on expressways and all the problems associated with the unreliable and unpredictable car. The service station owner testified that the car was not worth the money the Snyders had paid for it. The Snyders persisted against the world's largest auto manufacturer. They beat General Motors in court, winning a $2,500 judgment against General Motors plus court costs.

FINDING A LAWYER

In finding a lawyer, look for two things—competence and low cost. Sur-

130

prisingly, some of the best lawyers are free, because they work for programs designed to help the needy or for nonprofit organizations that look for test cases that can set legal precedents.

Similar aid may be obtained from law students who are participating in a legal clinic, such as the Law Students in Court Program in Washington, D.C. Call the nearest law school to find out whether there is such a program in your area. In many cases, a bright enthusiastic senior law student at a good law school may be more than a match for an overworked and unenthusiastic lawyer retained by a dealer. Legal assistance is available from neighborhood legal-service organizations or legal-aid societies, which are set up to help certain minority and low-income groups. Government-supported legal-service programs often provide legal services free of charge. These services are potentially very helpful, but only for those who meet rather strict eligibility standards. To be eligible in 1980 you had to show a poverty-level income, defined as a maximum of roughly $7,000 annually for a family of four.

For motorists with 1976 and later cars with warranty failures, look for a lawyer who will attempt to recover attorney's fees under the Magnuson-Moss Warranty Act. Under this act, the court may award attorney's fees as a part of the judgment. Traditionally, lawyers have been reluctant to handle lawsuits against giant corporations such as the auto companies, because the legal fees can easily be greater than the judgments awarded to the consumers. The Magnuson-Moss Act improves the economic feasibility for consumers to pursue remedies against the auto manufacturers in court.

For example, when Giuseppe Ventura's new car turned out to be a lemon, he sued the manufacturer for damages plus legal fees. He won both when the court ordered Ford Motor Company to refund the purchase price to the consumer and also pay his attorney's fees.

The New Jersey consumer bought his first new car, a 1978 Mercury Marquis Brougham, for $7,830.90 from a Plainfield dealer. The car over-heated and stalled, subjecting the Ventura family to several close-calls on the road. After eight trips back to the Ford dealer for repairs under the warranty, the car's problems simply were not fixed. Ventura sued Ford in January 1979, represented by attorney Mark Silber of Metuchen.

Silber prearranged with the consumer that he would not receive any payment other than a $350 good faith retainer fee (to avoid Canon of Ethics problems) unless he was successful in getting Ford to pay him under the Magnuson-Moss Warranty Act. This is the first known case where an attorney took a lemon auto suit into court under the Magnuson-Moss Act on the basis of receiving payment only if there was a court award of attorney fees. When Judge David Furman handed down his decision in 1980, he awarded $7,000 in damages to Ventura and $5,000 in fees to attorney Silber, all of which are to be paid by Ford Motor Company.

If you do not have a Magnuson-Moss warranty case and do not qualify for or cannot find good, free legal assistance, look for a lawyer who is willing to take the case on a contingency or percentage basis, where payment depends on winning. (See "Legal Fees" below.)

To find a competent attorney, look around. Contact consumer groups or faculty members of a law school in your area for guidance in finding a

131

good lawyer. In some states you may call a local judge's law clerk for assistance in finding a competent lawyer. Ask friends or business associates to recommend an attorney. Contact the local lawyers' referral service if one exists in your area. The state bar association can also provide you with such information.

A national directory, "Martindale-Hubbell," contains short biographical listings of many attorneys. Available at most public libraries or county law libraries, this and other directories provide valuable information about attorneys. In evaluating attorneys whom you do not know, ask them if they have ever sued an auto company or dealer and what happened. Look for interest as well as experience. Too many disinterested lawyers agree to represent consumers in auto cases only to drop the client later. One sign of interest is willingness to take the case on a contingency basis.

WHAT TO EXPECT FROM A LAWYER

In order to handle your case, the attorney needs to know all the facts—exaggerations or distortions will not help you. When you visit the attorney's office, bring all the receipts and records you have collected, documenting your case. Be sure not to mark up or alter any documents.

LEGAL FEES

Ask the attorney to describe the methods of payment so you have a clear understanding of how you will be paying attorney's fees and other expenses. Attorneys base their fees on many considerations, including the time required, the difficulty of the case, chances of winning, the amount involved, the method of payment, and the attorney's experience, reputation, and expertise. The most common fee arrangements include:

1. Contingent fee—this fee is a percentage of the damages collected where payment depends on winning. If the case is lost, there is no fee, other than out-of-pocket court costs. The contingent-fee basis of paying is often used when the client seems to have a good claim but cannot afford to pay a flat fee or an hourly rate. Consumers can negotiate with attorneys over the percentage of the recovery the lawyer gets. In negotiating the percentage, be sure you and the attorney understand which of you will pay the investigation and court costs. These expenses are independent of attorneys' fees. Most lawyers' fees require one third of any reward obtained if the case goes to trial and up to one fourth if the case is settled before trial. Such an arrangement should be entered into only where filing a lawsuit is inevitable—as settlements arising out of a simple attorney letter should be billed on an hourly basis.

2. Flat fee—this fee is based on the attorney's experience with similar cases. Usually applied in routine matters such as drafting a will, the flat fee is not generally used in cases concerning auto problems.

3. Hourly rate—this method of payment varies a great deal from one lawyer to another, from city to city, and from case to case. Rates generally range between $25 and $100 per hour, with $50 the average rate. For example,

132

settlements arising out of a letter written to the dealership about the client's auto problems should be billed on an hourly basis. If you think the lawyer's hourly rate is too high, shop around. Ask the lawyer for a memo stating the nature of the fee arrangement.

ATTORNEY-CLIENT PRIVILEGE

A good attorney-client relationship is based upon trust. If you do not like or do not trust an attorney, find someone else. You must feel free to discuss everything with the lawyer. A lawyer should be fully informed of all the facts of the case in order for his or her client to obtain the full advantage of our legal system.

The conversations between a lawyer and his or her client are protected by the "attorney-client privilege"—a technical term used in keeping the client's confidences and secrets out of the evidence in court. The conversations are also protected by the ethical obligation of a lawyer to guard the confidences and secrets of his or her client. These restrictions on the lawyer's use of a client's private matters help maintain a balance between the nature of the legal system and respect for an individual's privacy.

KEEPING INFORMED

Be sure the attorney understands that you expect to be informed of the progress on your case, including deadlines that must be met. A mistake made by many lawyers is the failure to keep the client fully informed. That does not mean daily reports, but it does mean advising the client of what is being done. Ask that copies of the following be routinely sent to you as they are produced:

1. All correspondence
2. Memoranda of fact and law
3. Pleadings and briefs
4. Responsive papers from the other parties involved, including the court

COMPLAINTS AGAINST ATTORNEYS

Before they are admitted to practice in every state, lawyers must take an oath to uphold the law and comply with the rules of ethics approved by the courts and bar associations. Unfortunately, they do not always live up to this oath. If you have been unfairly treated by an attorney, first try to work out disagreements with your attorney in case they arise from misunderstandings. If you are not satisfied, report him or her to the state bar association. Attorneys are subject to disciplinary proceedings by the state bar upon charges of unethical conduct. If an attorney made a fundamental error, such as failing to file suit before the statute of limitations expired, you can file a malpractice suit against the attorney.

133

CHAPTER 9 *When All Else Fails: Telling the World About Your Lemon*

PICKETS WIN TONY BETTER DEAL
Pioneer Volkswagen Takes Back "Lemon"

Twenty-five neighbors and coworkers of Tony LaSalata helped him get a better deal on a used car he bought from Pioneer Volkswagen of Watertown by picketing the auto dealer for two hours on a Saturday.

Harold Epstein, owner of the dealership, agreed to take back the [used] 1969 Toyota Crown LaSalata bought last August in exchange for any other car on the lot with the same price.

LaSalata had asked the dealer to give him a full refund on the car after he had trouble with it for over five months. Within two weeks after he bought the car he said he found that the horn, courtesy lights, stop lights, and brakes went out and the car began to stall at intersections. The car was returned to the Pioneer Volkswagen for service for twelve days while the dealer "waited for parts." The car was fixed seven days before the 30-day warranty ended. Shortly after the warranty ended the lights, horns, and brakes broke again. By the time he and his friends picketed Pioneer, the car had had over $200 in repairs and still needed repairs of the gas line, muffler, and clutch.

When LaSalata, neighbors, and coworkers from the regional office of the United Auto Workers in West Hartford showed up at the dealership at about 10 A.M., Epstein told police that he "paid taxes in this town" and asked them to make the picketers leave. Watertown police said that the picket line could stay as long as cars could "come and go" from the Pioneer parking lot.

According to picketers, Pioneer employees drove cars in and out of the Pioneer lot to disrupt the line. One picketer said that an employee had taken the same car for a "test drive" five times.

At 10:30 A.M. Epstein agreed to discuss LaSalata's complaint with LaSalata and Paul Keene, director of the Buyers' Action Center of Hartford.

Epstein offered to fix the car, but LaSalata wanted to return the car for the $1,800 he paid for it. After about 90 minutes of tense discussion Epstein agreed to either repair the car to "perfect condition" or "give you what you paid for the car in trade on any car in this organization." LaSalata said that he would return the car and pick out another one from the Pioneer lot. He said that he was "satisfied" with the deal. "All I want is a car to drive to work," he said.

Several of the picketers said that they had decided to help LaSalata because they had had similar troubles with cars they bought. Another

134

picketer said that he did not know LaSalata or Pioneer Volkswagen, but had joined the picket line because he had had trouble with a car bought from another auto dealer. "Consumers have to stick together," he said.*

INTRODUCTION

When writing letters does not help and lawyers want too much money, take your case to the public. Dealers fearing the financial repercussions of adverse publicity are often willing to reconsider complaints to clear the air.

The right of consumers to tell the world about their lemons is rooted in the First Amendment of the U.S. Constitution and in most state constitutions. The First Amendment protects the individual's or group's freedom of expression or "free speech." By making their lemon problems known to the public, consumers occasionally receive replacement cars or refunds from embarrassed dealers.

But picketing and the use of lemon signs, like other tactics that have proven effective against business interests, are controversial ones. Businesses claim a competing right—the right not to be injured in the conduct of their business. Thus, dealers have occasionally invoked the authority of the courts and the police in attempts to halt its use. The courts are divided in upholding the right of consumers to use lemon signs and picket dealerships. The cases frequently turn on a minor point, such as whether the picketers were on dealer property or interfering with consumers trying to enter the dealership.

Lemon owners have used many techniques in informing the public about their lemons. The most frequently used tactics include picketing and lemon signs, classified advertisements in newspapers, and flyers handed out to prospective customers at the dealership. A few local consumer groups specialize in picketing dealers. Many successful consumers and groups who have used this tactic have encouraged others with similar complaints to organize "lemoncades," lines of cars covered with lemon signs, driving slowly around the block where the uncooperative dealer is located.

PICKETING

Group picketing and demonstrations are most effective because they dramatize the fact that many consumers share a dissatisfaction with the dealer's unresponsive attitude toward the lemon owner's plight. Some consumer groups have organized on a local basis to provide their members with participants whenever picketing is necessary to protect a member's rights.

One group, Consumers Education and Protective Association International (CEPA), of Philadelphia, has frequently picketed uncooperative dealerships with success. Over its twelve-year experience with complaint handling, CEPA has developed a three-step grievance procedure for use in

---

*"Fair Deal" (Buyers' Action Center of Hartford), February 29, 1972.

135

lemon or other consumer complaints: (1) investigate, (2) negotiate, and (3) demonstrate.

For example, CEPA members picketed an unresponsive foreign-car dealer to settle their fellow member's complaint. When Larry Pizzi purchased a Triumph Spitfire in June 1976, the dealership (Buzz Marcus in Glenside, Pennsylvania) misrepresented the insurance coverage, underquoting the price by $1,767. Negotiations with the firm's attorney were unproductive. After CEPA members picketed the showroom, the dealer took the car back, paid off the balance due at the bank, and refunded two thirds of the down payment. The car had been driven 11,000 miles.

LEMON SIGNS

Lemon signs alone frequently bring success to consumers. For example, attach large lemon signs to your car reading: THIS FIRE-EATER IS A $5,500 LEMON, BOUGHT FROM SHADYDEAL MOTORS. MANUFACTURER'S DEALER CAN'T FIX. If your gripe is against the dealer as well as the manufacturer, you might add to the sign: SEE ME BEFORE YOU BUY. Then locate your car conspicuously near the dealer's showroom (but not on his property). This expresses your plight in a way that cannot fail to bring fast reaction.

The lemon sign tactic has the advantage of being a very flexible device. You can drive around town with the lemon signs prominently displayed, or you can park the car in a public place near the dealership's entrance and go off to work. Or you can stand beside your lemon to explain the signs and pass out leaflets or flyers about your lemon experience.

One successful consumer who painted lemon signs all over his defective car had reached a point where he could no longer put up with the cost and inconvenience of owning a lemon. W. L. Lanzone, Jr., of Long Beach, California, said his troubles began the day he took delivery of the new 1972 Chevrolet Blazer. In his May 30, 1972, letter to the Chevrolet Motor Division owner relations manager, Mr. Lanzone complained about his four-wheel drive lemon:

> Since the purchase of the Blazer on March 13, it has been nothing but trouble. At the end of this coming week it will have been in for repair not less than 38 days.
> So far they have removed the transmission three times, trying to locate an oil leak. They have replaced the valve cover gasket, rear-end seal, rear-end housing, rear bearings, two relay horn switches, new oil pan, and three new oil-pan gaskets. In addition, two weeks ago part of a front spring fell off while driving on the freeway and [last week] . . . the left front shock absorber became detached from the frame.

Mr. Lanzone followed the above lemon sign suggestions in the Center for Auto Safety's first edition of this book, *What to Do with Your Bad Car: An Action Manual for Lemon Owners*. He painted on the side of his Blazer:

136

This $5,000.00 LEMON! Courtesy C. Cannon Chevrolet. This is tough as . . . JELL-O LEMON.

and on the back of the vehicle:

This $5,000.00 LEMON! Please RETURN FALLEN PARTS! This CHEV . . . A 4-letter word!

Lanzone drove around town with this custom-lemon paint job announcing to everyone that his Blazer was a lemon. Not long afterward, he succeeded in getting a new Blazer from the dealership to replace his lemon.

HOW TO PICKET AND PROTEST WITHIN THE LAW

If you decide to picket or use lemon signs, there are certain guidelines which you should follow to remain within the law. This will help you defend your actions if the dealer requests a court order prohibiting the signs, picketing, demonstrations, or other activity, or simply calls the police. First, do not picket or otherwise protest until you have tried to negotiate with the dealer or manufacturer. When this fails, picket.

The purpose of your protest is twofold: to announce to the public that you have been treated unfairly and to settle your complaint. If your goal is to interfere with the dealer's business activity or to put him or her out of business, your demonstration, picketing, or lemon signs can be legally enjoined or stopped by court order. Thus, avoid statements that might be interpreted as attempting to coerce the dealer into a course of action or into paying you money. Direct your disparagement at the vehicle, rather than at the dealer personally.

The key to legal picketing is to be nonviolent, nonobstructive, and honest. It is advisable to notify the local police and news media ahead of time. Do not interfere with the operation of the dealership's day-to-day activities. Be careful not to block traffic in the street or to prevent people from entering the showroom. You may distribute flyers or leaflets to explain and clarify the message on your signs and car. Above all, do not interfere with the free flow of customers. Let them come to you or to your display.

The location of the picketing is as important as the purpose. Generally, you have to remain on public property, such as city sidewalks. If you picket or park your car with lemon signs on the dealer's property, you can be thrown off for trespass.

Picketing a dealer's home or corporate executive's residence may work, but it can get you in trouble with the law. If you want to try residential picketing and are willing to fight it out in court, be aware that private residences are generally heavily shielded by the courts when confronted with the issue. Courts weigh the competing interest of a consumer exercising his or her rights of free speech against the individual householder claiming his or her right to privacy and domestic tranquility.

The law does not protect acts of flagrant coercion, physical intimidation,

137

and destruction of another's property. The courts attempt to find a fair balancing point between the First Amendment right of the picketer to speak out and the property rights of the business being picketed. When First Amendment rights are exercised peacefully and all statements are true, they are most often upheld. (The Appendix traces the history of protest law in greater detail.)

Recognizing that court orders against picketing are difficult to obtain, some dealers resort to libel and slander suits alleging large damages in efforts to get consumers to back down on their protest activities and demands. By and large, these are spurious suits, particularly if consumers observe the above guidelines for picketing legally.

Consumers can turn these harassing lawsuits to their advantage if they refuse to back down and instead counterclaim for their damages. For instance, in 1970 Mr. and Mrs. J. Waterbury of New Rochelle, New York, were sued by their dealer, Tappan Motors of Westchester County, New York. They had parked their Volvo stationwagon in front of the dealership with a large sign affixed to the car describing the repair history of the automobile. Ultimately, the dealer dropped his suit. The Waterburys settled for a new Volvo worth approximately $4,550, as well as all expenses incurred in the ownership of the original car.

A handbook on when and how to protest and picketers' rights, called "Consumer Picketing," is available from CoPIRG, Univ. Memorial Center, Room 420, University of Colorado, Boulder, Colorado 80309.

NEWSPAPERS AND TELEVISION

In addition to picketing there are other effective ways of conveying your lemon story to the public. If your lemon story has an unusual twist to it, or if you have devised a novel way of getting results, it might be deemed newsworthy by the media. Certainly any dramatic reactions to lemon signs you get from local dealers or manufacturers could be material for a consumer-oriented feature writer or TV newsperson.

Unfortunately, the news media are reluctant to run lemon feature stories because they do not want to threaten their lucrative automotive advertising business. For example, K. Schoenberg of Great Neck, New York, called the local newspapers before she put lemon signs on her car and picketed the dealership, Jamaica Lincoln-Mercury Corp. She described her frustrating experience in a letter to the Center for Auto Safety:

> The newspapers did not seem to want to touch [it]. The *N.Y. Post* took pictures and a complete statement. It was never printed. The enclosed ad is no doubt the reason. [A large ad was placed by the Jamaica dealership in the *New York Post* classified ad section. Part of the ad read, "We're furlongs in front when it comes to pleasing the customer."]

If the major newspapers in your area refuse to run what they admitted was a newsworthy story, send a "letter to the editor" challenging this policy.

138

Send copies of the letter to the Center for Auto Safety and the Federal Trade Commission.

NEWSPAPER ADVERTISEMENTS

If the press will not do a feature on your lemon struggle, try placing an advertisement to generate publicity of your own. A. G. Southern ran the following ad in the *Cornell Daily Sun* in Ithaca, New York:

MY RENAULT STINKS
Does yours? Are you disgusted with your Renault and local authorized service? Add your name to the list of dissatisfied owners. Maybe we can rectify the situation. Call 555-1111 (days) or 555-1112 from 5 to .7 P.M.

Besides announcing your lemon story to the public, the classified advertising tactic is valuable in rounding up other owners of the same model lemon. As a group, you can picket the local dealership, form a lemoncade and drive through the town, or file a lawsuit against the manufacturer of the lemons.

Vikki Huff of Wilton, Connecticut, used the following advertisement to locate other Chrysler lemon owners who could help protest. Their resultant lemoncade received national news coverage including a major story in the *New York Times* (March 5, 1978).

ATTENTION! Aspen and Volare owners. Consumer group forming to seek redress for all manufacturing defects in our 1977 cars. Please call 555-3308 for details.

Advertisements can also be used simply to tell others how defective your car is, as opposed to gathering other lemon owners to form a consumer group. The following ad appeared in the "Import, Sports Cars" classified section of the *Detroit Free Press* on May 30, 1971:

'70 CORVETTE, this flawlessly finished, dark gray convertible, with contrast black leather int. and matching hardtop is equipped with FM stereo, ice cold air, pwr. steering, pwr. brakes and auto. trans. This handcrafted beauty must be sacrificed due to the following: There have been several electrical failures and 2 electrical fires, a leaky gas tank. There were failures in air-conditioning, stereo, safety warning lights, windshield wipers and washers. The front and rear bumper and other metal parts are rusted. There is front-end shimmy, faulty exhaust system, and defective tires. This car is a real collector's item and must be seen and driven to be believed. 555-1212.

This strategy, like lemon signs and picketing, is protected by the First Amendment right to freedom of expression—as long as you stick to the truth.

139

A highly publicized lemon advertising campaign was run by David Merrick, the well-known Broadway producer of such shows as *Breakfast at Tiffany's, Irma La Douce, Oliver,* and *Promises, Promises.* In 1967 Merrick spent $14,000 on a Chrysler limousine which proved to be defective. After owning the car several years and investing more than $6,000 on repairs, he realized the company simply could not keep it in running order. So he placed an ad on the front page of the *New York Times*: "My Chrysler Imperial Is a Pile of Junk. [signed] David Merrick." When further negotiations with Chrysler failed, he had a cartoon ad prepared of a horse pulling a Chrysler into a junkyard. The caption read "Good Riddance!" and his signature was across the bottom. Of the eleven papers he submitted it to, the *Miami Herald* was the only one to run it. He had no success whatsoever in placing a third ad. Then, *Harper's Bazaar* ran a full-page photo of a young couple emerging from a car, captioned: "Whatever David Merrick says about Chrysler Imperial, I like it." When asked whether Chrysler placed the full-page photo, *Harper's* said that it was part of an editorial spread on women's attire. After creating a lot of bad publicity for Chrysler, Mr. Merrick sold the lemon Imperial for $3,750 and switched to taxis.

MAKE A GIFT OF YOUR LEMON TO THE MANUFACTURER'S CHIEF EXECUTIVE

John M. Robertson of Oneonta, New York, devised a last resort which was imaginative, but not exactly suitable for the average new-car buyer.

When Mr. Robertson's new $6,900 Chrysler Crown Imperial turned out to be a lemon, he decided to make a gift of it to Chrysler chairman Lynn Townsend. He dropped it off at his local dealer together with a check for $94 to cover shipping charges, so that the car would be delivered directly to Mr. Townsend in Detroit "with my compliments."*

THE SLOW BURN

Eddie Campos of La Habra, California, had saved for five years to buy his 1970 Lincoln Continental. Despite innumerable trips to different Ford dealers, he could not get his lemon fixed. Problems with the car began the day after he bought it when the entire ignition system fell out. Other problems occurred repeatedly with the ignition, air-conditioner, electrical system, power windows, carburetor, and front-end alignment.

On August 31, 1971, after a year of "constant agony" with the car's mechanical problems, Campos drove the car onto the middle of the lawn at the Ford Motor Company assembly plant, poured gasoline inside, and set it ablaze. A sheriff's deputy on the scene said of Campos: "He was perfectly sober, perfectly rational, and completely disgusted."

The Wall Street Journal, July 21, 1965, p. 1.

140

Campos later hauled the remains of the car to his Los Angeles office and put signs on it reading, "Eddie Campos has a BETTER idea" and "We want cars, NOT Lemons." He also cut a hole in the car's roof and stuck a lemon tree through it. After he set fire to his lemon, Campos received over 120 letters and telegrams in support from other irate lemon owners from at least thirty different states. Many consumers even enclosed contributions.

THE TRIP TO THE ZONE OFFICE

Another unusual effort to publicize dissatisfaction with cars was undertaken by a group from the Hartford Auto Research Center, an offshoot of the Nader-sponsored Buyer's Action Center. On March 22, 1972, over twenty disgruntled Chevrolet owners decorated a bus with signs about the manufacturer's unresponsive attitude and went to the Chevy zone office in Tarrytown, New York. The surprised and embarrassed Chevy people promised to devote serious attention to all the problems described.

AUTO SHOWS

Take your lemon, appropriately labeled, to your local armory or amphitheater the next time the annual auto show is presented. Ask for a prominent location to ensure that visitors get a balanced view of what it can mean to own a new car. If you are refused entry, park your lemon near the entrance.

Steven Israeloff of Forest Hills, New York, took his $3,800 Dodge Challenger to the International Auto Show at the New York Coliseum on April 8, 1970, and parked in front. He put a sign in the window reading "4-sale. Please buy this car. It's a lemon and my Chrysler dealer won't fix it." The *New York Times* (April 9, 1970, p. 82) reported:

> To a rapt consumer audience, Mr. Israeloff . . . detailed the misfortunes that had befallen him since he took delivery. Only seven of the eight cylinders worked, the distributor was defective, the oil pan was cracked, the water pump broke.
>
> As Mr. Israeloff finished listing his car's ailments, a policeman approached. "I think you'll have to move that car out of here," he said gently.
>
> "I don't know if it will start," said Mr. Israeloff.

Before he left, Mr. Israeloff won a promise of an investigation from a Chrysler official attending the show.

LAST-RESORT RESULTS

Many car owners outraged in this way have come up with these and other inventive last-resort measures. Politic and impolitic, we have presented them

141

all here with the hope that one or more may be appropriate for you when all else has failed.

If you have suggestions to add to this list, and for possible inclusion in future editions of this book, mail them to:

Center for Auto Safety
1223 Dupont Circle Building
Washington, D.C. 20036

Imaginative last-resort measures might succeed for you. However, they fail to bring about any basic change in the situation giving rise to the problem in the first place. To score successes benefiting wider numbers of consumers, and to bring about changes in the system that generates the abuses, it is absolutely essential to broaden your base, to join others, and eventually to organize.

APPENDIX—CHAPTER 9

A History of Protest Law

Businesses which want to stop the picketing usually go to a court seeking an injunction. This is a court order prohibiting some specific activity either on a temporary or permanent basis. The forbidden activity is supposed to be unjustly injurious to the party requesting the injunction. State courts commonly enjoin violent picketing, mass picketing, obstructing entrance to or egress from public and private property. In addition, peaceful picketing which is either conducted for an unlawful purpose or fraudulently misrepresents the facts may be enjoined.

In the past, courts were liberal in granting injunctions to dealers and manufacturers. A 1937 court enjoined a man from displaying his automobile near the dealer's place of business. It was decorated with lemons and signs reading "Don't believe what they say, this car is no good; I have tried to have it fixed and they will do nothing about it," and "This was no good when I got it; don't be a sucker, this car is no good but it looks all right." [*Menard* v. *Houle*, 298 Mass 546, 11 NE2d 436 (1937).] The court said this was an unjustified and wrongful attack causing damage to the plaintiff's business. The following year, a court equated the use of similar signs on a car with attempts at physical obstruction to interfere with the dealer's business, and granted an injunction. [*Saxon Motor Sales, Inc.* v. *Torino*, 166 Misc 863, 2 NYS2d 885 (1938).] In *Carter* v. *Knapp Motor Co.*, an Alabama court stopped a man from exhibiting the car on which he had painted a white elephant, characterizing the act as a wrongful interference with lawful business. [*Carter* v. *Knapp Motor Co.*, 243 Ala 600, 11 So2d 383 (1943).]

Beginning in 1950, an emerging social concern with consumer rights began to surface in the courts. In *McMorries* v. *Hudson Sales Corp,* [(1950, Tex Civ. App) 233 SW2d 938] a dissatisfied consumer painted his car and parked it near various Hudson dealers. The signs boasted "Frame out of line when purchased new, Hudson refuses to make good," and "Another dissatisfied Hudson owner." Although the manufacturer initially won an injunction, a higher court reversed the order, stressing that in the absence of any proof that the statements were untrue or represented an attempt at intimidation or coercion, the injunction was a violation of First Amendment rights.

Courts now tend to examine picketing along the lines of classical cases on the rights of free speech under the Constitution. This was clearly set forth by a Washington State court:

> [W]herever one has a lawful right to express an opinion on the street, on the platform and in the press, such person has the same right without abridgment to express it on the picket line. . . . Peaceful picketing is a manifestation of the exercise of freedom of speech and it can be restrained only upon those grounds and conditions which warrant re-

straint in any other case involving freedom of speech. [*State ex rel. Lumber and Sawmill Workers* v. *Superior Ct.*, 24 Wash 2d 314, 164 P2d 662, 669, 672 (1945).]

At present courts analyze the breadth and effect of the limits on picketing to determine whether injunctions are proper. While picketing and parading and the use of the streets for such purpose are subject to reasonable time, manner and place regulation, such activity may not be wholly denied. [*Shuttleworth* v. *Birmingham*, 394 U.S. 147 (1969).] Thus injunctions which serve to completely prohibit communication of the consumer's views and experiences, rather than simply restricting the means and time of this expression, are unconstitutional. In overturning an injunction against consumer picketing, a Wisconsin federal district judge said the following about the group's peaceful, educational picketing in *Concerned Consumers League* v. *O'Neill*, [371 F. Supp. 644, 648, 649 (1974)]:

> They clearly have an interest in matters which affect their roles as consumers, and peaceful activities . . . which inform them about such matters are protected by the First Amendment. . . . The method of expression used . . . in this case is probably the most effective way, if not the only way, to inform unsophisticated consumers, i.e., by direct contact at the particular place of business.

Although courts in the past often granted injunctions when (they felt) the picketers were attempting to coerce business people, this aspect of favoritism for business interest is also undergoing a change. In dissolving a preliminary injunction against picketing an auto dealer, a Pennsylvania court held that "all picketing is to some degree 'coercive' if it is successful," and "peaceful attempts to persuade the public not to deal with a merchant [except for defamation] does [sic.] not constitute an unlawful act." [*Book Chevrolet* v. *Alliance for Consumer Protection* (Ct. of Common Pleas, Allegheny Cty., PA (Jan. 21, 1971).] Another court which refused to grant an injunction said that it still would refuse to do so even if the statements were intended to have a coercive impact and even if they were untrue. [*Stanbury* v. *Beckstrom* (1973 Tex Civ App) 491 SW2d 947.] Finally, it has been established that "so long as the means are peaceful, the communication need not meet standards of acceptability." [*Organization for a Better Austin* v. *Keefe*, 402 U.S. 415, 419 (1971).]

Many consumer organizations are set up to help supply members with sympathetic participants for picketing activity. The right to enlist the aid of outsiders was clearly established by the court in *Individual Retail Food Store Owners Assn.* v. *Penn Treaty Food Stores Assn.* [33 Pa D & C 100, 111 (1938)], which stated:

> [I]t is immaterial that the pickets are hired by defendants and have no personal interest in the dispute. The hired advocate is not novel, and the hired picket may likewise walk in the stead of his employer and do the same things the latter might lawfully do.

144

The written and oral assertions made while picketing are subject to careful scrutiny. Although a court cannot enjoin picketing merely because false statements are made, if a dealer feels your allegations are untrue and defamatory, he may successfully sue for libel or slander. If you are honest there is no need to be intimidated by such lawsuits. Truth is a defense in suits for libel or slander (defamation) in the great majority of jurisdictions. [Restatement (Second) of Torts § 581A (1977); W. Prosser, Law of Torts § 116 (4th ed. (1971); *Cochrane* v. *Wittbold,* 359 Mich. 402, 102 N.W. 2d 459 (1960); *Craig* v. *Wright,* 182 Okl. 68, 76 P. 2d 248 (1938), affd. 184 Okl. 371, 87 P. 2d 317 (1939).] This means that if you can prove the statements were true, you should not lose the case.

CHAPTER 10 *Before Buying a Car*

June 1, 1977

Dear Mr. Nader:

I purchased a 1969 Oldsmobile in 1969 as a new car and paid new-car price. I still have the written contract and bill of sale. Lately, Miss America decals have been showing through the paint on both car doors of my convertible! I went to the dealer from whom I bought the car and asked what they would do about this. I was told to have my lawyer contact theirs. I feel either the dealer from whom I bought the car, or GMAC, has defrauded me by selling me a new car which was obviously used in a Miss America pageant of some sort and therefore should have been represented on my written contract and bill of sale as demonstrator, or other classification other than new.

Yours truly,
/s/
A. L. Draughon
Huntington, W.Va.

Consumers experience auto problems of all types. Some problems show up right away. Others show up many years later, as did the Miss America decals in the above letter. Some auto ownership pitfalls can be avoided through wise and prepared shopping. Other problems simply cannot be anticipated, even by the most prepared consumer.

Before buying a new or used car, one should decide whether a car is needed at all. In these days of soaring insurance, gasoline, parking, and car prices, a second car or even a first car may cost too much. Individuals living in large urban areas may well find it cheaper and easier to rely on public transportation, taxis, and rental cars than to buy a car.

COST OF OWNERSHIP

The escalating costs of buying, owning, and operating a car push many consumers to the edge of their resources. The top expense in owning a car is a hidden toll—depreciation, the difference between the price paid for a vehicle and its trade-in value. According to a study by the Department of Transportation (DOT), depreciation accounts for fifty-two percent of the cost of running a brand new car the first year. A study by the Hertz Corporation, the car-rental company, estimated the total depreciation cost for all U.S. cars in 1975 at $48.9 billion, or about five cents a mile. The DOT study showed a depreciation of $1,215 for a standard-size 1976 model car bought new for $4,899 and sold or traded at the end of the first year, when it had been driven 14,500 miles. DOT recommended using a thirty percent depreciation rate as a working figure when calculating expenses.

According to Hertz's annual estimate, the average cost of owning and

146

operating a typical new U.S. car in 1978 rose more than 10 percent to 33.1 cents a mile, 3 cents above 1977's 30.1 cents outlay. These figures are for a normally equipped, intermediate-size two-door sedan driven 10,000 miles a year and kept three years.

The longer a car is kept and the farther it is driven, the lower the cost per mile to own and operate. For example, if the typical intermediate 1978 model is traded annually, the cost per mile averages 34.9 cents. If the car is kept for five years, the costs fall to 28.9 cents with an annual driving of 10,000 miles. The lower depreciation rate for an older car offsets higher maintenance expenses.

Other expenses of owning a car include gas and oil, maintenance and repairs, insurance and registration, finance charges on auto loans, parking, and tolls. The cost of running a small car is much less than that of operating a standard-size auto. DOT found that the operating costs for a standard-size 1976 car during its anticipated ten-year life will total $17,878.96 or 17.9 cents a mile; for a 1976 compact car, $14,561.46 or 14.6 cents a mile; and for a subcompact, $12,638.35 or 12.6 cents a mile, during the same period. These costs were based on conditions in suburban Baltimore, Maryland, and are not national averages.

For car owners who wish to reduce new-car purchase and operating costs: use radial tires, join a carpool, shop around for interest rates before getting a loan, keep your car well tuned, obtain insurance tailored to your particular needs, and look for reduced insurance rates for safety performance. Also, avoid adding power-robbing features to a small car, in order to take advantage of the small car's improved fuel economy.

Copies of the DOT study, "Cost of Owning and Operating an Automobile—1976," may be obtained from the Federal Highway Administration, U.S. Department of Transportation, HPA-1, 400 Seventh Street, S.W., Washington, D.C. 20590.

One way to reduce the costs of car ownership is to buy a used car, since most depreciation on a car occurs during the first three years. Buying a three- to four-year-old car and keeping it for three years will save a consumer at least $4,200 over buying a new car and keeping it for the same period.

MATCHING A CAR WITH YOUR NEEDS

"Buying a car is an easy thing," according to Detroit, which drowns consumers with images of the perfect car. The dealer tries to reinforce the image and brings forth a car not only as virile, or lush, or demure as you had imagined but even a little better, and costing only a little more. However, all reference to safety, quality, and the dealer's responsibility to prepare the car properly and honor the warranty is usually glossed over with glowing generalities. It is up to you to introduce these criteria into the dialogue.

One of the foremost factors in selecting a new car is size—full size, intermediate, compact, or subcompact. Choosing the right-size car is presently a compromise between, on the one hand, economy and maneuverability (which you get with small cars), and, on the other hand, more comfort, capacity, and safety (with the larger cars). As a general rule (passenger-restraint systems aside), larger and heavier cars are safer than smaller and lighter ones. There are a few exceptions, such as the VW Micro-bus, which uses the driver as a bumper—it is a middleweight car, but it is grossly unstable; and there is nothing but thin sheet metal between the driver and what he or she runs into.

Small cars, particularly the subcompact, used to be thought very unsafe. However, there is no reason why small cars cannot be made safe. For example, Mini-Cars, a California company that does safety research under government contracts, modified a 1974 Pinto by filling the open sections under the hood and in the doors with plastic foam, an effort which considerably improved the crashworthiness of the car without adding much weight (see Chapter 15, "Auto Safety").

A good example of a safer subcompact car is the Volkswagen Rabbit, with "passive" or automatic shoulder belts. The accident fatality rate for passive-belt VW Rabbits is only one half of that for Rabbits with regular seat and shoulder belts, according to the Department of Transportation. The fatality rate for VW Rabbits with passive belts is less than one fourth of that for other types of cars with regular seatbelts. The passive or automatic harness wraps around front-seat passengers when the door is closed. Regular seat and shoulder belts have to be fastened by the occupant, and are not used by eighty percent of vehicle occupants.

For most consumers, an intermediate-size car is the largest they will need. In fact, consumers will find that a well-designed compact car will provide more than adequate internal space while being most economical to operate.

General information on buying a car can be found in the April issues of *Consumer Reports*, and a Department of Transportation booklet, "Common Sense in Buying a New Car." See also Chapter 11 and the section "Sources of Information on New- and Used-Car Buying."

SELECTING THE CAR: SAFETY FEATURES

Despite the lip service that auto designers pay to safety, many features of "modern" cars cause accidents or maim and kill a large proportion of accident victims. Even now, with the results so plainly evident, the auto makers build and advertise "hard tops" (which are not really hard enough to protect in a rollover), recreational vehicles without seatbelts for all seats, eyelid headlamp covers that stick shut, and many more deadly features. The trivial gimmickry of hidden windshield wipers creates a cavity which clogs up with snow, ice, and debris; the raised sheet-metal edge that forms the top of the cavity may slice rearward as a neck-level guillotine in a serious crash. Most of these suicidal options were originated by stylists, and heavy advertising has led an unsuspecting public to pay stiff extra costs for them willingly.

The enormous cost of motor vehicle accidents arising from the lack of safety is readily seen in the National Highway Traffic Safety Administration's estimate that in 1978 the cost of motor vehicle accidents was $43 billion.

148

This estimate includes such costs as wages lost, medical expenses, insurance administration costs, property damage, legal fees, and court costs. The enormous cost of motor vehicle accidents reflects the outrageous number of people maimed and killed—on our nation's roads and highways, an accident involving injury occurs every eighteen seconds, while one involving death occurs every eleven minutes. Each year, about 50,000 people die in motor vehicle accidents.

Safer cars not only will reduce this awesome toll but also will save consumers money. Some insurance companies (Allstate is one) are now offering lower insurance premiums for cars that have less severe accidents. If consumers are in an accident with a safer car, the likelihood of severe injuries and costly medical bills is reduced. Safer cars in general mean lower taxes to support police, ambulances, public hospitals, children orphaned by accidents, paralyzed adults who must go on social security, and fire departments which clean up after accidents.

Although all cars must meet minimum federal safety standards, some cars, like the 1971–76 Ford Pinto, are much less safe than others. Unfortunately, consumers have no published guide as to the safety of different cars. In the near future, the government may provide ratings of the relative crashworthiness of vehicles and the cost of repairs. In 1972 Congress passed the Motor Vehicle Information and Cost Savings Act, which required the government to operate such a ratings system. The program has been stalled because of the absence of government interest and funding. But when the system is finally set up, it will provide car purchasers with information as to the relative safety and repair costs of various models. (For sample data from preliminary tests, see Chapter 15.) Until the system is operating, consumers can refer to the safety rankings of cars published by groups such as the Highway Safety Research Center, University of North Carolina, Chapel Hill, North Carolina 27514, and the Highway Loss Data Institute, 600 Watergate, Washington, D.C. 20037.

In order to buy a car with safety features that put it above the minimum federal standards, use the following checklist.

1. Visibility for the Driver

a. *Adequate Field of Vision*

The driver should be able to see a small child standing fairly close to any part of the car. In backing up the car, wide panels between the rear window and the side windows require as much use of the ears as the eyes and make lane changing unnecessarily dangerous.

b. *Distortion*

Vision through all windows must be clear and undistorted. The rakish angle of many windshields seriously obstructs vision. Fastback rear windows also often distort vision, and easily collect dirt and snow.

c. *Reflections and Glare*

When sitting in the car in the sunlight you should see no reflections (in front and rear windows) of the dash or the rear deck. There should be no glare from the wiper blades or other chrome ornaments. In many cars, when the sun is shining from overhead, reflections become so bad that safe vision

149

is impossible. Even when reflections are minor, they can increase eyestrain and fatigue dangerously.

d. *Rear Window Defroster*

The rear window should be equipped with an electric defroster (optional on some cars, standard on others) and, if available, a rear wiper.

e. *Rearview Mirrors*

The outside mirror should be far enough forward to let you use it without turning your head too far to the side. The inside mirror must be high enough not to obstruct forward vision, and low enough to allow you to see through the rear window when the trunk is loaded. (Have two people sit on the rear bumpers to check this.)

f. *Nonobstructing Headrests*

Headrests should not block the line of vision through the rearview mirror, nor should they be bulkier than necessary. The Volvo ladder shape is an example of a good design for added visibility.

g. *Windshields*

Fully tinted windshields (as distinguished from those with a band of tint running only along the top edge) are unacceptable because they drastically reduce dusk and night vision, making pedestrians and obstacles hard to see. The combination of a windshield with standard tinting and the usual sixty-degree tilt cuts incoming light by thirty-five percent—and worse yet, it cuts red light (important to the partially colorblind) by fifty-one percent. Cars can usually be ordered with clear-glass windows, unless tinted glass is standard in those vehicles.

2. Visibility of the Car

a. *Raised Taillights*

The higher the taillights are, the better. Stop lights at roof level (as on school buses and Citroëns) and those at rear deck level (custom-installed on some cars) can help to prevent rear-end chain collisions.

In a recent Washington, D.C., study, the use of an eye-level brake light in taxicabs cut the rear-end collisions of those vehicles in half. According to the National Highway Traffic Safety Administration, those taxis with a single brake light mounted on the trunk and centered beneath the rear window, in addition to the standard brake and signal lights, experienced a fifty-four percent drop in rear-end collisions in road tests. The collisions that occurred were less costly. The cabs equipped with these brake lights averaged only $194 in repair costs per collision, compared with the conventionally equipped taxis' $317 average.

b. *Turn Signals*

Side, front, and rear turn signals must be large enough to be plainly visible and, like taillights, must be as high as practical.

c. *Color*

Light-colored, single-tone cars are more easily distinguished from the surroundings by other drivers. Studies made by the New York Port Authority have shown that light-colored cars have significantly fewer collisions. According to one study released by the Minnesota Department of Safety, the safest color for an automobile is a greenish yellow shade. As a general rule,

150

red and black are worst; cream, yellow, and white are best.

3. Operating Equipment

a. *Brakes*

The brakes must be able to stop the car repeatedly from high speeds without any noticeable deterioration in effectiveness. Brake fade must be low enough that the weakest driver will still be able to stop the car with ease. Ideally the brakes should be strong enough to bring the car to a controlled stop from high speeds even with the gas pedal pressed to the floor, as if the accelerator were stuck.

The oldest and simplest rule for brake design, which has been used for many years to calculate *minimum* values of braking strength, states that brake horsepower must be greater than engine horsepower. This means that the brakes should be capable of stopping the engine even when the gas pedal is floored. (We do not advise testing your brakes for this capability—you'll be in trouble if the brakes flunk the test.) Larger engines, of course, require larger brakes; however, many cars built with large V-8 engines break this rule by using standard or inadequate brakes. The brakes must be stronger than the engine, not only when the brakes are applied, but also until the car comes to a complete stop. If the brakes fade, they must still be able to stop the car, even with a fairly weak driver.

Disc brakes are virtually universal on the front wheels of cars, vans, and light trucks sold in the U.S. These tend to resist fading and improve directional stability when compared with all-drum brakes. Power assist may be a useful option, if brake effort seems excessive without it. Four-wheel disc brakes are standard or available on several vehicles and are worth considering, especially if the vehicle will be driven hard or used to tow a trailer.

b. *Suspension*

American cars used to be so heavy that they needed heavy-duty, police-car-type suspension to be safe for emergency maneuvers. Now that cars are being made smaller because of regulations on fuel economy, a spinoff benefit is that heavy-duty suspension is no longer necessary. The suspensions of downsized vehicles are much tighter, thus improving their emergency handling.

c. *Power Steering*

Only large cars should be ordered with power steering. To determine whether power steering would be a good option, try parking the car in a line of cars parallel to the road. If you can easily back in and pull out without power steering, that particular car does not need power steering. If the car requires a gorilla to turn the wheel in this parking maneuver, then power steering would be a good option. Cars with power steering must be easy to steer if the engine stalls when driving since stalling causes the power steering assist to fail. This is fairly easy to test—while coasting through a large empty parking lot, with *plenty* of extra room to spare, shut off the engine and attempt to maneuver the car quickly.

d. *Tires*

From the vehicle's load capacity, which is usually listed on the side of

151

the driver's door or on the inside of the glove compartment door, determine the passenger and luggage load capacity for the size of tires on the car. Allow at least 150 pounds per passenger and fifty pounds for a heavy suitcase. Some cars, especially stationwagons, are delivered with tires of such a low weight-carrying capacity that the cars can only be partly loaded before an unsafe tire load is reached. For more information on tires, see Chapter 14.

e. *Gauges and Controls*

All gauges and warning lights must be placed, marked, and lighted so that they can be easily read day and night. You should be able to reach all the controls easily with your shoulder belt fastened and to operate them without taking your eyes from the road.

f. *Seat Adjustments*

If unusually short or tall drivers will be using the car, make sure the seat can adjust to accommodate all of them for both vision and pedal reach.

g. *Engines*

Large V-8 engines with displacement of 400 cubic inches or more have disappeared with overweight 5,000-pound cars. Smaller engines, properly tuned, provide enough reserve power for safe passing maneuvers. An over-powered car is uneconomical and can be unstable during hard acceleration or uncontrollable if the accelerator sticks. Since the auto companies began to eliminate hundreds of pounds of unneeded weight in their cars in 1977, a V-6 is adequate for all automobiles—even those equipped with air-conditioning. A four-cylinder engine is adequate for compacts and subcompacts. If you need to pull heavy loads frequently, a small V-8 such as a 301- or 305-cubic-inch engine should be satisfactory.

4. Minimum Crash Protection

a. *Bumpers*

Bumpers should be solid enough to withstand pushing and low-speed collisions. If the bumpers are up against the body of the car, minor collisions will push the bumpers into the sheet metal, causing expensive damage.

Bumpers on 1979 model-year automobiles were required to meet a new federal safety standard that prohibits damage to new cars in five-mile-per-hour front and rear barrier impact tests and three-mile-per-hour corner impact tests, but does permit some damage to the bumper itself and to its attachments. A second phase of the standard forbids damage in those tests to the bumper as well as to the rest of the car starting with the 1980 model year.

b. *Seat and Shoulder Belts and Passive Restraints*

The best restraint system available until the 1982 model year is the self-actuating or passive-belt system of cars such as the VW Rabbit. A passive restraint is a device that protects occupants of a car without requiring them to buckle up or take any other action. They are connected to the door so a passenger gets in and automatically puts them on.

When available, the highly publicized airbag will be the best passenger-restraint system when used along with a lap belt. Advanced airbag systems will better protect occupants in much higher-speed crashes than will seatbelts because airbags absorb the crash forces better.

After years of delay, the Department of Transportation ordered auto

152

manufacturers to phase in passive restraints in all cars starting with 1982 full-size cars and ending with the 1984 compact cars. (See Chapter 15, "Auto Safety," and page 232 for further discussion on passive-restraint systems.) Meanwhile, fasten your seatbelts. Seat and shoulder belts make driving about five times safer than driving without the belts. And even the seatbelts alone, without the shoulder belt, make driving about twice as safe.

5. Other Features
a. *Pedestrian Gougers*
About twelve years ago a nine-year-old girl was riding her bicycle near her suburban home outside Washington, D.C., when she struck the rear bumper of a parked automobile. The collision hurled her flush into the sharp, protruding tail fin on the car. She was fatally impaled. Such tragedies are not unusual accidents. Hundreds of thousands of pedestrians, cyclists, and motor-cyclists are injured every year in collisions with vehicles—stationary and moving—whose sharp exterior ornamentation inflicts additional injury. These protruding ornaments—bladelike front fenders, cutting grill patterns, sharp headlike eyebrows, and other designs—are not only hostile to pedestrians, but also purely stylistic in purpose. While many of the worst protrusions, such as Cadillac's lethal tail fins of the late 1950s and early 1960s, have disappeared, there are still sharp protrusions which should be barred at a cost saving to consumers.

No new-car buyer plans on running into any pedestrians, but few can avoid the pedestrian who runs into them. Your chances of striking a pedestrian are much higher than you might expect—in 1978 about 8,000 pedestrians were killed by automobiles and 100,000 more were injured. Avoid models with sharp corners or protrusions on the front end. High front ends on cars tend to push pedestrians under the wheels, so cars with lower flattened bumpers should be chosen.

b. *Gas Tanks*
Gas tank location is an important safety consideration on any car, new or old. Two gas tank locations are generally acknowledged as safer than others. One of these is behind the rear seat area, above the rear axle. This design also requires some kind of firewall to separate the fuel tank from the rear seat lest fuel escape from a ruptured tank into the passenger compartment. The other preferred location is under the rear seat, ahead of the rear axle. Many subcompacts with front-wheel drive use the latter design, which locates the fuel tank far forward of the rear of the car. Avoid designs that locate the fuel tank close to the rear of the car or near potential puncture sources. The Ford Pinto is an example of a car with this kind of poor gas tank design. Also, stay clear of vehicles that have exposed fuel lines or fittings within the trunk area, or a vulnerable fuel filler location. Some compact and midsize Fords from 1960 to 1971 actually used the top of the gas tank as the floor of the trunk.

UNNECESSARY OPTIONS

Optional equipment on cars all too often just adds to the price of the car and

153

causes excessive repair bills. The auto industry pushes options because they boost profits. Even a president of the National Automobile Dealers Association, Hugh R. Gibson, criticized many options as wasteful and unwanted by consumers but forced on them by the auto manufacturers:

> Another way for our manufacturers to cut the price of cars to the consumer is to stop putting unneeded and unwanted accessories and gimcracks on cars, regardless of whether the public needs or wants them.
>
> These are what the manufacturer calls "mandatory options." That's a funny phrase, isn't it? "Option" means you have a choice. "Mandatory" means "you have to." So, "mandatory option" means there is a choice but it is the "manufacturer's choice" and the public *has* to accept it.
>
> A typical car with radial tires, bumper guards, side moldings, day-night mirrors, and fancy interiors can run up the price $400 to $500 higher than it needs to be.
>
> I call on our manufacturers to stop loading their cars with fancy gadgets that add hundreds of dollars to the cost.

Avoid delicate options with a high frequency-of-repair record, such as power seats, air-conditioners, automatic speed controls, eyelid headlamp covers, power windows, power antennas, sunroofs, and moon roofs. (See Chapter 11 for further discussion on "delicate options.")

One method of selling options is to offer them in "packages" or "groups." You end up paying for unwanted frills in order to get the equipment you really want. Often the only new cars available from the dealer's lot are "loaded" with options. If you are willing to wait for delivery, you can specially order a car with only the options you really want instead of settling for the extravagantly equipped cars available for immediate delivery. This simply means planning a month or two ahead on buying a new car. The wait will mean an initial saving of hundreds of dollars in the price of the car and a later saving of costly repair trips to the garage.

Service Contracts. Optional extended warranties or service contracts are available through many dealerships. There are different types, including those offered by auto manufacturers and independent insurance companies. Coverage and costs vary from plan to plan. For example, some auto companies offer extended warranty coverage to thirty-six months or 36,000 miles for a onetime payment of about $100 to $300, depending on the make and model. Some insurance companies offer renewable yearly contracts. Basically, these plans are a form of insurance in case the need for a costly repair occurs after the regular warranty expires. If you live in a strong consumer protection state, such as Maryland, with statutes preventing car companies from limiting their implied warranties, you are better off without the service contract.

When considering service contracts, you should ask the following questions:

154

1. What repairs does the policy cover? What is excluded from coverage?
2. What is necessary to file a claim?
3. Is the policy transferable to a subsequent buyer of the car during the coverage period?
4. What are the requirements in vehicle maintenance and repair parts before a claim is honored?
5. Where can you get repairs under the contract?
6. Does the policy begin with the purchase of the car or after the manufacturer's written warranty expires? Remember that the car comes with a written warranty for at least 12,000 miles or twelve months, whichever comes first.
7. Does the company have the option to drop the service contract when your car gets older and more in need of repair?

WHAT VALUE TO GIVE TO EPA FUEL ECONOMY RATINGS?

All new cars should have an EPA or DOE fuel economy label on the window. Before 1979 the label gave estimated fuel economies for both city and highway driving. When the EPA ratings first came out in 1975, they were good estimates of consumer fuel economy. But by 1979 the auto companies had learned how to beat the ratings system so well that EPA dropped publication of the *highway* ratings and began using only the city rating as a single rating. Highway ratings may be reinstated in the future.

Until the EPA gets an accurate test for fuel economy and requires the auto companies to test cars that correspond to the ones consumers buy, as opposed to finely tuned prototypes, the Center recommends that consumers use the single rating (or only the city rating on pre-1979 cars, which have both city and highway ratings listed) with caution. This rating will accurately rank cars that are 5 mpg different in ratings. But it is not accurate enough to distinguish between cars that are less than 3 mpg apart.

HOW TO CHOOSE A DEALERSHIP

The best possible dealership is one which is convenient to your home or place of work and has a solid reputation in sales and service. The number of trained or licensed mechanics can be a good indicator of efficient service. A good dealership performs warranty work when it is needed without giving consumers unnecessary delay. If you are still not sure, ask the dealer a few questions, such as:

- Do you give customers copies of warranty repair work orders?
- Is warranty work as high a priority here as nonwarranty work?
- Do you fully prepare every new car before delivery? Do you give customers copies of the work sheet when it is completed? How much does it cost the customer?
- When a car is clearly a lemon, how do you handle it?

155

- What do you do if the car is delivered with many differences from the one the consumer ordered?
- When a car is recalled, do you have any trouble obtaining parts?

See if you can get any answers in writing. Such questioning provides the consumer with more information to consider before ordering the car from that dealer.

If you choose a dealership that is thirty miles away just to save $100 on the purchase price, you may regret having done this when you must drive out there every time the car needs warranty work.

Many local consumer groups keep listings of recommended dealers. So check with such groups before you buy. Other sources of information on dealers include state and local consumer protection offices as well as the experiences of your friends and business associates. Check with the local Better Business Bureau if no other source of reliable information is available. An excellent example of how a local consumer group can help is the Washington Center for the Study of Services, which publishes a report, *Washington Consumers' Checkbook on Cars*, on the quality and cost of repair at local dealers and independent garages.

CHAPTER 11 *How to Avoid Buying a Lemon*

CHRYSLER'S WOES

PUBLICITY ON RECALLS,
STIFFER COMPETITION
HURT NO. 3 CAR MAKER

SALES OF VOLARE, ASPEN SAG
AS AUTO MARKET SOFTENS,
OTHERS OFFER COMPACTS

ANGER AT "LEMONS" AWARDS

By Leonard M. Apcar

Last summer Vikki Huff of Wilton, Conn., embarked on a six-week vacation that she won't forget. She loaded her two young children and camping gear into her sparkling yellow, four-day-old Dodge Aspen stationwagon and headed west.

But within 100 miles of starting out, she says, the Aspen engine's rocker arms began to rattle, and eventually had to be replaced. As she drove along a Kentucky highway at about 50 miles an hour, the hood flew up, blocking the windshield.

In Colorado, the horn, lights, and turn signals all conked out at once. In Iowa the transmission gears jammed, and twice along the way the battery went dead. Mrs. Huff says she spent a major part of the vacation hopscotching around the countryside from one dealership to another 10 in all—of Chrysler Corp., maker of the Aspen.

"My kids saw more of Chrysler showrooms than the sights of the United States," she says.*

When Vikki Huff returned home, she took out a local newspaper ad soliciting complaints from other Aspen and Volare owners. She received a huge response. The owners banded together, holding a "lemoncade" protest, then a "lemonstration," and finally began to prepare a class action lawsuit against Chrysler Corporation.

Even the most knowledgeable and prepared shopper can end up with a lemon. But careful preparation and planning can improve your chances of avoiding a lemon. Learn all the important facts about the car you are considering before entering the dealer's showroom.

Try to find a dealership that is conveniently located and has a solid

---

Wall Street Journal, January 18, 1978, p. 1.

157

reputation for service. (See Chapter 10 for tips on finding a good dealership.) Do not rush into a deal—the salesperson may try to pressure you into buying a car. Take the time to shop around and test-drive the models you are considering. Do not hesitate to ask the salesperson for a full breakdown of the cost. A consumer has the right to ask as many questions as he or she wants to. If the salesperson does not cooperate, go somewhere else.

Sources of Information on New- and Used-Car Buying. *Available for free* from the U.S. Department of Transportation, National Highway Traffic Safety Administration, Office of Public Affairs and Consumer Services, Washington, D.C. 20590:

"Common Sense in Buying a New Car"
"Common Sense in Buying a Safe Used Car"
"Consumer Protection Under the Federal Odometer Law"

Available from Consumers Union, Book Department, Orangeburg, New York 10962:

Guide to Used Cars. Sums up Consumers Union's advice on which models to consider and which to avoid, where to buy and how to inspect a used car. Detailed reports on 131 cars, CU's ratings of 250 cars, and predicted repair incidence for 287 cars are included. ($5.50 plus 50 cents postage-handling) "How to Buy a Used Car." Consumers Union pamphlet on what points to check, how to check them, and what to have a mechanic look for. (75 cents)

Available in magazine or bookstores:
Consumer Reports Annual Auto Issue (April of every year). New-car buyers should study the "CU Judges the Cars" before entering the dealer's showroom. Both new- and used-car buyers should read "Frequency-of-Repair Records," based on readers' replies to CU's annual questionnaire.
Consumer Reports Annual Buying Guide Issue (December of every year). The 1978 issue lists inspections that individuals can perform in buying a used car.

The Compleat California Consumer Catalogue (1976). Available by mail for $1.00 from: Publication Section, P.O. Box 20191, Sacramento, California 95820.
The Car Buying and Selling Book. For a free copy, write Shell Oil Co., Consumer Relations, One Shell Plaza, P.O. Box 2463, Houston, Texas 77001.

ORDERING A NEW CAR

Because of an imbalance in bargaining positions between car makers and car buyers, many of the usual steps that a consumer would follow when a new product turns out to be defective are closed. It is almost impossible to return or exchange a new car without trouble. Almost any other product you purchase must work or it can be returned, but not cars. One reason: the contract you sign for a new car deprives you of *most* of the rights and powers that you would otherwise have (see Chapter 6 for those rights you *do* have).

Though it is unlikely you will succeed (let us know if you do), you can protect your rights by substituting the Consumer's New-Car Order Form proposed in Appendix A for the dealer's form. Unfortunately, the dealer's freedom to vary the terms of the contract with you is limited by the franchise imposed by the manufacturer. This proposal to substitute forms tells the dealer that you are not happy with the contract offered and will suggest ways in which the contract can be made more acceptable to consumers. After all, why should dealers write the contract all in their own favor? Exert some old-fashioned bargaining power as a customer.

There are other less ambitious precautions you can take when you order which may help you avoid a lemon.

1. *Avoid New Models*

Any new-model vehicle in its very first year of production usually turns out to have a lot of defects. Often the manufacturer is not able to remedy the defective design problems until the second, third, or even fourth year of production. For example, although the Volkswagen Rabbit in its first year (1975) was one of the top-rated subcompacts tested by Consumers Union (*Consumer Reports*, July 1975), the car was downgraded in its second year because of technical bugs that appeared in use. Later, in its third and fourth years, the manufacturer was able to work out most of the bugs. If the manufacturer has not been able to work out a new car's problems by the third year of production, the car will likely be a lemon forever. A classic example is the Chevrolet Vega, which was first introduced in 1971.

2. *Avoid New Cars Made During the First Three Months of a Model Year*

Most car companies close down their assembly lines every year to make the annual style changes that result in the next model-year cars. In addition to adding hundreds of dollars to the price of a new car, the annual style change will introduce new defects into the cars that first come off the assembly line in the new model year. It takes several months to iron these bugs out so it is better to avoid these cars.

3. *Delicate Options*

Avoid delicate options with a high frequency-of-repair record, such as power seats, air-conditioners, automatic speed controls, eyelid headlamp covers, power windows, power antennas, sunroofs, and moon roofs. Ralph Nader obtained an internal list of warranty repairs on 1978 model Fords that listed moon roofs, manual sunroofs, electric sunroofs, and power windows as first, third, fifth, and sixth in frequency of repair.

Not only do options inevitably need costly repairs, but they also needlessly run up the sticker price and operating costs of a car. For example, air-conditioning costs $500 and can detract 4 mpg from a car's fuel economy. Vinyl roofs not only cost up to $200 but also absorb the sun's heat so well that air-conditioning may become a necessity. For a good discussion on desirable versus undesirable options, see *Consumer Reports*, April 1976, "Choosing the Right Options."

As modern cars get smaller and lighter because of improved designs to

159

meet fuel economy standards, some options such as power steering and power brakes may no longer be necessary, except in the largest cars. One of the best ways to tell is to drive a dealer's demonstrator car without those power accessories.

4. *Dealer's Checklist*

Request a copy of the dealer's predelivery service and adjustment check sheet (or make-ready list) at the time your new car is delivered. Write the request directly on your new-car order. This request informs the dealer that you are aware of the dealer's responsibility to check your new car for defects. This may result in the performance of a more careful predelivery inspection when your car arrives. If the salesperson professes ignorance of the checklist, show him or her a copy of the list reproduced in Appendix C.

5. *Warranty*

As explained more fully in Chapter 6, "Your Legal Rights," the Magnuson-Moss Warranty Act requires all written warranties to be easy to read and understand, but does not require them to be fair to consumers. As a result, auto warranties are still clearly anticonsumer.

Since the warranty, like the new-car order form, deprives consumers of many of their rights, ask the dealer to use a fairer warranty, such as the one proposed in Appendix B. Although the dealer may say the manufacturer won't allow it, press anyway, and tell us if you succeed. Some dealers will give a longer-lasting warranty, valid at those dealerships as a sales pitch.

6. *Tire Warranty*

Most major manufacturers do not give warranties on tires. The tire policies of the Big Four domestic companies are similar—the tires are warranted by the tire manufacturer. Specific warranty information and tire adjustments must be obtained from the tire manufacturer's distributors, dealers, or retail stores. Ask the auto dealer for a copy of the tire warranty.

PICKING UP YOUR NEW CAR

1. *Is It Ready to Drive? The Make-Ready Procedure*

The dealer is the final step in the auto manufacturer's inspection procedure. The supposedly finished cars often arrive at the dealership in such poor condition that they are commonly referred to by dealers as "build-it-yourself kits." Many of these cars are also illegal—they have maladjusted parts, and poorly tuned engines which violate pollution standards set by the U.S. Environmental Protection Agency.

A 1978 EPA survey of twenty-five Ford and Lincoln-Mercury dealerships in Washington, D.C., and Atlanta, Georgia, found that the dealers were not making emission-related checks and adjustments required by law to prepare new vehicles for delivery. Not one dealership performed all ten procedures investigated. The only procedure performed by all twenty-five dealerships was the fluid check, and only two dealerships tested the choke setting on the new cars. Ten failed to perform the hose connection check, and three dealerships did not even bother to test-drive the new vehicles.

Have the salesperson or another authorized representative of the dealer

160

get and initial the predelivery service and adjustment check sheet (make-ready list) as an assurance that the make-ready was actually completed. This is one way to reduce the more than twenty defects found in the average new car by Consumers Union.

The important thing for a consumer to realize is that a new (or used) car may be so defective that the consumer should "reject" the car as soon as he can. "Reject" the lemon before, or even after, taking physical possession of the car, as long as "rejection" occurs within the reasonable time necessary for adequate inspection (usually the first week or so). Or "revoke acceptance" of the car after the reasonable time for inspection has expired. (The legal right of "rejection" is discussed later in this chapter, while "revocation of acceptance" is discussed in Chapter 6.) Once the consumer takes delivery (physical possession) of a lemon, the consumer in most cases will not be able to return it or get the purchase price back without a legal struggle. At the point the consumer takes possession of the car, he or she loses the best leverage over the dealer—the threat of buying an acceptable new car elsewhere.

There are three ways to determine the condition of a car: (1) a diagnostic inspection, (2) a test drive, and (3) a thorough self-inspection in broad daylight at the dealer's lot. Unfortunately, most new-car dealers will refuse to let a consumer take a new car for a test drive, let alone a diagnostic inspection. But every consumer has the right to an inspection of a new car at the dealer's lot and the right to refuse to take a new car that is not in excellent condition.

The excuses that a dealer gives for not letting a consumer test-drive a new car are numerous. For instance, one dealer incorrectly told a consumer:

> We can't let you take it out on the road until there are plates on the car. We can't put your plates on until the title passes to you, which of course doesn't happen until you've either paid or signed the financing agreement.

If your dealer objects, point out that the law allows the buyer a "reasonable opportunity to inspect" a prospective purchase before he or she is bound to accept it. The Uniform Commercial Code, which is the law in all states except Louisiana, states: "Acceptance of goods occurs when the buyer after a reasonable opportunity to inspect the goods signifies to the seller that the goods are conforming or that he will take or retain them in spite of their nonconformity." See the *Zabriskie* case, discussed in Chapter 6, where the court held: "It is clear that a buyer does not accept goods [a car in this case] until he has had a 'reasonable opportunity to inspect.' "

2. *Inspection at the Dealer's Lot*

The following checklists cover the most common defects that you can recognize in parts or make-ready adjustments in an inspection at the dealer's lot. The specific problems listed are discussed in detail in Chapter 14, "What Usually Goes Wrong."

a. Brakes

Push hard on the brake pedal for at least a minute. If it sinks toward the

161

floor, there is probably a leak in the brake system which could lead to sudden brake failure.

b. Tires

Check for cuts, bulges, or other signs of injury. Some assembly plants subject tires to extreme abuse before the car leaves the factory. Check particularly the tread and inside walls of the tires.

c. Steering

Turn the steering wheel back and forth to see how much free play there is before the front wheels start to turn. If the rim of the steering wheel can be moved two inches (one inch to either side) or more before the wheels move, the steering gear is too loose for safe operation (with power steering, run the engine).

d. Latches, Doors, Lids, and Windows

Check to see that the outside doors, the glove compartment door, the hood, the trunk lid and all windows close securely. The hood has a double latch which should keep the hood down even if it is not quite closed all the way. To test this, open the hood a crack and let go of the hood release lever. Then try to pull the hood open; it should open only about an inch. Misaligned windows not only let in the wind and rain but also cause excessive noise in the interior. Run each window from the fully opened to the fully closed position. If the window sticks or is difficult to move, there is a problem that needs correction. If there is a gap at the top, there is also a defect.

e. Body Damage

Many cars are damaged in transit and, when possible, repaired and sold as new. Telltale signs include spray paint in out-of-the-way places such as on the front of the sideview mirror or on the underside of the car, slightly discolored portions of the exterior surface (imperfect color match), and hard-to-close doors, trunk lids, or hoods. Sighting along the length of the car can help detect paint problems and variations in the sheet metal that indicate damages that were repaired. It is absolutely necessary to do this inspection in full daylight as many paint problems or repair signs cannot otherwise be detected.

f. Options

Make sure that all the options you ordered are there, especially safety ones. Certain options, such as air-conditioning, that are supposed to be installed by the manufacturer can be disastrous if installed by the dealer. Cars with *factory*-installed air-conditioning units are designed to accept the extra loads: front springs may be heavier, the cooling system may have greater capacity, tires will be oversized where needed, and the air-conditioner will be integrated into the car's fresh-air system. Many options, such as engines or transmissions, can be substituted or switched without the consumer's noticing. For example, manufacturers will sometimes substitute a smaller or larger engine than that ordered if the proper engine is not immediately available on the assembly line. In one case, General Motors even put Chevrolet engines in thousands of Oldsmobiles without telling the purchasers.

g. Engine, Transmission, and Brake Leaks

Even a new car can have an oil, a transmission, or another system-fluid

162

leak. The first check is simply to look for visible leaks in the engine compartment—oil on the engine and fluid on brake, radiator, power steering, and other hoses and connections. After doing this, drive the car to a clean spot on the lot and leave it running for a few minutes at a fast idle. Then move it and look for any fresh marks that indicate leaks on the spot where the car was.

h. Body Water Leaks

Ask to have the car washed just before you take delivery. Then look and feel for water leaks around all the windows and doors, in the trunk, and under the dash. There is no better test than this to determine whether a new car has water leaks, which frequently will cause an unsuspecting new-car purchaser unending trouble.

i. Miscellaneous

Operate all controls and accessories to be sure that they work (heater, radio, brake and turn signals, windshield wipers, lights, etc.).

Check to see that a new-car label is attached to the car (usually on the side window), as required under the federal Automobile Information Disclosure Act. Each label is required to list certain information, such as: the make, model and identification number, the manufacturer's suggested retail price of the vehicle and each item of optional equipment on the car, destination charges, and the final assembly point.

3. *Test Drive*

It would make a major difference in the car-selling business if buyers as a routine matter were to test-drive their cars before making a final commitment. Although such pretesting is permitted by some dealers (particularly small dealers, who have to try harder to make a sale and who will, therefore, bend over backward to meet many customer requests that large-volume dealers can afford to refuse), it is not a general practice. If a dealer lets you take a test drive, do not limit yourself to a spin around the block. Take it out on a turnpike to see that it performs correctly at all speeds.

Most people would never think of asking to test-drive a brand-new car, on the assumption that if it is a new car, it must be close to perfect. Though most new cars appear roadworthy, many nevertheless have serious defects that become apparent during thorough testing.

Many letters like the following have come to us from people who have experienced first- or second-day breakdowns.

August 17, 1978

Dear Mr. Nader:

On May 5, 1978, my husband and I bought a new 1978 Grand Prix. The very next day the drive shaft broke with less than 200 miles on the car. We are still having all kinds of problems with our car. Our car has been in service five times already and has to go in for more. The items listed below are just some of the things we are having trouble with.

1. Front-end alignment
2. Right and left caster

163

3. Steering

[Nos. 4 through 14 include problems with door locks, windshield wipers, weather stripping, carpeting, and choke.]

/s/
J. and A. Behof
Westmont, Illinois

March 23, 1978

Dear Mr. Nader:

On January 11, 1978, I purchased a [new 1978] Plymouth Horizon. On January 12 I was to pick up the car but was told that due to a rattle of an undetermined nature I should leave the car. On Jan. 16 I returned, picked up the car, and drove it as far as three miles when it broke down. The car was towed to the dealer and I was told that the clutch had burned out of it. On March 10, on the way to Cumberland, Maryland, my friend, who was traveling with me, found that the lock on the passenger side was faulty and had to enter the car through the driver's side. When I went to close the door on the driver's side, the handle came off in my hand. As if that were not enough, upon entering into Cumberland, I stopped the car for a few minutes, and when I started up again I found that I had no gear shifting.

I called to a local resident for help and when he looked under my car he called to me to look under also. The horror I felt when I looked, words cannot express. My drive shaft was completely dismantled and hanging on the ground. As I looked away from the car, I found parts strewn up and down the street. My friend and I collected as many as we could, placed them in my litterbag, and gave them to the servicepeople at Potomac Motors. The odometer read 280.6 miles.

/s/
N. Sturtz
Alexandria, Va.

Many car buyers pass up a test drive or ignore its results, believing that, even if defects reveal themselves, the warranty will cover them or the dealer will assume responsibility for repairs. This is all too often just a delusion. Letter after letter received by the Center for Auto Safety and Ralph Nader indicates that such repairs are simply not that easy to obtain. For example, the following consumer failed to attach enough importance to a test run that showed the car was defective:

March 2, 1977

Dear Mr. Nader:

I am writing this letter with great aggravation, frustration, and disgust. It all started on July 8, 1976, when I purchased a new 1976 Ford LTD from Gilboy Ford-Mercury. Since then I have had nothing but trouble with the car and with the dealer.

First, the car stalls, cuts out, and backfires. It did this even when I took it on a test run before I bought the car. The salesman assured me

164

it would be taken care of if I bought the car but it wasn't alleviated. This is one of the major problems of the car till this day.

Sincerely,

/s/

J. P. Toth

Whitehall, Pennsylvania

Dealers, even if their intentions are the best, find it difficult to remedy new-car defects because of overloaded repair shops, inadequate compensation from manufacturers for warranty work, unskilled mechanics, defects which simply elude diagnosis or are unrepairable, and poor design.

4. *Professional Diagnosis*

Because the make-ready operations are rarely performed and are not covered by warranty, and because a test drive provides but a partial indication of how well your car runs, have a mechanic or a diagnostic center check the car before accepting it. (You have the legal right to such an inspection as explained above.) The investment can prove to be a wise one. Many large cities have diagnostic "clinics" or "lanes" equipped with elaborate machinery to analyze every phase of the car's performance and condition. The quality and honesty of diagnostic centers vary widely, so it is necessary to pick a center with a good reputation. If the diagnostic center has ties to a repair facility, inform the mechanic or service writer that the repairs will be performed elsewhere (in order to eliminate the incentive to add unnecessary repairs to the diagnosis). (For more on diagnostic clinics, see Chapter 13.)

BUYING A USED CAR

A used car can save a consumer money. Hertz, the car-rental company, reports that savings in operating costs of a one-year-old car, as compared with savings in operating a new car, can be fifteen to twenty percent. On a three- to four-year-old car, the saving is roughly fourteen cents a mile—about $4,200 less than the costs of operating a new car for three years at 10,000 miles a year. The greatest saving is depreciation, since the original owner already absorbed the heavy depreciation that accompanies a new-car purchase.

A key factor in buying a used car is finding a safe and reliable one. A defective used car can be dangerous to your safety and pocketbook. Good preparation and patience cut the risk of ending up with a bad used car. Without adequate care, a consumer can end up with someone else's lemon. To help consumers in purchasing a used car, the Federal Trade Commission has proposed a rule, discussed later in this chapter, requiring a disclosure statement to accompany all used cars sold by dealers.

Consider buying a used car through the classified advertising section of a local newspaper. You can usually get a better price when buying from a private owner, since there are no commission charges, overhead costs, and other expenses that a dealership would have. The private owner should be able to give a detailed description, including repair records, of the mainte-

165

nance history of the car. But there are pitfalls, including the fact that most private owners do not offer warranties. You can write out a contract of sale, though, with provisions specifying who will pay for repairs if the car breaks down within a set time period. Be prepared to handle the paper work in transferring the title and getting new license plates.

Selecting a Used Car. Many of the same rules apply in selecting a used car that apply in looking for a new car. Unless you're prepared to pay extra, stay away from sport and luxury models. Not only do you have to pay extra for many needless frills, but also these cars are the ones most likely to rattle, squeak, and have other defects. Avoid models with power-operated windows and seats, and similar convenience features. Such features are troubleprone; they're expensive to repair, and they raise the price of the car. Steer clear of "orphans" (makes and models no longer in production), very old models, and uncommon imports. Parts and service for such cars may be costly or difficult to find.

In selecting a used car, a consumer must frequently question the dealer or owner in depth to get enough information on which to base a decision to purchase. Even where the consumer does ask questions, often the answers are insufficient or inaccurate. For example, consumers can expect to receive little information from dealers about the safety or other mechanical condition of a used vehicle they are considering for purchase. As a matter of fact, many used-car dealers intentionally cover up mechanical faults in order to sell the cars. According to the Federal Trade Commission:

> [T]he consumer shopping for a used vehicle is confronted with immaculate vehicles and smooth-talking salespeople who strive to assure the customer that the gleaming beauties are in "mint condition" or "dependable transportation" while maintaining a wall of silence about defects which may lie beneath the surface.

Used-car dealers often "misrepresent that used vehicles are defect-free or that substantial repairs have been performed." Such dealers promise to fix any defect that develops, but when confronted with a problem at a later date, they deny having made any promises. These oral assurances have all too often proven empty rhetoric to the buyer of a lemon.

Mechanical Inspection. The lack of reliable information on a car's operating and safety condition is why a thorough mechanical inspection of the car before purchase is so important. Always take a used car to a diagnostic center or a good mechanic for an overall inspection before you buy it. If the used-car dealer refuses to let your own mechanic inspect the car, go to another dealer. Nor should you buy the car if refused a test drive with you at the wheel. Offer to take the dealer's mechanic along with you to the diagnostic inspection. Ask to see copies of all repair orders and other maintenance records, particularly if buying from a private owner. Not only does this tell how well the car has been kept up but also indicates whether it has needed such frequent repairs that it is a lemon.

166

Before taking a used car to a diagnostic center or mechanic for inspection, some simple on-the-lot and on-the-road tests can eliminate many bad used cars. Do these tests in good weather and during daylight. Some of the worst lemons have been sold at night, in the rain, or under other conditions that discourage consumers from thoroughly examining the car inside and out. For your convenience, we have included the following checklist from *Consumer Reports* to use in inspecting a used car. *Consumer Reports* offers an illustrated pamphlet, "How to Buy a Used Car," and an extensive "Guide to Used Cars," which includes information on frequency of repairs by make and model, lists used models that are good buys, and tells of specific models to avoid.

This checklist indicates the most important tests that should be done before deciding on a used car. If possible, bring someone along to help with those tests. On the lot, check the body for appearance items such as rust spots, blisters in the paint, flaking paint, ripples in the metal, and different shades of paint. Such tests performed by close visual inspection can reveal anything from major corrosion to evidence of a prior accident.

While on the lot, check to make sure that the car's lights, indicators, and accessories are all in working order. Start the engine and listen for unusual noises. Inside the car, make sure that the instrument-panel lights work, also testing the windshield wipers and washers, fuel gauge, turn signals, horn, and radio (if there is one). Then with the help of someone standing outside the car, make sure that each of the car's exterior lights work.

Get out of the car and push up and down on a fender to check the car's shock absorbers. When pushed in such a manner, the car should go up and down once and stop—in a middle position. If the car tends to keep on bouncing, it may need new shock absorbers. Shake the top of each front wheel—in and out—to check for looseness and noise that may indicate bad wheel bearings or worn suspension joints.

As with the on-the-lot tests, certain defects will be readily apparent by driving the car for about a half hour on the road. If the seller refuses a road test, look elsewhere for a car. The automatic transmission should engage smoothly when put into drive and then shift itself smoothly into higher gears as the car speeds up. A manual transmission should also engage smoothly as you shift gears without the clutch grabbing. Look for smooth pickups from low speeds without pinging or knocking to check for a good engine. The brakes should stop the car three times from 45 mph without any swerving or the pedal feeling soft. When accelerating hard from low speeds, look for thick clouds of blue smoke, which indicate worn piston rings. Finally, check for handling and stability, particularly over rough roads. If any item seems questionable, check it with your mechanic during the shop tests.

If the car passes the on-the-lot and road tests, arrange for a good auto mechanic to do some shop tests, including checking the engine compression, brake and exhaust system, battery, and any suspected defects. The mechanic should be a person who will be working for you and not for any dealer. Expect to pay the mechanic at least $20 for the shop tests; it's money well spent if it saves you from buying a lemon or a car with low compression that needs a $600 engine overhaul within the first 5,000 miles.

Besides checking out the following, you can use the list to enter estimated costs of repairs. The total figure for repair costs can give you a better idea of the real price of a particular car.

On-the-Lot Tests — Estimated cost of repair

— 1. Interior wear and tear $—
— 2. Worn tires (including spare) $—
— 3. Bad rust spots, flaking paint $—
— 4. Malfunctioning windows and doors $—
— 5. Worn front-wheel bearings or worn suspension joints $—
— 6. Brake-fluid leaks $—
— 7. Defective lights, indicators, accessories $—
— 8. Worn shock absorbers $—
— 9. Damage to body and frame $—

On-the-Road Tests

—10. Wheels out of line or out of balance $—
—11. Smoothness of engine pickup $—
—12. Problems with transmission $—
—13. Problems with brakes $—
—14. Problems with steering $—

Estimated cost of repair

—15. Worn piston rings $—
—16. Need for repairing shock absorbers, front end, or suspension $—
—17. Overheating of engine $—

In-the-Shop Tests

—18. Problems with engine compression (valves, piston rings) $—
—19. Problems with brake drums, discs, linings, wheel cylinders, master cylinder, front-wheel bearings, or parking brake $—
—20. Worn or broken seals, rusted or broken muffler or exhaust pipe $—
—21. Defective battery; other problems $—

These precautions should enable you to avoid even such lemons as flooded cars which frequently look like good buys. For example, cars damaged by saltwater flooding during the Boston area's severe blizzard of 1978 were being resold as "good" used cars in Maine, according to *Automotive News*. About 5,000 cars had been judged total losses by insurance companies and "were not worth a quarter," according to car experts. Although insured owners had been compensated for their losses, the cars were still being sold at salvage pools in southern New England for resale to unwary used-car buyers. The following special hints to avoid buying a flooded used car were offered by an insurance company executive:

- Check for sand, silt, or salt deposits under the carpeting in the passenger compartment. A stagnant odor also may be present.
- Ask to remove a seat cushion, then drop it bottom side down on pavement. If salt falls out, beware.
- Check recesses in the intake and exhaust manifold and other crevices for indications of sand deposits.
- Check for sand in chrome headlight rims.
- Check wiring for signs of corrosion. Note copper connections: They turn green when exposed to saltwater.

- Ask to see the title to determine if it has been stamped "submerged" or "flood car."

Generally, your best bet in a used car is one that is two or three years old. If cars only a few years old were properly cared for by their previous owners, they still have a lot of life left. If you find several cars within your price range that fit your particular needs, consider the one with the least mileage on the odometer and best general overall condition.

Used-Car Warranties. Although every new car comes with a written warranty, many used cars come without any warranties at all. These cars may be sold "as is" or "with all faults." Often cars without warranties are sold by private parties or by organizations that have no service facilities, such as banks or finance companies.

Where warranties are given, they often differ. One warranty may cover parts and labor for thirty days. Another warranty may cover only parts for ninety days. Or another may be a 50-50 warranty, with the buyer paying half the cost of parts and labor for a certain period of time. Since some of these are clearly better than others, it is important to shop around for a good warranty.

The reputation of the dealer can be more important to the buyer than the used-car warranty. Even with a complete warranty for parts and labor for sixty days, a dishonest dealer can give a consumer the runaround for two months without actually fixing the car. If the warranty or the deal itself sounds too good to be true, or if the dealer looks like a fly-by-night, check with local consumer protection agencies and the Better Business Bureau on the dealer's reputation.

Whatever the warranty, make sure it is understandable and in writing before buying the car. The warranty should specify the actual terms of its coverage and duration. In other words, the warranty should spell out the parts and labor guaranteed and the length of time of the warranty. The words "sixty-day warranty" by themselves do not mean anything. Specific components or systems such as the engine must be listed to give the warranty meaning. Otherwise, one could get a warranty that covers only the most extreme failures.

If the used car is a recent model, the original manufacturer's warranty may still be in effect. Check to see if coverage is transferred to you before purchasing the car. This transfer should include a warranty book with the name of the new-car dealer who originally sold the car.

Federal Help for Used-Car Buyers. A few federal laws, regulations, and services make used-car buying just a little easier. Additional help may come from state laws and regulations.

Auto Safety Hotline. After selecting a used car, call the auto safety hotline of the National Highway Traffic Safety Administration (NHTSA) to verify the safety-defect and recall history of the vehicle. This hotline is toll-free, serving the citizens of every state except Hawaii and Alaska. The number

169

is 800-424-9393. In the Washington, D.C., area, the number is 426-0123. When calling, be prepared to give the make, model, year, and vehicle identification number of the car.

If you find the car was recalled, check with a mechanic to see if the defects were fixed by the previous owner. If not, make arrangements with a franchised dealer of that model to have the car repaired for free under the recall. If the mechanic is not sure whether a recall repair was done, have a franchised dealer check with the manufacturer, which keeps a computerized list of serial numbers of cars that have not been fixed in a recall.

The Odometer Law. The federal odometer law, part of the Motor Vehicle Information and Cost Savings Act, makes it illegal for anyone to tamper with a vehicle's odometer to show the wrong mileage. Neither the vehicle owner nor anyone else may turn back or disconnect the odometer, except to perform necessary repairs. This law protects car buyers from a seller concealing a car's true mileage by turning back or disconnecting the odometer. The law recognizes that true mileage is an indicator of a vehicle's condition and value. Odometer fraud is a widespread practice used against unsuspecting buyers by dishonest sellers of used motor vehicles. Rolling back odometers to disguise the true vehicle mileage has cost consumers an estimated $1 billion a year, according to the Department of Transportation.

The federal law requires the seller to give the buyer a written statement of the mileage before the sale of any vehicle, except antique vehicles and heavy trucks. Under the law, a person who has been victimized by odometer fraud has a private right of action against the violator. If you sue the seller in state or federal court and win, the court will award you $1,500 or three times the amount of damages, whichever is greater, plus court costs and reasonable attorney's fees. Consult an attorney if you suspect the odometer has been changed. Report violations to the state attorney general's office, which can bring civil actions on behalf of consumers. The federal government can bring civil and criminal actions against violators of the law. In order to report a violation to the federal government, contact the National Highway Traffic Safety Administration, Office of the Chief Counsel, 400 Seventh St., S.W., Washington, D.C. 20590.

For a free copy of a pamphlet on odometers, "Consumer Protection Under the Federal Odometer Law," write the National Highway Traffic Safety Administration, Office of Public Affairs, Washington, D.C. 20590.

The Used-Car Rule. The Federal Trade Commission has a regulation concerning the sale of used cars by dealers. Under the regulation, dealers may decide whether or not to inspect each car offered for sale. Some dealers will choose not to inspect each car as a way to avoid having to tell consumers about any existing defects. Therefore, consumers should look for dealers who are willing both to inspect the used cars and to inform the consumer about its condition on the FTC-required window sticker, as explained below. Used cars which have been inspected and are rated "OK" on major components should be more reliable purchases.

170

If the dealer does inspect the car, the actual condition of the car must be disclosed to potential buyers by a window sticker. For each category of potential vehicle problems (for example, brakes, steering, transmission), the inspecting dealer would have to check the sticker either "OK" or "Not OK" or "Don't Know." Items marked "OK" would have to function properly for a reasonable time after the purchase or the consumer could get a refund under state law. If a car has been inspected, but has many major items marked "Don't Know," chances are the car will not be reliable since "Don't Know" may be used to disguise a "Not OK" rating. If the dealer chooses not to inspect the car, he must disclose that no inspection was made, by indicating "Don't Know" on the sticker.

A used-car dealer would also be required to disclose on the window sticker the duration and terms of any express warranty. If the car were being sold "as is," without any warranty at all, the dealer would be required to state this fact on the disclosure sticker with an explanation of the legal significance of an as-is sale; that is, there is *no warranty* at all—the purchaser must pay the costs of all repairs. But if the dealer had checked something "OK," he or she would be obligated to fix it if it were in fact defective. (Note: in some states, as-is sales are illegal; see Chapter 6.) The name and address and phone number of the dealership and the person responsible for handling consumer complaints would be included on the sticker.

The used-car rule may be useful in helping consumers avoid used cars with hidden defects. When shopping for a used car, remember that dealers are not required to inspect the vehicles. Therefore, ask the dealer for a car that has been inspected. Since the dealer is allowed to inspect the car and still check "Don't Know," look for inspected cars with "OK" or "Not OK" indicated on the required window sticker.

The purpose of the regulation is to encourage comparative shopping by providing consumers with important information about the condition of used cars and the extent of any warranties. The disclosure requirements will also encourage dealers to make needed repairs before offering a used car for sale.

To inquire about the used-car sales regulation, write the Federal Trade Commission, Bureau of Consumer Protection, Washington, D.C. 20580.

YOUR FIRST DAYS DRIVING THE CAR

The period permitted to complete a "reasonable inspection" of the car includes the first days of possession. After this period, the consumer is said to have "accepted" the car and further efforts to return the car must be based on "revocation of acceptance." If for some reason you were unable to test-drive the car or subject it to a mechanical check before taking delivery, put the car through its paces and get it to a diagnostic lane or a mechanic as soon as you can.

If the car turns out to have serious defects within the reasonable inspection period, you have the legal right to "reject" the new or used car—unless it is a used car that was sold "as is." "Rejection," which is similar to "revocation of acceptance" (discussed in Chapter 6), works best

171

in cases where something serious goes wrong during the first few miles, as in the *Zabriskie* case (Chapter 6), or within the first week or so of ownership. Revocation of acceptance, on the other hand, is a legal strategy that can be used months after accepting a new or used car if it takes that long for major defects to appear.

In *Zabriskie*, the car broke down only a few minutes after leaving the dealership, and the consumer immediately notified the dealer of his rejection. He stopped payment on the check and notified the dealer that the sale was canceled. The dealer, nevertheless, sent a wrecker to the consumer's home, brought the vehicle in, and made the necessary repairs. But the consumer continued to refuse acceptance of the new car. When the dealer sued the consumer for the purchase price, the court upheld the consumer's right to reject the car.

If you have paid other than by check, or the check has cleared before the lemon showed its true colors, you can reject the car in the same way and demand your money back from the dealer. If the dealer refuses, a lawsuit may be necessary to receive a refund. Many cases have upheld the consumer's right to reject the car, and they have ordered the dealer to return the owner's money.

If you decide to reject the car, follow these general guidelines:

1. Begin rejection as soon as the defect appears. This should be within the first week after delivery of the car. (If you have had the car for more than a week, many courts would conclude that you have "accepted" the car—in which case, follow the similar strategy of "revocation of acceptance" discussed in Chapter 6.)

2. Notify the dealer *in writing* that you are rejecting the car and explain why. Demand your money back, or inform the dealer that you have stopped payment on the check, whichever applies. Send this notification and demand by certified mail with return receipt requested. Keep a copy of this letter with all other records relating to the car purchase.

3. Return the car to the dealer's lot, noting the mileage. Offer the certificate of title and car keys to the dealer. If he or she does not accept them, just hold onto them and mention in the letter that the dealer can have the title and keys anytime he or she changes his or her mind. If the dealer does take them back, this helps prove that rejection has been agreed to by the dealer.

4. Remove the license plates if they are in your name. If they are the dealer's plates, just leave them on. Return your plates and registration to the Department of Motor Vehicles.

5. Notify your insurance company in writing that you have rejected the car, but do not cancel the insurance until the dispute is resolved. Ask the company to reduce the premium to the minimum needed to protect you while the car is on the dealer's lot.

6. If the dealer has financed the car or has arranged the financing for you, stop making payments on the car. Notify the finance company or bank in writing that you have rejected the car, explaining why. If the dealer or finance company sues you for the balance of the payments, you will need

172

an attorney to represent you. Show him or her the section on the Federal Trade Commission's holder-in-due-course rule, discussed in Chapter 6, which allows the consumer to withhold payments in many cases where the new car is a lemon.

This tactic worked perfectly for M. P. McCollough of Alexandria, Virginia, who purchased a used 1973 Toyota with dealer-arranged financing. When the car's fuel line broke within a few miles of the dealership, the consumer asked the dealer for a refund of the purchase price. The dealer wouldn't budge, so the consumer notified the finance company that she was rejecting the car and explained why. The finance company responded by stopping payment to the dealer on the car. The dealer finally gave in and offered to reimburse the consumer for the full purchase price of the car.

CONCLUSION

Without some basic changes in the way automobiles are sold, it will be difficult to detect certain types of lemons before being stuck with them. But you can take precautions which will reduce the chances of your new or used car's being defect-ridden. Perhaps the most important precaution is to avoid, if possible, putting yourself in the position of having no choice but to take the car you ordered even if it is not just right. This may be difficult to do if you have traded in your only car in order to get the new one. But if at all possible, arrange to have some form of backup transportation available, so that if the car is a lemon, you will be able to return it to the dealer.

APPENDIX A—CHAPTER 11

Consumer's New-Car Order Form
Conditions of the Agreement
(rewritten to preserve some basic consumer rights)

1. If vehicle ordered by purchaser cannot be delivered or tendered for delivery to purchaser within 15 days of delivery date specified hereon, purchaser reserves the right to cancel this order. Dealer shall be liable in event of cancellation for the return in full of deposit, in amount specified hereon.

2. If purchaser revokes order before delivery to purchaser of vehicle ordered, dealer reserves the right to retain deposit.

3. Price of new vehicle ordered is governed by this order. Any increase by dealer in price of vehicle ordered over the price specified hereon shall create in the buyer the right to obtain any vehicle offered for sale by dealer at the price stated hereon. Purchaser shall not be required to pay dealer more than price agreed upon as specified hereon, except for the cost of options or features ordered by purchaser after the signing of this order.

4. Vehicle offered in trade (hereinafter "trade-in") shall be delivered within 30 days of the date of this order or within 30 days of trade-in delivery date, if such date is specified, but in no case later than date new car is accepted by purchaser. If trade-in is not so delivered, dealer reserves the right to reappraise trade-in. If trade-in is not delivered to dealer in substantially the same condition as when it was appraised, dealer may reappraise the trade-in. If trade-in allowance is substantially reduced by dealer after initial appraisal for any reason, purchaser may terminate this order, and in the event of such termination, dealer shall retain advance deposit or $25, whichever is less.

5. In the event purchaser terminates this order before delivery of the new vehicle, but after dealer has sold trade-in, dealer may retain as a sales commission 15 percent of trade-in allowance specified in this order, plus reasonable itemized costs for repairs to the trade-in, but in no case shall the total of sales commission and repair costs exceed 35 percent of said trade-in allowance.

In the event purchaser rightfully revokes or terminates this order after the delivery of the new vehicle to purchaser, but after trade-in has been resold, purchaser shall receive from dealer 100 percent of resale price of trade-in.

6. Purchaser certifies he is over 18 years of age and under no legal disability and has right to dispose of trade-in, if any, and to assign to dealer certificate of title to said trade-in.

7. Dealer may cancel this order if purchaser fails to take delivery of ordered vehicle and make settlement (payment, or arrangements for time payments) within 15 days of the time dealer notifies purchaser of readiness of ordered vehicle for delivery, in person, by telephone, or in writing to address of purchaser specified hereon. In the event purchaser fails to make such settlement, dealer reserves the right to retain deposit.

174

8. Above and beyond all warranty protection provided to purchaser, dealer agrees to remedy all defects or malfunctions in new vehicle reported to dealer within 90 days of date of original retail delivery, at no charge to purchaser, unless the need for such repair is the result of misuse or racing of new vehicle, accident, fire or other casualty (unless the accident, fire, or other casualty is itself the result of a factory defect).

If within 10 days of date purchaser tenders vehicle to dealer for repair and provides dealer with written notice of defects or malfunctions in new vehicle, dealer has not corrected all such defects or malfunctions to the satisfaction of purchaser, purchaser reserves the right to have such corrections made at location of his choice, and if purchaser exercises this right, dealer agrees to reimburse purchaser for reasonable, itemized costs incurred in obtaining necessary repairs at location other than dealer's.

If the purchase of vehicle is a credit transaction, buyer may withhold payments to dealer or to any third party to whom the dealer referred the buyer, or who furnished forms to the dealer, or has taken paper from the dealer, until such defects have been remedied and outside repairman is paid in full.

9. If defects which substantially impair the safety or operating condition of said vehicle are not corrected to purchaser's satisfaction, purchaser reserves the right to revoke his acceptance of new vehicle in accordance with the provisions of the Uniform Commercial Code and/or other applicable laws.

If purchaser so revokes his acceptance of the vehicle, dealer shall refund within 10 days to purchaser all payments plus any interest payments made by purchaser for said vehicle, regardless of to whom paid. Such refund shall become payable upon delivery of vehicle to dealer's premises, and shall be adjusted only to the extent of (a) cost of repairing damages to vehicle or vehicle equipment resulting from purchaser's abuse or negligence, or from accident, fire, or other casualty not themselves caused by a manufacturing or dealer-repair defect, and (b) cost of replacing parts or equipment removed from vehicle if any after initial retail delivery.

10. In the event purchaser revokes acceptance of said vehicle under section nine of this agreement, all obligations of purchaser to third parties to whom the dealer referred the buyer, or who furnished forms to the dealer, or has taken paper from the dealer, for payments on said vehicle shall terminate on written notice to such third party of such revocation, except that purchaser shall remain liable to such third party for any amounts due to third party prior to date third party receives notice of such revocation. Dealer hereby agrees to assume any and all obligations to such third parties in excess of amount due to such third parties prior to date third party receives notice of such revocation.

11. If within three weeks of the date of delivery of new vehicle to purchaser, vehicle is rendered inoperable and cannot be removed under its own power because of a defect in said vehicle, unless shown by dealer to have resulted from accident or negligence or abuse on the part of purchaser, purchaser may revoke his acceptance of said vehicle, regardless of any efforts on the part of dealer to cure such defects. In such event, dealer agrees to refund all

payment made for such vehicle in full upon return of vehicle to his premises.
12. Nothing herein shall be construed in any way as limiting, waiving, or otherwise affecting rights of purchaser under any warranties, express or implied, created by the operation of the law or otherwise, pursuant to or as an incident of this agreement.
13. Nothing herein shall be construed in any way as limiting, waiving, or otherwise affecting the rights of the dealer to secure from the manufacturer appropriate reimbursement for expenses incurred by dealer in curing or attempting to cure defects or malfunctions attributable to manufacturer workmanship or manufacturer materials.
14. Any controversy or claim, except personal injury claims, arising out of or relating to this agreement, the breach thereof, or the goods affected hereby, whether such claim is founded in tort or in contract, shall be settled by arbitration under the rules of the American Arbitration Association, provided, however, that upon any such arbitration, the arbitrator(s) not vary or modify any of the provisions of this agreement. If any award is made to purchaser, dealer shall pay arbitration costs.

APPENDIX B—CHAPTER 11

Consumer's New-Vehicle Warranty

FIRST WARRANTY

(Name of Manufacturer and Dealer) warrant this (year and make of vehicle) to be fit for normal and anticipated uses for 5 years or 50,000 miles, whichever shall first occur.

SECOND WARRANTY

(Name of Manufacturer and Dealer) also warrant this new (year and make of vehicle) to be free from defects in material, workmanship, design, and assembly for the duration of its useful life.

LIMITATION

Repair or replacement of any part which fails as a result of noncompliance by owner with the schedule of maintenance operations specified by the manufacturer in the owner's manual for the (year and make of vehicle) shall not be covered by these warranties.

THIRD WARRANTY (Not Subject to Above Limitation)

In addition, during the first 90 days following the delivery of the new vehicle to purchaser, the manufacturer will provide, free of charge, at any (name of make) dealer, any adjustments and services required to maintain the vehicle in reasonable working order (unless the need for them is clearly the result of accident, vandalism, fire or other casualty, misuse, or racing) including, but not limited to:
- lubrication as needed
- wheel balancing, wheel alignment, and removal of all vibrations in the suspension
- headlight alignment
- cleaning of fuel, cooling, and brake systems
- addition of engine coolants, power steering, brake and air-conditioning fluids, and engine oil
- tightening of nuts, bolts, and fittings
- adjustment to carburetors, valves, belts, transmission, clutch and brake systems, hood, deck and door-closing mechanisms
- repair or replacement of soft trim and external appearance items damaged by normal exposure

177

LOANER CAR

If the car needs warranty repair work and "same-day" (morning to evening) service cannot be completed as promised or if warranty repairs require that the vehicle be kept overnight, the dealer will provide purchaser with a free loaner car until the car is ready.

APPENDIX C—CHAPTER 11

Manufacturer's Predelivery Inspection Checklist

Dealer	R.O. No.	Stock No.
	Complete Vehicle Identification Number	

1978 BUICK/OPEL
New-Vehicle Inspection
Procedure

Check, Inspect, and Perform the Following Operations:*

1. ☐ Under Hood:
   - All components for proper assembly, operation and leaks.
   - Test coolant protection.
   - Battery test indicator—green dot should be visible.
   - All fluid levels.
2. ☐ Body—Chassis:
   - Interior and exterior lights for proper operation.
   - Headlight aim (adjust if necessary to conform with local specifications).
   - Doors, hood, and compartment lids for proper operation, and adjust strikers or latches if necessary. (Includes checking all locks for proper operation.)
   - Install shipped parts of optional stationwagon luggage rack.
   - Install shipped parts air dam and mirrors—Opel sport coupe pkg.
   - Install license plate bracket—Skylark.
3. ☐ Under Vehicle:
   - Axle lube level.
   - Adjust tire pressure to specifications.
   - Install wheel covers and trim rings.
   - All fluid lines and couplings for leaks. Tighten as necessary.
   - For proper assembly of steering, suspension components and exhaust system.

4. ☐ Road-Test & Inspect for Proper Operation:
   - Steering column ignition lock.
   - Starter safety switch.
   - Instruments and gauges.
   - Brakes (including parking brake and warning light).
   - Throttle controls for free operation.

179

- Engine and transmission performance (including downshift).
- Steering.
- Windshield wipers and washers. Adjust washer aim as necessary.
- Heater and/or air-conditioning.
- Horn.
- Factory-installed accessories and options.
- Install clock fuse—Opel.
- Remove squeaks and rattles.

5. ☐ Appearance:
   - Wash vehicle and detail cleanup as required (exterior trim, moldings, and paint finish). Touch up paint as required (brush or aerosol spray can). Hand-polish surface blemishes.
   - Remove key number slugs and place with spare keys.
   - Remove protective covers, and inspect interior trim and moldings.

*Reference wall chart, 1/1/77, for additional details.

DELIVERY REPORT
OWNER-DEALER-VEHICLE DATA

☐ Imprinted authorized-selling dealer plate on back of New-Car Warranty Information folder. Typed owner's name, address, vehicle identification no., delivery date, and vehicle mileage on front of New-Car Warranty Information folder.
☐ Reviewed New-Car Warranty Information folder with owner.
☐ Explained Vehicle Maintenance Schedule to owner.
☐ Consumer Information folder delivered to the owner.
☐ Demonstrated operation of all accessories to owner.
☐ Presented keys to owner.

Above service and adjustments performed by_____ Date_____
                                             (Technician Name)

Delivered by_____ Date_____

180

CHAPTER 12 *Maintaining Your Car*

WHAT ITEMS ARE NOT COVERED BY THE WARRANTY?

● Racing, overloading, road hazards, other misuse or negligence. The owner also is responsible for proper maintenance of the vehicle including the cost of parts and labor. Examples are the addition of oil, the replacement of wiper blades, and adjustments required because of use. Recommended maintenance schedules are listed in the Owner's Guide.*

WHAT IS NOT COVERED BY WARRANTY

● Damage due to lack of proper maintenance as described in the Maintenance Schedule.

RECOMMENDATIONS FOR MAINTENANCE SERVICE AND REPLACEMENT PARTS

THE WARRANTY OBLIGATIONS ARE NOT DEPENDENT UPON THE USE OF ANY PARTICULAR BRAND OF REPLACEMENT PARTS. THE OWNER MAY ELECT TO USE NONGENUINE GM PARTS FOR REPLACEMENT PURPOSES.

MAINTENANCE SERVICE CAN BE PERFORMED BY ANY QUALIFIED SERVICE OUTLET: HOWEVER, WARRANTY SERVICE MUST BE PERFORMED BY AN AUTHORIZED CHEVROLET DEALER. Receipts covering the performance of regular maintenance should be retained in the event questions arise concerning maintenance. These receipts should be transferred to each subsequent owner of this car.**

The average car during its useful life will require some $3,664 worth of repairs and maintenance (excluding gasoline and oil purchases). Proper care and maintenance of a car are essential to its safe performance, reliability, and efficiency. An improperly maintained car wastes money, fuel, and the owner's time, and can even endanger the owner's life through defects that proper maintenance would catch. A properly maintained nonlemon car should provide trouble-free driving of 100,000 miles or more. While warranty service must be performed by an authorized dealer, regular maintenance and repairs not covered by the warranty can be serviced anywhere. For guidelines in choosing a competent service facility, see Chapters 3 and 13.

Even during the car's first few years of operation, the manufacturer's warranty obligations do not cover regular maintenance items arising from

---

*Warranty Facts Booklet, Limited Warranty 1978 New Car and Light Truck, Ford Parts and Service Division.
**Warranty Information on 1978 Chevrolet New Cars.

181

normal wear and tear, such as tune-ups, oil changes, and replacement of worn-out brake linings. It is up to the vehicle owner to care properly for and maintain the car. Any car problems resulting from the owner's failure to do so will not be covered by the manufacturer as they are regarded as "owner abuse." Proper maintenance is necessary to protect your warranty rights. If a car owner can prove that the car has been properly maintained, the manufacturer cannot rightly claim "owner abuse."

DIAGNOSTIC AND SAFETY INSPECTIONS

Studies have shown that defects help cause from five to eighteen percent of all accidents. Periodic safety inspections are designed to catch defects and reduce accidents. Many urban areas either have or will have emission inspections which can be done at the same time as safety inspections. Emission inspections not only lower vehicle emissions, but improve fuel economy by catching improperly tuned vehicles that waste gas.

Another type of vehicle inspection is the diagnostic inspection—a more thorough check, often using special sensors and computers. Diagnostic inspections run a series of tests on a car, giving the consumer a status report on its overall condition or a specific problem. A diagnostic report serves as a prescription for getting proper repairs.

Diagnostic inspections can be obtained in independent diagnostic centers or clinics. In most large cities, there are repair shops that have diagnostic lanes. Of course, diagnostic centers that operate in conjunction with repair shops do not offer the same type of objective, disinterested advice as do government-operated or otherwise independent centers.

At present, there are only a handful of such independent centers. One of the most successful centers is run by the Auto Club of Missouri, which operates diagnostic clinics for its members and the general public in St. Louis and Kansas City. At the clinic, consumers pay a small charge (about $20) to have their entire vehicle diagnosed. For about $1, consumers can return after repairs have been made in order to verify that they were done correctly. If repairs have been made improperly or not at all, the club will mediate complaints with the repair shop.

The Automobile Club's former director of membership services, John N. Noettl, described the club's ten years of experience with diagnostic inspection:

> Our own conclusions on the benefits of diagnostic clinics that give an unbiased appraisal of one's car, seem to be supported by reports from the DOT, EPA, and other organizations. Namely: (1) lower repair costs; (2) more safe cars; (3) less polluting cars; (4) more safety consciousness on the part of the motorist; and, (5) information feedback to the government regulatory agencies and the manufacturers concerning the "real world" benefits of safety regulations and design changes.
>
> We have recently completed a study for the DOT in which 288 collision-damaged vehicles were inspected for damage to their safety

182

and engine exhaust emission systems, as well as for precollision noncompliance with established standards.

The program data revealed that many types of information are accessible and a thorough evaluation of vehicles involved in accidents is available from this type of program. It appeared that a statistically large number of accident-involved vehicles had poor components in their brake system. The friction material [brake pads and linings] was thinner than considered a safe level on 27 percent of the vehicles; 31 percent had low brake fluid. Also, 33 percent of the vehicles exhibited alignment problems.

Testifying before the U.S. Senate Commerce Committee in March 1978, Mr. Noettl advocated making independent diagnostic centers available nationwide at low cost to the motor public with government assistance if need be. According to Noettl, the clinics are usually self-sustaining, since the cost of operations is supported by fees paid by car owners. "Aside from the benefits to individual motorists, the societal benefits in cleaner, safer, more economical, and energy efficient cars would be incalculable."

The National Highway Traffic Safety Administration found that national diagnostic motor vehicle inspections would save consumers $1.4 billion. NHTSA's recent report, "Motor Vehicle Diagnostic Inspection Program," concluded that car owners can achieve greater safety, lower pollution, improved gas mileage, and lower repair and maintenance costs for their cars by using diagnostic inspections. This report was based on pilot diagnostic inspection projects set up in Alabama, Tennessee, Arizona, Puerto Rico, and Washington, D.C. The projects carried out 125,000 in-depth diagnostic inspections of safety-related and exhaust emissions systems of cars during 1975 and 1976, using a sample of 1968 to 1973 cars.

In the NHTSA project, consumers whose cars were diagnosed as defective had the repairs performed at a repair shop. After repairs, a car owner would return to the inspection station with repair bills to see that the proper repairs were made. Consumers relying on the diagnostic inspections achieved better-quality or lower-cost repairs than owners of cars going through pass/fail inspections, particularly where more complex repairs were involved. For example, the diagnostic group spent an average of 5.7 percent less on emission-related repairs than the nondiagnostic group for the first periodic inspection. The diagnostic group had a forty percent lower failure rate on reinspection, indicating that they were getting better-quality repairs than the nondiagnostic group. NHTSA specifically found that owners of diagnostically inspected cars had an average improvement in fuel economy of 4.7 percent right after repairs. The failure rates for safety systems like brakes dropped by about fifty percent.

NHTSA reported that consumers reacted positively to the diagnostic inspection program—93 percent said that they would rejoin it if they could; 85 percent felt that the inspection should be required by law; 63 percent said they would pay $10 or more for the service; and a third said they would pay $15 or more. Inspection helped auto repair shops around the diagnostic center, too. Aided by a diagnostic status report on the car, the shops could fix only what was needed and do it right the first time.

One of the NHTSA projects included an analysis by the University of Alabama, which gave further evidence as to the value of diagnostic inspection. Alabama found that its inspected cars had twelve percent fewer accidents than uninspected cars, after adjusting data for sex, age, and income.

DO-IT-YOURSELF MAINTENANCE

Some consumers regularly perform their own maintenance, such as changing the oil and filter in their cars and performing tune-ups. According to a recent survey conducted by the Automotive Parts and Accessories Association (APAA), at least one member in over sixty percent of the car-owning households practices some form of auto maintenance and repair. After consulting the manufacturer's owners manual and other guide books, many of these consumers are successful at performing proper maintenance. The major advantages of performing your own maintenance are: saving money and eliminating the time required to go to a repair shop. The major disadvantages of self-maintenance are: do-it-yourself mistakes can be costly in time and money spent in repairing the errors; certain mistakes can constitute "owner abuse," thus eliminating otherwise guaranteed warranty repairs; and complex and sophisticated electronic gadgets on new cars take some expertise to maintain.

Familiarity with auto maintenance and repair can be best developed through learning from an experienced friend who does his or her own maintenance, studying repair manuals, and attending consumer car repair courses. Some consumer groups, YMCAs and YWCAs, community centers, local colleges, and recreation departments conduct courses like "Auto Awareness," "Driveway Mechanics," and "Basic Auto Repair" to educate car owners on automobile maintenance and repair. Several do-it-yourself books are available, covering such topics as auto tune-ups for beginners and the mechanics of specific auto models. See Appendix for a list of some titles.

As a result of the rising trend in self-maintenance and repairs, some other specific consumer aids have become available. One is the "rent-a-bay" garages which have opened in some areas, providing ambitious consumers with tools, space, lifts, and even expert advice. By some estimates, there are more than 100 rent-a-bay garages in the country, with the number likely to grow. Mobil Oil Corporation and Shell Oil Company have entered the field, and some independently owned rent-a-bays are making franchising arrangements.

Another aid to consumers who want to do their own maintenance is a membership organization that specializes in providing members with tools, advice, and facilities. CAR Club, Inc., of Baltimore, Maryland, is an example of such an organization (see Chapter 5). Consumers pay a $10.00 membership fee, which entitles them to use the CAR Club's facilities for $3.50 an hour. At their disposal are tools, hydraulic lifts, and technical assistance from the club's managers as well as other club members. The club's director estimates that members spend fifty percent less to repair and maintain their cars at the

184

club than if they paid professional mechanics to do the work.

Before rolling up your sleeves and buying your own supplies, carefully weigh the disadvantages and advantages of self-maintenance. For example, one consumer found himself in a warranty dispute with General Motors after changing the car's oil on his own. G. P. Montoro of Redwood City, California, had changed the oil and filter on his 1977 truck when the mileage was 1,865. Over three months and almost 3,000 miles later, the truck experienced engine failure. After towing the truck into the dealership, he was informed that the service department had found the oil filter loose and they had determined that this resulted in a loss of oil leading to the failure. He was also told that it would cost about $1,600 to repair the damages.

According to his October 18, 1977, letter to General Motors—copy to the Center for Auto Safety—Montoro was told by GM that the manufacturer was not responsible for the engine damage, since the consumer had installed the oil filter. According to Montoro, the fact that he changed his own oil filter was automatically used against him. He said it was the only reason GM refused to make full warranty repairs. He stated that the manufacturer service manager "was very closed-minded in considering any other possibilities for the engine failure other than that what [the dealership] had contended."

Montoro then took the truck to a mechanic at an independent garage to examine the engine and determine the cause of the failure. The mechanic came up with a different explanation from GM's as to why the engine failed. Although the consumer had this statement of an independent mechanic and evidence from the truck to prove there was no "owner abuse," GM would not give in. GM did offer to install and supply a short block for the truck if the consumer paid $500. But Montoro refused because "I was convinced that the failure was mechanical and I had proof to show just that."

185

APPENDIX—CHAPTER 12

Do-It-Yourself Maintenance Guides

AUTOMOTIVE TUNE-UP FOR BEGINNERS.
By I. G. Edmonds. 184 pages, hardcover.
Macrae Smith Co., $6.50.

BASIC AUTO REPAIR MANUAL.
384 pages, paperback.
Petersen Publishing Co., $3.95.

BASIC AUTOMOTIVE TROUBLESHOOTING.
By Richard Bean. 144 pages plus fold-out diagrams, paperback.
Petersen Publishing Co., $2.95.

FIXING CARS, A PEOPLE'S PRIMER.
By Rick Greenspan et al. 191 pages, paperback.
The San Francisco Institute of Automotive Ecology, $4.95.

HOW TO KEEP YOUR VOLKSWAGEN ALIVE.
By John Muir, 329 pages, paperback.
John Muir Publications, $7.50.

MONEY-SAVERS' DO-IT-YOURSELF CAR REPAIR.
By LeRoi Smith. 408 pages, hardcover.
Macmillan Publishing Co., Inc., $11.

THE TIME-LIFE BOOK OF THE FAMILY CAR.
357 pages, hardcover.
Time-Life Books, $14.95.

CHAPTER 13 *Repairing Your Car*

The owner of a 1969 Chevrolet Impala had been to several repair shops to complain of a knocking noise in the engine and backfiring when he accelerated.

"They just kept tuning the engine and replacing parts, but the engine kept making the same noises," he told the staff at the St. Louis Diagnostic Car Clinic operated by the Auto Club of Missouri.

[Finally, after wasting hundreds of dollars on ineffective repairs, the car owner was referred to the clinic by one of the repair shops.] "He wanted to keep the car if we thought the whole car was worth fixing," recalls Larry Pipes, manager of technical services for the club.

They did find repair was worthwhile. Using its $125,000 worth of equipment, the clinic performed an exhaustive check of the car—including not only the engine but also brakes, lights, horn, electrical system, transmission, tires, alignment. And they gave him a detailed prescription of what should be done to put the car in top condition.

The main source of the engine noise, it turned out, was a flat lobe, or bump, on the camshaft which opens and closes the valves that feed the engine a mixture of air and fuel and take away exhaust.

The owner took the car back to a repair shop and had the prescription filled—and this time the problem was cured.

It cost him another $620, but he didn't have to buy a new car as he had feared.

The Auto Club's Larry Pipes calls this "a classic example of how a diagnostic clinic can help a consumer."*

AUTO REPAIR ABUSES

Proper repairs are vital to vehicle safety, reliability, and cost of operation. Yet auto repairs are number one on almost every complaint list across the country. Testifying at hearings on auto repair problems held by the Consumer Subcommittee of the U.S. Senate Commerce Committee in March 1978, Joan Claybrook, administrator of the National Highway Traffic Safety Administration (NHTSA), estimated that consumers lost over $20 billion in 1977 on inadequate, incompetent, unnecessary, or fraudulent auto repairs and maintenance. Claybrook reported that almost forty cents of every dollar spent on car repairs is wasted. Most witnesses at the hearing agreed on the extent of the auto repair problem. The controversy lay in what to do about it.

Another cause of wasted consumer auto repair dollars is the "flat-rate" system of charging for repairs, used by most repair shops around the country.

Consumer Transpotopics (Department of Transportation, Office of Public and Consumer Affairs) 7 (April 1978).

187

According to a study by a subsidiary of the National Automobile Dealers Association, mechanics can beat the time listed in flat-rate manuals on seventy-five percent of all jobs. A 1972 study by the Wisconsin attorney general concluded that over a one-year period, consumers were charged for 61,887 more hours than were worked. At $12.50 per hour, this amounted to $773,587 of overcharges.

DIAGNOSTIC INSPECTION CENTERS

In many cases, diagnostic clinics help consumers spot needed repairs, as in the example at the beginning of this chapter. The St. Louis Diagnostic Car Clinic is a diagnostic clinic which does not perform repair work. Thus consumers can have more confidence in the results of the diagnostic tests, since there is no profit-making incentive to find unnecessary repair problems.

Other diagnostic clinics are not so helpful to consumers. Most diagnostic clinics also do repairs, so they profit from the problems they find. Other clinics are simply incompetent. Studies by consumer groups, government agencies, and others have reached a conclusion similar to the following from the Washington Center for Study of Services: "*Checkbook*'s experience at Washington area diagnostic centers proves that the centers are not necessarily the answer to the motorist's prayers."*

After collecting extensive data on 212 Washington area auto repair shops, *Checkbook* found that shops which offer diagnosis, as well as repairs, may overdiagnose as a way of creating repair business; that diagnosticians vary widely in skill; and that the use of sophisticated testing instruments does not eliminate the skill element.

But this is not to dismiss the value of competent diagnostic centers that happen to be affiliated with repair shops. Despite the bad experiences with diagnostic centers as reported by various studies and consumers, many car owners have saved money by using clinics before getting repairs. One precaution can help you avoid being taken by clinics connected to repair shops. When you want a diagnosis to help decide what repairs to get at a repair shop, let the diagnostic center know, in no uncertain terms, that any recommended repairs will be done elsewhere.

In the following situations, a repair-connected diagnostic clinic will see no incentive to overprescribe repairs:

- When the car's warranty is running out, a diagnosis can catch major problems before the warranty actually expires.
- In checking out a used car before purchase.
- When taking delivery on a new car.
- Before settling an insurance claim for damage to the car.

In these situations a diagnostic center is an easy, inexpensive place to get a checkup. It is likely to be better equipped, better organized, and

---

Washington Consumers' Checkbook on Cars (1976), p. 92.

188

more willing to give you a quick assessment than an ordinary repair shop would be.*

STATE AUTO REPAIR LAWS

A number of state and local governments have attempted to reduce auto repair problems through one of three basic types of auto repair laws: (1) disclosure, (2) shop licensing, and (3) mechanics licensing. Disclosure laws give the consumer a right to certain information about the auto repair being performed. Shop-licensing laws require auto repair shops to avoid fraud, deceptive practices, and gross negligence or face losing the license which permits them to do motor vehicle repairs. Mechanics-licensing laws require that persons performing repairs meet certain competency standards before being permitted to repair motor vehicles.

Disclosure and shop-licensing laws may help decrease the number of fraudulent repairs, but they are not directed specifically at competence, as are mechanics-licensing laws. Only a few jurisdictions license mechanics—District of Columbia, Hawaii, and Michigan. The licensing of motor vehicle mechanics has been opposed by a number of groups, particularly the automobile, tire, and oil industries.

There are other types of auto repair laws that help the consumer. These laws vary in approach and scope among states. On the whole, the best auto repair law is in California. This law requires written estimates before the repairs are performed, return of replaced parts to the consumer after the completion of repairs (only if the consumer requests them), and a sign placed in a conspicuous place at the repair shop containing the address and telephone number of the state agency that handles consumer auto repair complaints. The act provides for state enforcement of the auto repair laws.

FINDING A RELIABLE REPAIR SHOP

A reliable garage is one that performs only those repairs that are necessary, performs them properly, and does not overcharge. Finding a repair shop that fits all three criteria is not easy. For example, a study conducted by the Colorado Public Interest Research Group (CoPIRG) showed that the majority of repair shops make unnecessary repairs. In *An Investigation of Market Conditions of the Auto Repair Industry*, the researchers took a 1971 Volkswagen bus to eight repair shops that specialized in VWs in Boulder, Colorado. A loose drive belt was intentionally put in the VW, after the CoPIRG mechanic performed a tune-up and prepared the vehicle for the survey. Of the eight shops, only one shop solved the problem and charged a reasonable amount to fix the drive belt—$6.50. Four other shops fixed the problem, but they also did costly unnecessary repairs, such as a tune-up, charging from $34.64 to $63.38. Two others charged $5.00 and $7.80 respectively but did not solve the problem. The eighth shop, a VW dealership, charged $8.00 for an in-

---

Ibid.

189

correct diagnosis and did not perform any repairs. Similar test studies in other cities have turned up virtually identical results.

Many experts on consumer auto repair abuses agree that small, independent garages that pay their mechanics a straight salary, as opposed to following the flat-rate manual, often offer the best repair work. Since, on the whole, independent shops are usually the most reliable, consider one even if the mechanics are paid by flat rate. The reliability of independent garages is increased because they usually survive on reputation only, as opposed to a big-name shop like Sears or General Tire or a car dealership, which attracts many customers on the basis of its name alone.

Most surveys show greater consumer satisfaction with the performance of independent shops when compared with dealerships. One survey in Washington, D.C., found that eighty-two percent of customers at the average independent shop were satisfied with the way the shops fixed their cars, compared with only fifty-four percent at the average dealership. Large retail outlets such as Sears, Roebuck and Montgomery Ward received a sixty-six percent satisfactory rating. Similarly, fifty-eight percent of the independent shops had no complaints filed with Better Business Bureaus or a "very low complaint rate," compared with only thirty-two percent of the dealers with no complaints sent to Better Business Bureaus.

The National Highway Traffic Safety Administration offers the following generally good tips on choosing an auto repair shop:

- Reputation
  —Consult with your friends and neighbors.
  —Check with your local consumer office, Better Business Bureau, and voluntary consumer groups.
- Qualifications
  —Are the mechanics certified or licensed?
- Facilities
  —How long has the shop been at its present location?
  —Does the shop appear to be well equipped?
  —Is it clean and organized?
- Repair Practices
  —Will the shop give you a written estimate?
  —Will it advise you on additional costs?
  —How does it handle complaints?
  —Does it guarantee its work in writing?
- Cost
  —Do the shop's prices seem competitive?
- Convenience
  —Is it close to where you live or work?

Also consider these guidelines, as suggested by Arthur P. Glickman and Donald A. Randall in *The Great American Auto Repair Robbery* (Charterhouse, 1972):

Independent shops—The independent garage is the best place for the consumer to get his or her car serviced because it does not sell anything but service. It depends on the customer's coming back.

190

Mass merchandisers—Many repair shops are operated by mass merchandisers with branch operations such as Sears, Penney's, Montgomery Ward, K Mart, and the major tire manufacturers. These shops push fast-moving and profitable items such as tires, batteries, and accessories. They are usually interested in selling parts, not service. Although the price may be right for tune-ups, alignment, brake jobs, and the like, watch out for unneeded repairs or more repairs than you anticipated.

Franchise operations—Some repair shops are operated under a franchise with a controlling company, such as AAMCO Transmissions, Midas Muffler, and General Tire. Be careful of advertised specials. They often attempt to sell you more expensive repairs.

Gasoline stations—If you can establish yourself as a regular customer at such a service station, your chances of being satisfied increase—if there are competent mechanics employed there.

New-car dealers—Most car dealers sell cars, not service, to make money. The service department primarily supplements the car sales business. But where a relatively new car requires complicated repairs to the engine, transmission, or electrical system, often the dealer's service department has the most expertise. A dealer's service department generally has the right equipment, as well as familiarity with manufacturer service bulletins and circuit diagrams not always available to nondealer shops.

In judging the competence of a repair shop through its mechanics, you can be somewhat assured if the mechanic has been certified by the National Institute for Automotive Service Excellence. NIASE was established in 1972 by the domestic auto manufacturers and auto dealers to improve mechanic competence. The NIASE program gives voluntary tests and certifies mechanics who pass. But just because mechanics are not certified with NIASE does *not* mean they are incompetent. If the mechanic does wear the NIASE seal of approval, then you know that the mechanic at least passed a competency test. Since 1972 over 100,000 mechanics have each been certified in at least one area of automotive repair. NIASE publishes a booklet listing repair shops employing NIASE-certified mechanics. The booklet, "Where to Find Certified Mechanics for Your Car," is available for $1.95 from NIASE, 1825 K Street, N.W., Washington, D.C. 20006. Or you can request a free list of only the shops in your state.

One helpful aid is available to consumers in the Washington, D.C., area and could be adopted by consumer groups in other areas. The Washington Center for the Study of Services, a private, nonprofit consumer organization, researched the quality and cost of auto repair services in the metropolitan area. Then the Center published the results in a book called *Washington Consumers' Checkbook on Cars*, mentioned earlier in this chapter, which rates different repair shops in the Washington area. The ratings are based on consumer surveys, Better Business Bureau complaint records, local consumer office files, and investigations of repair facilities' equipment and personnel. For information write the Washington Center for the Study of Services, 1518 K Street, N.W., Suite 406, Washington, D.C. 20005.

HOW TO TALK TO A MECHANIC

The best customer is the fellow who comes in with a list of work to be done, leaves the car for three days while he's out of town, and tells the service writer to drive the car home several evenings to make sure everything works right.*

Although it is not always convenient to leave a car for three days at the repair shop, there are other ways to help the shop employees. If you know what needs to be done, such as a wheel alignment, new brake linings, or an oil change, simply give the mechanic or service writer a written list of the work to be done. Taking the car to an independent diagnostic clinic first is a good method of finding out just what is wrong for the repair shop to fix. Communication is the key to getting your car properly repaired and avoiding unnecessary repairs.

If you do not know what repairs are necessary and have been unable to find a good diagnostic clinic, do not guess. Simply describe the symptoms. If the symptoms are difficult to describe, ask a friend who knows about cars or the mechanic at the shop to take the car for a test drive. The more you are able to narrow down the symptoms, the better are your chances of getting the car fixed right the first time. Give details and description of the symptoms as precisely as you can:

- What are the sounds or smells? (clunking or burning, etc.)
- Where are they coming from?
- When do they occur? (hot or cold weather; right after starting the car; at 55 mph)
- How does the car feel to drive?
- How long has the problem occurred?

Write down each repair to be performed and all the symptoms of problems to be fixed before going to the shop. Keep a copy for yourself for later reference.

As mentioned in Chapter 12, consumer auto courses are frequently given by community colleges or local community groups. These courses are not held for auto mechanics, but are specifically aimed at teaching auto consumers more about their cars. Such training can be especially valuable for consumers who want to know more about the upkeep of their cars in order to avoid being taken by a repair shop.

HOW TO AVOID GETTING GYPPED

Always request a written estimate. The value of an estimate is that it does not give a dishonest shop blanket approval to run up a bill for unnecessary items. If overcharged, you can hold the repair shop to the figure in the

---

*Charlotte Slater, "How the Customer Looks to a Service Writer," *Washington Star*, January 22, 1977.

192

estimate, taking the written estimate to small-claims court to recover the overcharge if necessary.

Never sign a blank repair order. Unless you completely trust the mechanic, never tell him simply to "do *whatever* needs to be done to repair the car." Find out how long the repairs will take. Leave a phone number where you can be reached.

Ask that replaced parts be returned to you after the completion of repairs. Most good shops will agree to return replaced parts unless the parts must be returned to the manufacturer for warranty reasons.

Where the car needs a major repair, such as a transmission overhaul, call a few shops ahead of time to compare prices. Beware of bargain advertisements, especially for transmission, tune-up, or brake repairs. Many of these are used as "bait" by unscrupulous shops to get your car up on the lift so the service writer can talk you into unnecessary repairs.

When picking up the car, check over the repair order to see that everything was done and no extras were added. Test-drive the car to make sure all the work was done correctly. Keep copies of all repair orders, as discussed previously in this book. If the repair was not done right, discuss the problem with the repair shop first. If necessary, talk with the shop manager or owner. Many problems caused by a lack of communication can be resolved by talking to a person in authority at the shop.

Avoid having major repairs on auto trips, unless the car has broken down and you have no choice. Consumers who are away from home and anxious to be on their way are often victimized by a number of unethical repair shops that are located right off major highways. These highway bandits stock up on parts like air filters, tires, and batteries, and will try to sell the traveling consumer a new one whether necessary or not. For example, the mechanic may tell you how lucky you are that you stopped, because the air filter is too dirty and in need of replacement. Or the gasoline attendant may cut the fan belt, puncture the tires, or disconnect the battery cables and then try to sell unneeded parts and repairs.

To avoid becoming a victim of such tactics, get out of the car and watch the attendant carefully. Always take the name and (shop) address of the salesperson who tries to sell you a new tire or battery, and if he or she seems hesitant, take your business elsewhere. Consumers who do get swindled by a service station connected to a big oil company may have some recourse against the oil company that franchises the station. One way to prevent this form of highway robbery is to have the car thoroughly checked and repaired by a trusted mechanic before leaving on a motor trip.

HOW TO COMPLAIN

If the repair shop refuses to resolve your complaint, follow the suggestions in Chapter 4, "How to Complain," which discusses federal, state, and local agencies that may be interested in your complaint.

If further help is needed in solving the problem, consider using small-claims courts (see Chapter 7) and other strategies discussed throughout the

193

book. If your complaint is based on incompetence and the mechanics are certified by NIASE at the repair shop, send a copy of your letter of complaint to NIASE, 1825 K Street, N.W., Washington, D.C. 20006.

If you disagree with the repair bill, it is normally advisable to pay it first in order to get the car back. Then pursue your complaint later. Most states have what are called "mechanics' lien" laws. If a consumer refuses to pay a bill, no matter how outrageous, the shop can keep the car. In some states, you do not have to pay the bill to get back the car under a mechanic's lien. In those states a consumer can post a bond in court for twice the amount (in Florida, equal to the amount) of the disputed bill. The consumer can recover the bond by taking the case to court and winning. Consumers in states where no bond is permitted can pay and then sue to recover the overcharge. In cases of flagrant overcharge by the repair shop, a consumer can pay by check, drive away, then stop payment on the check that day.

Some states require written estimates and authorization for repairs. In those states, a mechanic's lien would be invalidated where the shop has failed to comply with these requirements. Check with a local consumer organization or agency or a lawyer to find out the law on mechanics' liens in your state.

Whatever your gripe against a repair shop may be, the act of complaining is usually essential to resolving the dispute successfully.

194

CHAPTER 14 *What Usually Goes Wrong*

Breakdowns can be caused by defects, abuse, or plain wear and tear. In a new car practically any malfunction can be called a defect. As a general rule, all parts of a car except routine maintenance items such as oil filters should last at least as long as the period of any written warranty. If, with normal wear and tear, a part breaks down during this period, then it is defined by the warranty to be defective. Major items such as the engine and transmission should last over five years or 50,000 miles.

Certain breakdowns are more common in new cars, others in particular makes and models, while some are very common in all cars. In this chapter we will describe the most important defects and the ways in which they affect the safety of the car, and, we hope, provide you with enough information to help you develop a sense of knowing whether they are repaired properly.

1. TIRES

Tires tend to be more defect-ridden than any other single part of a car, and the defects generally have more disastrous consequences than other car defects. Evidence of their frequency of failure can be seen along any major highway—chunks of rubber and damaged guardrails are left behind, although the rest of the debris may be towed away.

Defective tires can disintegrate at any time, regardless of the age, price, or general quality of the brand. Failure can be sudden and often total. Chances of failure are greatest at the precise moment when an accident would be unthinkably disastrous—when the car is filled with passengers and traveling at high speed.

If the tire is properly loaded and inflated, it is safe from disintegration only if there are no serious defects in the cords or other parts of the tire. To inflate a tire properly, you *must* check it with your own, pretested pressure gauge. (A pressure gauge, tread-wear gauge, valve caps, and safety booklet are included in a "Tire Safety and Mileage Kit" available from the Rubber Manufacturers Association, Publications Dept., 1901 Pennsylvania Avenue, N.W., Washington, D.C. 20006, for $2.25.) See the February 1980 issue of *Consumer Reports* for ratings of various tire gauges.

The rubber tread and sidewalls of tires are laid over layers of heavy ply which are called the *cord* of the tire. The plies, or layers of cord, give a tire its strength, so when the cord breaks or fails, the tire usually loses its air. On some tires the cord is poorly bonded to the rubber, and *cord separation* occurs. Cord separation causes heat to build up and may lead to ply or tread separation. You can easily spot tread separation. Pressurized air from inside the tire escapes through the plies of cord and forms a bubble beneath the stretchy rubber tread or sidewall.

Ply separation or disintegration, for which a single cause is not apparent,

195

usually occurs when the tire is being subjected to high speed or heavy loads for a long enough time to build up heat. Other common defects include tires that are not perfectly round (and therefore ride roughly and wear unevenly), tires that are simply too weak to withstand normal road hazards, and tires that are so far out of shape or size as to fit improperly on the wheels.

All of these defects have been found on tires bought and tested by the National Highway Traffic Safety Administration. This is particularly disturbing since the workout given to tires in the government tests is mild compared to the more strenuous use the tires get on the highway.

Defective tires have been discovered on the market in increasing numbers in recent years. The classic bad example is the Firestone 500 steel-belted radial. Of over twenty-four million made between 1972 and 1978, the Department of Transportation ordered some ten million to be recalled. Millions more would have been recalled, but the statute of limitations had expired before the government finally declared them to be defective in 1978.

Consumers who had a Firestone 500 steel-belted-radial blowout and lived will never forget the experience. M. E. Pitcher of Phoenix, Arizona, wrote:

> I wanted the best tires on my new car and paid extra money to the Ford dealer to have Firestone 500 steel-belted radials on my '76 Ford. I also feel that my family and friends are very lucky to be alive.
> I am very careful concerning my automobile, having the oil changed, tires checked and rotated regularly, etc. My car had less than 5,000 miles on it when the first tire went. Fortunately I was traveling below the speed limit. In spite of that when the tire blew out it completely lifted the rear end of the car off the road and flipped it over. My mother and a young child were in the car with me at the time. We landed upside down in the median between divided highways. By the time we stopped rolling, a tow truck was already there since the driver was at a station across the highway and heard the tire blow. The Highway Patrol even explained about the bad quality of the Firestone tires on my car. There was nothing left of the tire but powder on the road.

Similarly, D. Hance of Durham, Pennsylvania, wrote:

> There are no words that could express my feelings toward the Firestone Company. In my opinion they have completely defrauded the American public by supplying an inferior product and then refusing to face up to its shortcomings in the face of criticism.
> My family's experience has been with five (5) different sets of Firestone 500 tires. At least two tires of each set developed large bubbles on the sidewalls. Two tires had complete tread separation, one of which caused a major accident. All tires failed between 9,000 and 19,000 miles.
> Whenever the Firestone people were contacted they accused us of riding with the tires underinflated, which they say caused overheating resulting in bubbles and tread separation.

196

I am glad to see that someone has finally been able to do something for the American public in stopping a large organization like Firestone from cheating them.

After holding extensive hearings on the Firestone 500 steel-belted radial, Congressman John E. Moss of California concluded:

The record is clear that Firestone had early knowledge of the serious failure propensities of the 500. Its high adjustment rates in the early years, its unusually brisk activity in settling damage claims, and its energetic efforts to improve on the earlier tires all suggest its early knowledge.

These facts lead to but one conclusion. The Firestone Tire and Rubber Co. is and has been for some time in a position to avoid the devastating toll of human destruction which it knew its tires could cause. In the exercise of clear and conscious choice, it nonetheless permitted this destruction to take place.

2. BRAKES

Regardless of which American car you have, the brakes may well be either defective or dangerously inadequate under expected conditions of highway use, even when the car is brand new. "Even with passenger car disc brakes . . . prolonged braking with a heavily laden car is still a hair-raising experience," Karl Ludvigsen of *Motor Trend* wrote. In 1973 the Auto Club of Missouri's Diagnostic Clinic found defective brakes to be the most common cause of a car's failing the state motor vehicle inspection, accounting for 36 percent of all defects. Of the new 1973 cars tested, 32 percent had defective brakes. Brake repairs accounted for the largest percentage (22.5 percent) of all vehicle repair costs, ahead of tires and wheels (21.9 percent), in the Department of Transportation's Motor Vehicle Diagnostic Inspection Demonstration Program.

Usually brake failure is caused by leaks that allow the brake fluid to drain out. Other causes include water in the brake fluid which vaporizes when the brakes get warm, and (in cars with power brakes) engine stalling, which cuts power to both power brakes and power steering. Also, uneven brake drums often wear the brake shoes out quickly, and differences among the braking strength of the wheels can make the car swerve uncontrollably in a panic stop.

3. ACCELERATOR LINKAGE

The largest automotive recall in history, involving nearly seven million GM vehicles, resulted from a jammed-open accelerator, which occurs when the engine mount breaks and lets the engine move upward to pull the accelerator linkage open. When this happens, the gas pedal won't come up when you

197

release it, and the car will keep accelerating just as if the pedal were floored even though the pedal has been released.

Between September 1966 and March 1979, the throttling of eighty-two kinds of vehicles had sticking problems serious enough to require their recall. A failure record this high is unjustifiable. The function of the linkage is simple: it transmits the movement of your foot on the gas pedal to the carburetor, and in some cases shifts the transmission into passing gear. In most present cars, this is done with a haphazard system of levers, pivots, and springs which extend totally unprotected through the engine compartment. Whenever any piece of debris, or one of the many tubes that fill "modern" engine compartments, interferes with this system, the throttle can be held open. A much safer system, hydraulic or mechanical, and fully protected, could easily be developed by today's engineers.

4. ENGINE DEFECTS

The most common engine defects include poor tuning, cooling system defects or overheating, and excessive use of oil.

a. Tuning

Poor tuning (improper adjustments of the fuel controls in the carburetor and of the electrical impulses sent to the spark plugs) can cause poor performance, stalling, hard starting, or too fast an idle. Also, poor tuning allows partly burned fuel to go out the exhaust, causing air pollution and poor gas mileage at the same time.

Although tuning is part of the dealer's predelivery inspection responsibility, it is seldom performed because of the general inadequacies of dealer preparation. Once you've accepted your new car, tune-up bills are on you, although a manufacturer may provide (Ford does) adjustments to the carburetor free of charge on a onetime basis.

b. Overheating

Overheating is particularly a problem with air-conditioned cars. The air-conditioning puts an extra strain on the engine which the cooling system may not be designed to handle. In any car an obstruction may slow down the flow of coolant through the engine and radiator causing repeated overheating, which can usually be stopped by washing out the cooling system ("flushing") or ordinary replacement of parts. In any case, the repairs are covered by the warranty, and must be obtained immediately, before overheating can lead to serious engine damage. The 1971–74 Chevrolet Vega had so inadequate a cooling system that it led to warped engine heads and scored cylinder walls.

c. "Burning" Oil

Heavy oil consumption in new cars is often caused by leaky gaskets. If no leaks can be found, a dealer may doubt that you are leaking oil and will insist on proof of oil purchases before he checks further for causes such as faulty piston rings. As a general rule, a fully broken-in car in good condition should go over 1,000 miles for every quart of oil added. A quart of oil should normally last 2,000 miles.

198

5. FUEL SYSTEM LEAKS

FIRE! is the last cry made in many American automobiles. A brief tour of any junkyard will show how completely fire can sweep through an automobile. Occasionally a gutted hulk will be seen which does not even show signs of having been in an accident. Most "accident-caused" fires could be prevented, as well as nonaccident fires.

The two most common causes of nonaccident fires are electrical shorts and gasoline leakage near the hot engine where it easily catches fire. Any type of fire can result in a dangerous situation—the car may easily explode like a bomb if the fire is not quickly extinguished. Ironically, in many cases where a defect causes the fire, the burnt-out car is often junked with the consumer being reimbursed by the insurance company rather than the responsible party—the manufacturer. Even where the consumer does get reimbursed for the car, the depreciation deducted by the insurance company often requires the consumer to shell out more money in replacing the car with a new one. For example, P. Kenzel of Hawkinsville, Georgia, was very pleased with her 1979 Mustang ("a real beauty") until the lights kept shorting out. After three attempts by the dealer to repair the light failure, the consumer had the following frightening experience:

> I put the lights on for only a few minutes when I smelled smoke. Suddenly a flame could be seen through the air-conditioning vent over the headlight switch in the dashboard; within a few seconds the flames were spreading. I was driving about 55 or 60 mph and when I saw the flames I panicked and almost turned the car over; I lost control of the steering but luckily the car came to a safe stop. My car was burning up. A truck driver stopped and had a fire extinguisher and proceeded to put the fire out.
>
> We contacted Ford; they said for us to let our insurance company take care of it—that's what we had insurance for. . . .
>
> Even *if* Allstate decides to total the car, we'll only get $7,200.00 minus approx. $1,500. I can't buy another new Mustang for that.
>
> I feel Ford Company is at fault here; I almost get killed, lose money, and don't have my $7200.00 car.

In 1976 the U.S. District Court for the District of Columbia ordered General Motors to recall an estimated 375,000 model-year 1965 and 1966 Chevrolets and 1966 Buicks because of a fire hazard caused by faulty carburetor plugs; those vehicles were equipped with Rochester Quadrajet carburetors manufactured before March 28, 1966. The court also ordered GM to pay a $400,000 civil penalty to the U.S. for refusing the National Highway Traffic Safety Administration's order to notify owners of the safety-related defect. NHTSA had reports of more than a thousand fires resulting from these carburetor plugs falling out and spilling gasoline onto a hot engine.

Accident fires are often caused by ruptures in the gas tanks. Gas tanks

199

are presently made with only a single layer of steel, which can rupture in a serious collision. If the tank is placed between the bumper and rear axle as in the infamous 1971–76 Ford Pinto, fires can and will occur in low-speed rear impact crashes.

6. TRANSMISSION FAILURES

Whether it's an automatic or manual transmission, manufacturers usually blame failures on owner abuse and refuse to pay for the repair. Both types of transmissions have clutch plates that quickly wear out—if misaligned in the case of a manual transmission or inadequately lubricated in case of an automatic. Either will subject consumers to expensive repair bills.

Another common transmission problem occurs when an undersized transmission in a car leads to failure under moderate loads. When GM put the Type 200 Chevette transmission in its full- and intermediate-size cars in 1977–79, these transmissions failed by the thousands because they were not durable for cars larger than the Chevette. Consumers ended up paying $400 to $600 for replacements by 20,000 miles. A properly designed transmission should last at least 50,000 miles and with proper care, a full 100,000 miles. If you want to pull a trailer or other load with a new car, tell the salesman and ask for an adequate transmission. Even if you don't get a larger transmission, the salesman's representation can create an implied warranty that will be the basis for recovery if the transmission fails.

7. STEERING, ALIGNMENT, AND TIRE BALANCE

Faulty steering, poor tire balance, and improper alignment are present to some degree in nearly every new car. Often they can work together to make handling both unsure and unsafe. Vibrations are set up which allow the tires to shimmy on the road, ruining traction and rubbing off tread in uneven patterns. The resulting lumpy tires make the vibration even worse. In extreme cases the tire may overheat and eventually blow out.

Some cars with steering or alignment defects wander sideways on the road or always try to turn to one side, while others fail to straighten out promptly after turns. Some, running as if pigeon-toed, quietly erase the rubber from the tire in a few thousand miles. Because a symptom may indicate any of several front-end problems, the only way to diagnose many of these is to subject them to tedious, careful measurements and observations. Since these problems are difficult to detect, they often are noticed only after the warranty has expired.

Alignment of the wheels and steering involves adjusting all parts of the steering mechanism and suspension so that the front wheels stay parallel and flat on the pavement at all speeds with no scuffing or other unwanted action, and so that the feel and balance of the steering are even and the ride is stable.

The cost of a shimmy or vibration can be high if the problem is not corrected immediately. Along with the front tires, parts of the steering mechanism and the front suspension may be worn out. The cause is usually in the

200

adjustment of the alignment, or the wheel balance, both of which are included in the instructions to the dealer for preparation of the car before sale.

Since alignment and balance are not covered by the warranty, except by the ninety-day new-car adjustment policies of some manufacturers, the dealer has a financial incentive to do the adjusting after you buy the car rather than before. By skimping on the alignment and balancing, the unscrupulous dealer also misses an opportunity to correct any loose or defective parts, an omission that could cause a failure and bring on an accident.

One of the best ways to detect poor alignment in new cars is by measuring the wear on the front tires. Insert a tread-wear gauge into the grooves nearest the inner and outer edges of the tread on both wheels. If your four measurements indicate any noticeable differences in the depth of the tread, the alignment or wheel balance may be off.

Power steering on new cars sometimes fails when the rubber hoses that carry the fluid are cut by fan belts, wheels, or other parts. This happens because the hoses are placed too close to moving parts by sloppy designers or assemblers and the defect slips through inspection.

Sudden failure of the power assist to power steering because of fluid leakage or stalling of the engine does not make steering impossible—unless the surprise leaves you frozen and bewildered. But power failure does make steering so much harder that drivers may think that there is no steering at all; and even if they do realize what is wrong, the needed force may be more than they can muster.

Even more dangerous is the power steering spool valve that jams because of particles in the fluid and causes the car to turn sharply to one side or the other. Such hidden defects in the steering system can bring about accidents, the true cause of which is never determined.

8. SUSPENSION

The suspension consists of the springs, shock absorbers, and other parts that are designed to support the car and give it a comfortable, yet stable, ride. The suspensions of most large American cars provide plenty of comfort, but they are so soft that control of the car becomes very difficult in many emergency situations. Sudden swerves or bumps can throw the car so far off balance that it will go out of control. Suspension inadequacies are frequently the cause of single-car crashes, where no one lives to describe what happened, and where the police report often cites reckless driving as the cause.

What stability there is deteriorates rapidly with age. Shock absorbers often become useless after a few thousand miles, and the soft springs become even softer when they rust. To reduce these problems, a consumer can specify a heavy-duty suspension when ordering a new car. In an advertisement, Mercedes-Benz stated the problem well:

A passenger doesn't *need* suspension fit for a racer, argue some critics. . . . For everyday city driving, this is sheer engineering extravagance.

201

But some day you *might* have to get off the pavement, onto a stretch of potholed back road. You *might* have to enter a sharp curve or a turn-off faster than you intended. You *might* have to change course quickly while cruising on a busy turnpike.

And suddenly, you realize this engineering extravagance is no extravagance at all.

9. WIRING, SWITCHES, AND SOCKETS

The wiring, switches, and sockets of modern automotive lighting systems are generally of such cheap construction that failure is frequent. The plugs and sockets which connect the various parts of the lighting system are made of plastic, which melts whenever the overloaded wires and connections inside heat up. The moisture protection is inadequate, so water gets in the sockets and corrodes the metal contacts. As a result your headlights may go out when you hit the dimmer switch, your taillights may fail repeatedly, or your car's entire electrical system may short out with no warning at all.

British Leyland cars are notorious for their defective electrical systems, with recalls over the past few years to repair faulty lighting systems in 1973–76 Triumph TR-6s, 1969-73 GT-6s, and 1969–74 Spitfires; and electrical short circuits causing underhood fires in 1977–78 MGBs and headlamp failure in 1975–78 Triumph TR-7s. One unlucky 1973 Triumph TR-6 owner, B. Rumph of Newark, New Jersey, could not get a serious electrical problem properly repaired which resulted in frequent headlight failure. In her March 7, 1979, letter to British Leyland, she complained:

> The electrical system in the car appears to have a short in headlights. When lights are turned on, voltage goes from 15 to below 11 (particularly if the car is stopped). This problem has been in existence for approximately two years. No one seems capable of locating the short, which resulted in great loss of money.

She further explained in a March 23, 1979, letter:

> As shown by the enclosed receipts, three (3) different alternators were supposedly installed in the automobile. When the car was taken to Springfield Imports, I informed them of this; stating that perhaps something was draining the alternators.
>
> I picked up my car from Springfield Imports. The mechanic, who allegedly worked on it, informed me that I should not drive with the lights on.

10. CONCEALED HEADLIGHTS

The best of the new animal cars do their prowling only at night. During the day they close their glistening steel eyelids and purr quietly, awaiting the dusk when they can again snarl through the underbrush in pursuit of their imaginary prey. But sometimes, having overtaken the weaker animals on the

202

road, the beasts become tired; their eyelids droop, and they careen into the ditch for a long rest.

The most amazing thing about eyelids, or headlight covers, is that while they cost a small fortune, serve absolutely no useful purpose, require expensive repairs, stick shut so often that the auto manufacturers give instructions in their owner's manuals on how to rip them open by hand, and have been the subject of a recall campaign, part of the American public is still brainwashed into thinking they are a good idea.

11. AIR-CONDITIONERS

Air-conditioners are not only the most expensive of all options, but also one of the most popular. Given the high frequency of repair and increased service costs and fuel consumption, air-conditioning is an option that many consumers would do well to avoid. Because an air-conditioner takes so much power to run, it usually cuts down on gas mileage.

According to April 1979 *Consumer Reports*, air-conditioning can cut gasoline mileage by as much as 4 mpg when operated on a hot summer day. The car's engine, which must supply this extra power, heats up more as it runs harder. The engine's cooling system is sometimes not beefed up enough to remove this extra heat, so the engine can be damaged by overheating. This is by far the most common complaint in letters from owners of air-conditioned cars. The extra weight also strains already overburdened brakes. Freon leakage is common. Less frequent but more expensive are failures where the air-conditioner's compressor bearings seize up and stop the compressor.

12. GAUGES

Operation of all warning gauges, especially temperature, oil pressure, amperage, and fuel level, is vitally important for your safety and for prevention of unnecessary damage to your car's engine. The problem, now that warning lights have replaced many needle gauges, is that you can't always tell if they are out of order. The best way to be sure they are all working is to have them checked periodically by a mechanic or diagnostician.

Between checkups you can get a rough idea of how the gauges are doing by watching for the light when starting the car. For example, the oil-pressure light should glow when you turn on the ignition key. The light should go out shortly after the engine is started.

Speedometers and odometers are notoriously inaccurate. An inaccurate odometer which overregisters mileage can reduce your warranty by a thousand miles, and an inaccurate speedometer can get you arrested for speeding. The best way to test these instruments is to use the mileage markers on some highways. At an even 55 mph you should go a mile in one minute and five seconds.

13. SPEED CONTROLS

The automatic speed control, or "cruise control," which is available on

203

higher-priced cars, may well be one of the most dangerous luxuries available today. With a speed control you simply get the car going as fast as you want it to go, turn on the control, and take your foot off the gas pedal. You are now free to curl up in the driver's seat, needing only a finger to guide the car, and to settle into a peaceful state of drowsy relaxation, accompanied by stereo music.

Of course, you are an aware and careful driver, and you don't intend to be lulled into sleep by having so little to do—but can you help it? Cars are too pacifying as they are. And even if you *do* stay wide awake, your car's perfectly steady speed is a hazard if there is any traffic. Other cars often slow down momentarily, even if only a mile or two per hour. But you, with your automatic speed control, can't slow down unless you step on the brake to turn off the control, bring the car to a new "perfect speed," and turn on the control again. Unfortunately, it is far more convenient to maintain your speed and change lanes or pass, even though it is often more hazardous.

14. BODY LEAKAGE

Water leakage around the windows, doors, or other parts, while not as dangerous as most defects, can be more difficult to get repaired. Windshields that leak around the edges should be taken out to eliminate leaks, but few dealers do this. Other leaks around fittings or through missing plugs are difficult to spot. Even when a leak is found, dealers often don't check their repair by hosing it with water, so you may have to make several return trips to get the job completed.

15. LOOSE PARTS

Loose parts are so common that they are almost taken for granted. While most loose parts cause only rattles, some, such as loose glove-compartment doors, can cause serious injury in an accident or sudden stop and must be fixed immediately. Once loose parts are diagnosed, they can usually be fixed quickly; and a good dealer will fix them while you wait.

Since even the best maintained vehicle may still cause an emergency, it helps to know what to do when a malfunction occurs. A government pamphlet, "How to Deal with Motor Vehicle Emergencies," can be obtained for free by writing:

U.S. Department of Transportation
National Highway Traffic Safety Administration
Office of Public Affairs and Consumer Services
Washington, D.C. 20590

204

CHAPTER 15 *Auto Safety*

Motor vehicle accidents are one of our nation's leading causes of death. In 1978 more than 50,000 people met violent deaths in motor vehicle collisions while almost 2,000,000 more suffered disabling injuries. The cost arising from motor vehicle accidents in 1978 was a staggering $43 billion in the U.S. This figure reflects lost wages, medical expenses, ambulance and police services, funeral costs, insurance administration, rehabilitative expenses, and property damage from motor vehicle accidents.

Enormous as the highway traffic toll is, it would be even larger but for the passage of the National Traffic and Motor Vehicle Safety Act in 1966 and the imposition of vehicle safety standards in 1968. In 1966 the death rate per 100 million miles traveled was 5.48. Even though only a few of the original safety standards had been updated, the death rate dropped to 4.11 deaths per 100 million miles in 1973. With the imposition of more and more safety programs, the fatality rate per 100 million miles dropped to 3.27 in 1978. In the ten-year period from 1967 to 1977, over 134,000 lives have been saved by the imposition of safety standards.

One program that has saved thousands of lives was instituted not as a safety standard, but as a measure to conserve energy. The 55-mph national speed limit was established in late 1973 in response to the oil embargo and ensuing shortage of gasoline. At first, both speed of travel and the number of fatalities went down noticeably, with more than 5,000 lives saved each year in 1974 and 1975 which were directly attributable to the reduction in speed. But average speeds began inching up over 55 mph in 1976 with a corresponding change in the fatality rate. As more motorists disobeyed the 55-mph speed limit, fewer and fewer lives were saved by the law. Thus, by 1977 only 1,600 lives were saved by the 55-mph speed limit, whereas in 1974 over 5,000 lives were spared.

In spite of the lives saved because of safety programs, mass carnage still reigns on our highways; and forecasts of the traffic environment to the year 2000 are particularly bleak. The Department of Transportation has estimated there will be a seventy-one percent increase in fatalities and serious injuries because of the growth in the numbers of vehicles, vehicle miles traveled, and the number of drivers—unless further safety measures are adopted.

NATIONAL HIGHWAY TRAFFIC SAFETY ADMINISTRATION

The federal regulatory agency responsible for the development and introduction of safety standards and the duty to get the auto companies to build products with fewer safety-related defects is the National Highway Traffic Safety Administration. NHTSA was established by the National Traffic and Motor Vehicle Safety Act of 1966. The agency was empowered to establish motor vehicle safety standards for motor vehicles and equipment, to undertake and support necessary safety research and development, and to investigate and recall motor vehicles and equipment with defects.

205

FEDERAL SAFETY STANDARDS

Most of the federal safety standards first became effective for 1968 model-year automobiles. These standards governed the strength and quality of seatbelts and anchorages, safety glass, impact-absorbing steering columns and their rearward displacement in a frontal collision, safety door latches and hinges, location of dash instrumentation, padded dash and visors, and mounting of fuel tanks and filler spouts. Standards were also implemented that set performance criteria for brakes, tire tread, lights, windshield wipers, and other features.

Since 1968 only a few additional standards have been issued. These include standards governing windshield mounting, performance requirements for optional child restraints, strengthened side doors the better to resist side impact, improved crush resistance of vehicle roofs for better occupant protection in rollover accidents, the flammability of materials used in car interiors, and protection of the fuel tank in rear and side impacts.

After eight years of delay, NHTSA finally issued the most lifesaving safety rule in standard 208—Occupant Crash Protection. This standard specifies that all large passenger cars manufactured for sale or use in the United States must be equipped with front-seat passive-restraint systems to protect occupants from injury in crashes, beginning with the 1982 model year. In model-year 1983, all intermediate cars must be so equipped. By model-year 1984 all cars will be required to have front-seat passive-protection systems.

The design and type of passive-restraint system to be used are up to the manufacturer. Two systems have been developed that meet the performance requirements of the standards: the airbag and the passive belt. The airbag system has been extensively tested both on the road and in laboratories. The concept of the airbag is simple: in a collision, airbags inflate within thirty milliseconds inside the vehicle—so that the occupant collides against the bag instead of metal or glass. The airbag cushions the occupants and distributes the crash force more evenly over their bodies. Passive belts are a belt system that is designed to move into place when the front-seat occupants enter the vehicle and close the doors. There is no action required by the occupants. Passive belts first became available in the 1977 VW Rabbit and the 1979 Chevrolet Chevette.

The Department of Transportation conservatively estimates that 9,000 lives will be saved and 65,000 injuries prevented each year, once all cars are equipped with passive restraints. Although the estimated cost of passive restraints ranges from $90 to $235 for airbags and $25 to $75 for passive belts, these costs will be recovered several times over through reduced insurance costs and savings in lives.

DEFECTS INVESTIGATION AND RECALLS

Another primary mission of NHTSA is to investigate safety defects unknown to, overlooked by, or covered up by the vehicle and vehicle equipment manufacturers. Between 1967 and 1979 over 400 defect investigations were

206

conducted. During a defect investigation, the NHTSA checks consumer mail it has received, requires data on failures and other information from the automobile manufacturers, checks with consumer groups and repair facilities for further data, and issues consumer protection bulletins or public advisories to the media to generate further reports of failures from the public at large.

After gathering all the information pertinent to the defect, NHTSA makes an initial finding of whether there is or is not a safety defect. The manufacturer is informed of the finding and given notice of the time and place when a public meeting will be held so that the manufacturer and other interested parties may present their views. A notice is published in the *Federal Register* and released to the media to inform the public of the meeting.

After the public meeting, NHTSA reviews the material presented and makes a final determination. If the administrator determines that a safety defect does exist, a final letter is written to the manufacturer requiring the recall of all vehicles, tires, or vehicle equipment affected. Should the manufacturer refuse, the administrator can go to court to compel the recall action and impose a fine of up to $800,000.

PETITIONS FOR RULEMAKING

As explained in detail in Chapter 4, consumers may petition NHTSA to begin investigations into safety-related defects that the consumer believes may also occur in other vehicles.

In 1977 NHTSA received thirteen petitions from consumers urging that defect investigations should be conducted. One of these petitions resulted in a recall campaign and another resulted in a formal defect investigation. In response to all the petitions, NHTSA examined the information available before notifying the consumer that a basis for a defect investigation did or did not exist.

NEED FOR FURTHER IMPROVEMENTS

The need for further improvements in motor vehicle safety is abundantly clear. For example, passenger safety for light trucks and vans needs to be improved because these vehicles are being used more and more as substitutes for cars. As the population of these vehicles has increased, so has the number of deaths to their drivers and passengers and to occupants of other vehicles. Light truck, van, and multipurpose passenger vehicle occupant fatalities rose from 4,672 in 1975 to 6,585 in 1978, a 41 percent increase. During that same period, by comparison, there was a much smaller increase (7.4 percent) in passenger car occupant fatalities.

Currently, most vans, pickup trucks, and jeep-type vehicles are not required to meet most of the federal safety standards for passenger cars, and the automobile manufacturers have done little to provide protection for light truck and van occupants. Many of these vehicles lack energy-absorbing steering columns, crash padding, secure windshield mountings, head restraints, and other items that offer crash protection to occupants of passenger automobiles. In response to the rising death tolls in light trucks and vans, and specifically to petitions filed by the Center for Auto Safety and the Insurance Institute for Highway Safety, the Department of Transportation has proposed a rule to improve the braking systems of these vehicles. A final rule issued by DOT, effective in 1981, extends three safety standards to cover light trucks and vans. The standards require improving interior padding to protect occupants, steering wheels to absorb energy to cushion the driver's impact in an accident, and limiting the distance the steering wheel can move backward in protecting the driver in a crash.

To date, NHTSA and the automobile companies have done very little to reduce the likelihood of injury or death in pedestrian-automobile collisions. Many domestic and foreign automobiles have numerous exterior protrusions such as hood ornaments and bumper guards that localize the impact and cause extensive injuries. Each year, approximately 100,000 pedestrian accidents kill nearly 8,000 people and injure many thousands more. Pedestrian accident statistics indicate that seventy-seven percent of pedestrian impacts involve the front end of the car and that a majority of these impacts occur at speeds less than 20 mph. Research has shown that at 25 mph the human body can survive the impact if the front end of the car collapses one foot. Calspan, an automobile safety research corporation working under contract with NHTSA, developed a soft front bumper covering the full front face of an automobile that will pick up the pedestrian and carry him along until the vehicle stops, without throwing the pedestrian under the wheels or into the windshield. The bumper developed was designed to recover its original shape after an impact. The introduction of similar bumpers would prevent a large number of fatalities and reduce the costs of low-speed two-car collisions.

Occupant crash protection in higher-speed impacts must be improved if we are further to reduce our highway losses. Current automobiles provide impact protection of 25–30 mph in a barrier collision or 50–60 mph in an impact with a stationary vehicle of the same weight. Side impact protection is even worse, protecting only up to 12–15 mph. The technology is available to improve significantly the crashworthiness of today's average vehicle. Automotive safety researchers have developed subcompact-size vehicles that are designed to protect the vehicle occupants in collisions of up to 50 mph into a solid barrier or 100 mph into a parked car. These engineers have not used any exotic materials or processes, but have designed their vehicles with safety as their foremost goal. Not only are these vehicles extremely safe, but they are also very fuel efficient, comfortable, and stylish.

Thus the 30-mph protection assured by passive restraints in current motor vehicles can greatly be improved. Passive protection at 50 mph is easily attainable and will eliminate nearly 80 percent of the societal costs of frontal automobile accidents and 75 percent of the fatalities. Research has demonstrated that the side crashworthiness of vehicles can be significantly improved by the addition of reinforcements, increasing the thickness of the sheet metal, and substituting high-strength low-alloy steel for mild steel, which is commonly used. These improvements would increase the protection from the current 12–15 mph to a safer 40–50 mph in side impacts.

LARGE CAR vs. SMALL CAR

The adoption of strict fuel economy standards and the increasing cost of gasoline that will ensure more fuel-efficient and necessarily lighter automobiles have spurred a growing concern over the safety of small cars. By the mid-1980s small cars will make up more than half the vehicle population and will be responsible for more than sixty percent of the societal costs of accidents.

If large and small cars are constructed in the same way, the larger cars are safer. Large cars have greater areas of sheet metal to crumple and absorb crash forces, and more room in the engine compartment that make it less likely that the forces of the crash will push the engine through the firewall into the passenger compartment. Analyses of actual crash data demonstrate that large cars are safer than small cars by almost a factor of two. A 1968 New York State study based on more than 400,000 vehicles in reported crashes found a strong association between the weight of a car and the percentage of accidents in which there was a fatality or serious injury in that type of car. Results of that study show a large increase in the percentage of serious or fatal injuries with decreasing vehicle weight. A University of Michigan study reported that once a car is involved in an accident, the chance of injury in that car increases at the rate of about 2.5 percent for each decrease of 100 pounds in vehicle weight.

Small cars *can* be designed to be as safe as or safer than present large passenger cars. Contractors working for the Department of Transportation's Research Safety Vehicle Program designed and built 2,250-pound subcompact vehicles that have a higher level of occupant protection than is currently available in even the largest automobiles, of 4,500–5,000 pounds. These cars are able to withstand frontal barrier impacts in the 40–50-mph range while current automobiles are able to withstand only 30–40-mph barrier impacts without massive intrusion into the passenger compartment. Minicars, a California company which designed one of the Research Safety Vehicles, also altered a number of 1974 Ford Pintos with readily available techniques that could be used to make current small cars safer than current large ones. Similar results have been obtained by small foreign companies such as Volvo, Volkswagen, and Datsun on their own Experimental Safety Vehicles (ESVs). Volkswagen included many features from its ESV on the Rabbit when it was introduced in 1975. Indeed, the Rabbit with the passive seatbelt system is an excellent example of a safe small car, as it had one of the lowest fatality rates of any car in 1977.

Comparative safety ratings would provide consumers with the necessary information to select the safer small cars. Unfortunately, the auto companies never have systematically rated cars for crashworthiness and accident avoidance capabilities. Although Congress passed a law in 1972 requiring NHTSA to rate automobiles by make and model for susceptibility to damage, crashworthiness, and ease of diagnosis and repair, the ratings had been stalled for eight years for lack of funding from Congress and confusion and absence of purpose on the part of the agency.

In 1979, NHTSA finally crashed cars in comparative tests that showed a majority of the U.S.-produced autos and all of the imported cars tested would not provide good occupant protection in head-on frontal collisions. Of the thirty cars tested by NHTSA, five cars passed all of the tests:

Table 2
NHTSA: Best Cars

These cars passed the following tests:

35 MPH Frontal Impact: Occupant Protection, Windshield Retention, Windshield Intrusion, Fuel Leakage.
35 MPH Rear Impact: Fuel Leakage.

SIZE:	Subcompacts (2,151-2,650 lbs.)	Compacts/Intermediates (2,651-3,350 lbs.)	Standard/Full Size (3,351-4,050 lbs.)
MAKE/MODEL:	Plymouth Horizon* 1979	Chevrolet Citation 1980	Dodge Magnum** 1979
		Ford Mustang* 1979	Chrysler Cordoba** 1979

*Same construction in 1980.
**Similar cars—second car was used for rear impact test.

NHTSA used two dummies in the front seat wearing safety belts and loaded with instruments to measure the crash forces. The 35-mph speed of the tests was 5 mph higher than required by federal motor vehicle safety standards. Only high-volume sales cars were tested, so not all cars sold in the U.S. were represented in table 2. One car with a long reputation for safety, the Volvo 244DL, flunked the 35-mph occupant frontal collision test.
For more information on the above analyses, contact:

U.S. Department of Transportation
National Highway Traffic Safety Administration
Office of Public Affairs
Washington, D.C. 20590

Although the NHTSA test results are a good guide for informed consumers who want the safest cars, the test results are not meaningful for those who refuse to wear seatbelts. For nonseatbelt wearers, the following insurance accident report may be useful since it studied actual on-the-road conditions which reflect the fact that only eleven percent of occupants wear seat belts.

The Insurance Institute for Highway Safety (IIHS) (described in Chapter 4) releases an annual report through its related Highway Loss Data Institute (HLDI) which identifies the best and the worst of most cars sold in the U.S. The report analyzes insurance injury-claim frequencies for recent model cars each year. HLDI, in table 3, shows the relative injury-claim frequencies per 1,000 insured vehicle years for the 1977 and 1978 model-year cars with the best and worst loss experience in personal injury protection coverages.

210

Table 3

Relative Injury-Claim Frequencies per 1,000 Insured Vehicle Years

1978

	BEST CARS				WORST CARS		
HIGH VOLUME (At least 1% of total exposure)	Oldsmobile Delta 88	4-Door I	55	Honda Civic	2- Door SC	144	
	Chevrolet Caprice	4-Door I	64	Toyota Corolla	—* SC	142	
	Buick LeSabre	4-Door I	65	Datsun B-210	—* SC	140	
	Chevrolet Impala	4-Door I	75	Ford Mustang II	2-Door SC	133	
	Chevrolet Nova	4-Door C	79	Toyota Celica	2- Door SC	131	

1977

HIGH VOLUME (At least 1% of total exposure)	Oldsmobile Delta 88	4-Door I	73	Datsun B-210	—* SC	146	
	Buick LeSabre	4-Door I	76	Chev. Chevette	2-Door SC	136	
	Chevrolet Caprice	4-Door I	77	Toyota Corolla	—* SC	135	
	Dodge Aspen	SW I	77	Pontiac Firebird	Spec. C	127	
	Cadillac DeVille	2-Door FS	79	Chev. Camaro	Spec. C	123	
	Chevrolet Impala	4-Door I	79				
LOW VOLUME (Less than 1% of total exposure)	Chrysler Newport	4-Door FS	59	Datsun 200 SX	2-Door SC	183	
	Oldsmobile 98	4-Door 1	62	Plymouth Arrow	2-Door SC	161	
	Chev. Caprice Est. Wagon	SW I	63	Chevrolet Vega	2-Door SC	148	
	Buick Skylark	4-Door C	69	Honda Civic	2-Door SC	141	
	Pontiac Catalina Safari	SW I	69	Datsun 280Z	Sports SC	134	

SOURCE: Insurance Institute for Highway Safety.
Watergate 600
Washington, D.C. 20037

NOTES:

Results are standardized to the exposure distribution:

YOUTHFUL OPERATOR	NO YOUTHFUL OPERATOR
15%	85%

100 = 18.6 claims per 1,000 insured vehicle years.
= claim frequency for all 1977 model-year cars.
Subcompact (SC)—cars with wheelbases less than or equal to 101 inches.
Compact (C)—cars with wheelbases greater than 101 inches and less than or equal to 111 inches.
Intermediate (I)—cars with wheelbases greater than 111 inches and less than or equal to 120 inches.
Full-Size (FS)—cars with wheelbases greater than 120 inches.

*Body style not determinable from vehicle identification number.

The improved crashworthiness of automobiles is valuable but occupants still need to use the proper restraints—either "active restraints" such as seatbelts or "passive restraints" such as airbags or passive belts—to have adequate protection in a crash. The use of restraints greatly improves the safety of any vehicle. Researchers at the University of North Carolina have shown that the use of lap and shoulder belts was 57.4 percent more effective at preventing or lessening serious or fatal injuries than nonuse of these restraints. In automobiles under 3,600 pounds, the effectiveness of lap and shoulder belts is 51.9 percent; in larger cars, 64.5 percent. For airbag-equipped automobiles, the protection offered in frontal collisions is even greater.

Although government safety programs are necessary to reduce the mounting toll of motor vehicle–related deaths, injuries, and property damage, the cooperation of the auto industry and individual motorists is also essential to decreasing these losses. Human carnage on the highway would be reduced if the industry would put a greater emphasis on auto safety than on cosmetic styling and annual design changes. More lives would be saved if individual motorists would follow the 55-mph speed limit, wear seatbelts or use other available restraints, and avoid speeding, combining drinking and driving, and other unnecessary driving risks.

CHAPTER 16 *Auto Energy Use*

While environmental problems are still very much with us, we are now confronted as well by an energy crisis which continues to worsen and which threatens the security and economic stability of the country. And once again the automobile is front and center as the single largest source of energy waste in our society.*

The Arab oil embargo of 1973–74 demonstrated to the nation the great dependence of automobile transportation on the availability of petroleum sources. Almost all fuels used in transportation are derived from petroleum. The amount of petroleum used by passenger vehicles each year in the U.S. has grown from about thirteen percent in 1950 to about forty-four percent in 1978. In 1978, 10.09 million barrels per day, more than half the total U.S. petroleum consumption, were used in transportation. More than eighty-two percent of this amount was used by passenger vehicles. Despite serious adverse effects on our balance of payments and national security, we import approximately half of the petroleum we consume.

Given the increasing scarcity of petroleum products to the U.S., with rising prices and unstable sources, the federal government stepped in to encourage improvements in automotive fuel economy technology in order to ease U.S. dependence on foreign oil. In 1975 Congress enacted the Energy Policy and Conservation Act (Energy Act), which requires a 1985 new-car-average fuel economy standard of 27.5 mpg—double the average fuel economy of new cars in 1974. Since that time, the Department of Transportation has established fuel economy standards for 1978–84 model-year vehicles that will enable the 27.5-mpg requirement to be met in 1985 (see "Government Role in Auto Energy Use" in this chapter).

The government's task of setting standards for fuel economy has not been an easy one. One hurdle in promulgating stringent fuel economy standards has been the auto manufacturers' resistance and excuses as to why one type of vehicle should be exempted, a special class be set up for another and a lower standard be set because lead time and cost prohibit use of one technological development or another.

Such technological development is not necessarily going "forward"; instead, we are going back to a time when cars were not as large or so powerful and achieved better gas mileage than they do today. For example, in the 1936 Mobilgas economy run, the Willys 4, Chevrolet 6, and Chrysler 6 respectively achieved 32.2, 25.7, and 21 mpg. In 1955, the Rambler Super 6 got 27.5 mpg while the Ford 6 got 22.8 mpg.

The 1981–84 average fuel economy standards will save the U.S. an estimated 590,000 barrels per day in 1985 and 1.2 million barrels per day in 1995 over what would be achieved if the standards were held at the 1980

---

*Russell E. Train, former administrator, Environmental Protection Agency.

213

level of 20 mpg. Besides saving the country valuable petroleum, stringent fuel economy standards benefit consumers by saving them money over the long term with more fuel-efficient automobiles. By comparison with the average 1977 model-year cars, owners of the 1985 model-year cars can expect:

- An increase in fuel economy from about 17 to 27.5 mpg.
- A saving of about $2,770 in the cost of gasoline over the life of the car, computed at $1.50 per gallon.
- A saving of about $200 in maintenance costs over the life of the car.
- Net savings to the car owner will be approximately $2,870 after deducting the cost for the technology to meet the standards.

Downsizing, one of the primary means of manufacturing more fuel-efficient vehicles, should not adversely affect the cargo-carrying capacity of cars. Passenger and luggage space will remain the same. Consumers will still have a variety of models from which to choose. Even stationwagons can achieve good fuel economy, as shown by studies made by the Environmental Protection Agency. An EPA analysis of 1975 stationwagons found that the better-designed midsized wagons that averaged up to 30 mpg were capable of carrying seven to eight passengers.

WHY BE AN ENERGY SAVER?

There are many reasons why consumers should become energy savers. The two major ones are cost and resource availability. Over the twenty years between 1955 and 1975, U.S. dependence on imported oil more than doubled. Long-range projections show that, if present energy consumption trends go unchanged, world oil supplies will be insufficient to meet world demand for oil around the year 2000. In these circumstances, prices will rise sharply and available gas and oil may have to be rationed among all users, particularly hitting the auto owner. Conservation-minded consumers will help stretch oil supplies and ease the transition to energy sources other than oil. The other reason for becoming an energy saver is to save money. If you drive a gas guzzler that gets only 12 mpg, your fuel cost for the average 100,000 miles of useful driving life at $1.50 per gallon is $12,500. If you drive a car that gets 20 mpg, your fuel cost for the same number of miles driven goes down to $7,500—a saving of $5,000. If gasoline prices keep rising at the same rate at which they have been rising within the last two years, the saving from a more fuel-efficient car will continue to grow.

GOVERNMENT ROLE IN AUTO ENERGY USE

In requiring the Department of Transportation to set fleet average passenger and nonpassenger automobile fuel economy standards, Congress's primary goal was "the need of the nation to conserve energy." When enacting the Energy Policy and Conservation Act, Congress weighed various alternatives and settled on requiring standards that represented the "maximum feasible

214

average fuel economy." The act is geared not to any one manufacturer but to the industry as a whole. For those manufacturers unable to meet the standards, Congress carefully delineated an economic penalty system that would enable the manufacturer to stay in business by paying a civil penalty based on the magnitude by which the company missed the standards.

Yet the auto makers still resist meeting the government's standards. For example, in 1978 Chrysler told NHTSA that it could not meet the government's fuel economy standards for 1981 model-year vans and light trucks and that huge layoffs and production cuts would be likely unless the rules were changed. When the truck standard was announced by DOT in July 1978, it was a drastically lower figure than what the agency had proposed originally. But even after this relaxation, Chrysler and the other auto companies lobbied heavily for a still lower figure.

There is little doubt that the 27.5-mpg new-car-average fuel economy standard imposed by the Energy Act for 1985 can be met and exceeded. The prime issue in energy conservation is not achieving this standard but how to go beyond it. The Department of Transportation recognized this fact when it pointed out in June 1977 that it could not legally set a 27.5-mpg standard before 1985 even though "data analyses . . . appear to justify average fuel economy standards more stringent than 27.5 mpg by 1985." DOT's conclusions are not surprising since a large number of previous government and private reports established that the 1985 standard can be not only met but bettered.

With this in mind, Secretary of Transportation Brock Adams challenged the auto industry to "reinvent" the automobile—leading to 50 mpg by the year 2000. After studying the recommendations of three panels of technical experts on engines, fuels and powertrain systems, and structures and materials at a February 1979 DOT conference held in Boston, Adams expressed confidence that "a kind of fundamental breakthrough" in automotive technology is possible—that the auto makers could virtually double the average fuel efficiency before the end of the century. The secretary noted that "the auto industry over the past fifty years has relied on imitation, not innovation, and evolutionary instead of revolutionary thinking in manufacturing their cars." He added that imitation and evolutionary thinking are not sufficient today in order to "deal with the realities of a worsening energy situation."

Without government regulation setting these fuel economy standards, technology would have remained relatively stagnant and few goals in auto energy conservation would have been met. As is the case in other areas of government auto regulation, such as safety and emission control, the domestic manufacturers' policy seems to be a curious mixture of "wait and see" while not making any voluntary technological improvements. This wait-and-see policy is illustrated in the domestic industry's hesitation to enter the subcompact car market until spurred by the fuel economy standards and the import sales of nearly twenty percent, a market to which the industry still has not begun fully to respond.

The government role in auto energy use, through the fuel economy standards for both passenger and nonpassenger autos, is crucial to force the domestic manufacturers to produce more fuel-efficient and utilitarian vehicles in this country, thus contributing to the fuel saving necessary to meet the goals of the Energy Act as well as increasing domestic employment.

EPA FUEL ECONOMY RATINGS

In carrying out the Energy Act, DOT must coordinate closely with the Environmental Protection Agency, which is supposed to provide consumers with gasoline mileage estimates of individual models of automobiles. The annual "Gas Mileage Guide," published jointly by the EPA and the Department of Energy (DOE), gives the new- or used-car buyer information on the relative fuel economy performance of cars, stationwagons, and light trucks. Each new-car dealer is required to have free copies of the booklet in the dealer's showroom. The estimates are given in terms of miles per gallon on standardized EPA fuel economy tests. Cars are grouped into classes according to their interior size. Trucks are grouped by their capacity, by gross vehicle-weight rating.

In pre-1979 guides fuel economy estimates were given for city and highway driving and for a combined figure. When the EPA ratings first came out in 1975, they were good estimates of consumer fuel economy. But by 1979 the auto companies had learned how to beat the rating system so well that EPA dropped publication of the *highway* ratings and began using only a single *city* rating. Although this change was touted as an attempt to make consumer expectations more realistic, in reality it does nothing for the consumers who expect that the estimate should concur with the actual mileage they get on their cars.

The gasoline saving projected under the fuel economy standards will not be realized if the vehicles that consumers purchase do not achieve the fuel economy projected by EPA certification. This concern is reflected in the flood of consumer mail that our Center receives about misleading EPA fuel economy ratings. Many of these consumers state that they wanted to conserve gasoline by buying a vehicle with good EPA fuel economy ratings but ended up with a car that had substantially poorer fuel economy, which could not be explained by differences in driving practices.

Fundamental problems still exist with the EPA rating and labeling procedures, EPA itself has admitted, and these problems should be addressed in model years beyond 1980. The Center has encouraged EPA to reevaluate its test procedures for determining fuel economy estimates, rather than to switch the estimates around in the guide. Until then consumers are advised to take the EPA ratings conservatively and accept them as valid rankings of cars only when one car is at least 5 mpg better than another.

Another government program to limit energy use is the maximum national speed limit of 55 miles per hour. The 55-mph speed limit, enacted in 1975 by Congress, was originally adopted as a temporary measure under the Emergency Highway Energy Conservation Act. Besides saving fuel at the rate of about 200,000 barrels of gasoline a day, the 55-mph limit saves lives and dollars. One sure way to save costs in operating an automobile is to

216

observe the 55-mph speed limit. The Department of Transportation has estimated that the nation's consumers as a whole would save about $460 *billion* a year (at $1.50 per gallon) if all drivers observed the 55-mph limit. In addition, the 55-mph limit was the biggest single factor in saving an estimated 36,000 lives between 1974 and 1978, above and beyond the lives saved by the vehicle safety standards.

The federal government in cooperation with the states has developed another potentially useful energy saving program—"vanpooling," which is becoming more widespread around the U.S. as a means of commuting to and from work. Vanpooling is an arrangement where up to fifteen persons share commuting costs and save fuel by riding together in a passenger van. According to a Federal Highway Administration estimate, one vanpool provides about 120 person miles of transportation per gallon of gas used. Over one year, each vanpool can save 5,000 gallons of gasoline. During 1977 twelve states used some of their regular highway funds to assist vanpool projects. More than thirty-five vanpools are now operating in seven states, with many more being developed.

Other suggestions by which the government could encourage more fuel-efficient motor vehicles and consumer fuel conservation are:

- The making available, by NHTSA, EPA, and DOE, of impartial government testing for a significant number of fuel-saving devices proposed by inventors outside the auto industry.
- Development of inherently cleaner and more fuel-efficient alternative engines than the present internal combustion engine.
- Increased construction of bikeways in urban areas.
- Improvement of the quality and quantity of mass transit services.

FACTORS THAT AFFECT FUEL ECONOMY

Consumers can increase their fuel economy savings in many ways. For example, since summer temperatures over seventy degrees are better for fuel economy than winter temperatures, long trips can often be planned for the spring or summer rather than the winter. More important in saving gasoline is how you drive and the condition of the vehicle. For example, a vehicle that has been properly tuned gets approximately three to nine percent better fuel economy than one that has not been properly tuned. Underinflated tires can cause a fuel economy loss of up to ten percent, so check tire pressure often. Trip length also affects fuel economy. Trips under five miles do not allow the engine to reach its best operating condition, while longer trips do. Try to combine numerous short trips into a single, longer trip.

When purchasing a new or used car, remember that its size and weight affect the fuel economy. Use the EPA "Gas Mileage Guide" as a means of comparing relative fuel economy ratings. Normally, the smaller and lighter a car, the better the fuel economy. In 1979, for example, the diesel-powered Volkswagen Rabbit had the best fuel economy rating, at 41 mpg. The Datsun

217

210 was tops among 1979 model-year cars that use gasoline (not diesel fuel), getting a 35-mpg rating.

Other suggestions for saving gas:

DRIVING TIPS

- Avoid rapid starts. Accelerate gently. Smooth driving improves fuel economy. Try to avoid constant stops and starts.
- Anticipate stops. Rather than accelerating and braking right up to every stop, coast to a stop if you can stay within the flow of traffic.
- Drive at moderate speeds. Obey the 55-mph speed limit.
- Do not weave in and out of traffic lanes. Weaving just increases the vehicle miles traveled and can be hazardous as well.
- Save gas when changing gears. If you drive a car with a *manual transmission*, run through the lower gears gently and quickly for maximum fuel economy. Then build up speed in high gear. If you drive a car with *automatic transmission*, apply enough gas pedal pressure to get the car rolling, then let up slightly on the pedal to ease the transmission into high range as quickly as possible. More gas is consumed in the lower gears.
- Use the brake pedal rather than the accelerator to hold your car in place on a hill.
- Do not let the car idle for more than a minute if possible.

TRIP PLANNING

- Share the ride. Take the bus or schedule your trips to share a ride with others. For short trips, walk or ride a bicycle. Avoid driving to work if you work in a large city. Traffic jams can increase fuel consumption as much as fifty percent, as well as increase air pollution.
- When possible, drive when the roads are dry. Wet pavement demands more power to reach a given speed.

CAR MAINTENANCE AND CARE

- Use multigrade low-40 or 30-weight motor oils instead of single-grade 30-weight oils. This helps cut engine drag.
- Keep the wheels properly aligned.
- Use radial-ply tires.
- Avoid or do not overuse fuel-guzzling options such as air-conditioning. Air-conditioning reduces fuel economy by as much as four miles per gallon.
- Clean out the trunk. Avoid hauling around unnecessary objects that just add extra weight to the car.
- Check brakes for dragging—brakes that do not fully release when your foot is off the brake pedal.

218

For a more detailed discussion of the factors that affect fuel economy, write for:

"Factors Affecting Fuel Economy"
Public Information Center (PM-215)
U.S. Environmental Protection Agency
Washington, D.C. 20460

For additional copies of the "Gas Mileage Guide," write:

Fuel Economy Distribution
Technical Information Center
Department of Energy
P.O. Box 62
Oak Ridge, Tennessee 37830
(All new-car dealers are required to display prominently and have available copies of this guide in their showrooms.)

For single copies of "Tips for the Motorist: Don't Be Fuelish," write:

Consumer Information Center
Pueblo, Colorado 81009

CHAPTER 17 *Auto Emissions and Air Pollution*

SMOG SETS A RECORD AND IS GETTING WORSE
By Douglas B. Feaver

Eye-irritating, chest-tightening smog reached record levels for the Washington metropolitan area last summer and area officials say it is getting worse, not better.

The forecast comes in a year that saw four air pollution alerts, including one that had as its centerpiece the worst air quality day in the region's history.

Washington Post
December 28, 1975, p. B-1

DIRTY AIR ALERT FOR FOURTH DAY
By Calvin Zon

Like an unwelcome guest, the hot, dirty air which showed up here last Wednesday shows no inclination to leave town, and the second air pollution alert of the season has been extended into its fourth day.

For most people the hovering gray matter is only an irritation—a rubbing of watery eyes, perhaps, or a slight sting in the throat, or avoiding deep breaths.

But for others—including those with chronic respiratory ailments, the very old and the very young—the smog is serious business. Many such persons have taken refuge in their homes. Others were forced to enter hospitals.

By far the most hazardous element of the pollutants hanging in the still air is the gaseous substance called ozone. A precious boon in the upper atmosphere by shielding man and nature from the ultraviolet rays of the sun, ozone is most undesirable at ground level.

While stratospheric ozone is naturally produced, man-made ozone is an indirect product of combustion engine emissions. Specifically, ozone is formed by the action of strong sunlight on the nitric oxide and hydrocarbons of automobile exhaust fumes.

Ozone attacks the tissues of the lung and respiratory tract, making breathing more difficult. It also attacks cells that normally fight off infection, increasing one's vulnerability.

Persons with such respiratory ailments as asthma, emphysema and acute bronchitis—who comprise more than ten percent of the population nationally—are less able to cope when auto exhaust becomes trapped in masses of stagnant air.

"Our hospital is filled to capacity, which is extremely unusual this time of year. I'm sure many patients are here either directly or indirectly because of the air pollution," said Dr. Alfred Munzer, associate director of the pulmonary division of Washington Adventist Hospital.

Munzer said patients whose condition is aggravated during times of high pollution are treated with antibiotics and "other devices to support their breathing."

Washington Star
June 13, 1976, p. A-1

AREA GAGS UNDER ITS WORST SERIES OF POLLUTION ALERTS
By Gloria Borger

The hot, humid and dirty air that surfaced here two days ago will be with us at least another day, extending the area's seventh air-pollution alert of the year—the highest number ever recorded here.

There have been ten days this month that Washington area residents have had to bear the irritations of the pollution—the watery eyes, slight breathing trouble or perhaps even a slight sting in the throat.

"We get people calling us every morning to find out what the COG reading is so they can determine if they should go outside," said Dennis Bates, director of health and environmental protection at COG.

"All of us are affected in one way or another by this. We all feel a lot of discomfort and the heat and attendant humidity doesn't help much."

When pollution levels reach above a 100 rating—which indicates hazardous air quality levels—COG issues an alert to warn commuters, the elderly and those with respiratory and heart ailments to limit their activities. Most pollution in this area, according to COG spokesmen, is the result of sunlight reacting on vehicle exhaust to form ozone.

Washington Star
August 26, 1976, p. A-1

ANTISMOG RULES IMPOSED IN L.A.

Los Angeles (UPI)—One of the heaviest layers of smog in recent memory settled over Los Angeles yesterday, forcing officials to impose mandatory antipollution measures on business and industry for the first time in history.

Persons with respiratory problems or heart conditions were advised to stay indoors and avoid physical exertion. Children were warned against taking part in strenuous outdoor exercise.

The South Coast Air Quality Management District issued the tough antismog measures as the city stifled under an orange blanket of pollution.

The restrictions included a ban on the unloading of oil tankers, twenty percent production cutbacks for smog-causing industries and the closing of business parking lots to employes who fail to join carpools.

The regulations were to remain in effect until at least today as temperatures near 100 and lack of wind left little hope of the smog blowing away any sooner.

South Coast Deputy District Director James Birakos said compli-

221

ance by business and industry was "spotty," with officials planning to issue about forty violation notices.

Under voluntary provisions of the emergency episode plan, residents of the sprawling Los Angeles basin were asked to cut back on home electrical usage and avoid unnecessary driving.

Washington Post
July 15, 1978, p. A-12

The Washington, D.C., area, like many other large U.S. cities, has a serious air pollution problem. Automobile emissions account for an estimated eighty to ninety percent of its air pollution. Other U.S. cities, such as New York and Los Angeles, face even more severe air pollution situations. Automobile-related air pollution is an area of utmost concern to the residents of most major urban areas around the country.

The problem of air pollution is not limited to big cities. Studies have shown that air pollution can be hazardous to people who live fifty or a hundred miles away from major urban areas. This is because pollutants travel long distances from their sources. Some of the highest levels of smog are found not in the central cities, but downwind in suburban areas.

COSTS OF AIR POLLUTION

Pollution caused by auto emissions is responsible for up to an estimated 4,000 deaths and four million days of illness a year, according to the 1974 National Academy of Science (NAS) report, "Air Quality and Automobile Emission Control." NAS noted that these figures represent one eighth of the annual deaths for bronchitis, emphysema, and asthma combined, and one tenth of the total number of days lost from work each year because of respiratory illness.

The most serious of the automobile pollutants are carbon monoxide, the deadly colorless, odorless gas; hydrocarbons and nitrogen oxides, which combine to form photochemical oxidants, or smog, in the presence of sunlight. These pollutants affect all segments of the population and are responsible for the Los Angeles and Washington, D.C., types of smog that now affect most major urban areas.

Most severely affected by air pollution are the older- and younger-age groups and those people suffering from or susceptible to heart and respiratory diseases such as asthma, bronchitis, and emphysema. The effects of air pollution range from annoying to severe, and are experienced by healthy individuals as well. Symptoms include headaches, nausea, dizziness, eye irritation, visual disturbances, reduced tolerance for exercise, respiratory tract irritation, and impairment of cardiovascular efficiency. Nitrogen oxides have been statistically related to lung and breast cancer. Auto pollutants also cause damage to trees, crops, and other vegetation. Pollutants corrode telephone and other electrical contacts, and cause rapid deterioration in rubber, marble statues, and other materials.

Various scientific bodies and governmental authorities have found that

222

the benefits achieved from implementing stricter emission-control standards for automobiles are equal to or greater than the expected costs of tighter controls. The Environmental Protection Agency has found that federal pollution controls do not cost the country as much as dirty air. Douglas Costle, administrator of the EPA, said that the benefits of EPA's programs to curb air pollution far exceed the costs of the pollution. The NAS estimated that the benefits of cleaner air range from $2.5 to $10 billion annually. As more becomes known about the harmful effects of air pollution and as more efficient technology is developed by the auto industry to reduce emissions, the public benefits of tight emission standards become greater.

Furthermore, the American public values clean air highly and is willing to pay increased prices for better air quality. In an August 1975 survey made by the former Federal Energy Administration, consumers indicated a strong preference for cleaner air. When asked, "Do you think it is better to permit present levels of air pollution from cars OR to charge $250 per car to clean the air by another ten percent?"—the public chose higher prices and cleaner air by a *two-to-one* margin. The public obviously is willing to pay for the costs of cleaner air rather than to pay the costs of medical bills and suffering from needless respiratory illnesses and from unknown amounts of cancer. The costs of dirty air are also reflected in property values. One study of real estate values in Los Angeles suburbs found houses in highly polluted areas selling for an average of $20,000 to $50,000 less than similar houses in less polluted suburbs.

AUTO INDUSTRY RESTRAINT OF POLLUTION-CONTROL DEVELOPMENT

Although auto-related pollution costs the nation about $10 billion a year, the automobile manufacturers have resisted most efforts to clean up the air. This resistance can be traced back twenty-five years when the auto industry first began to restrain the development of pollution-control equipment for new cars. At that time the U.S. automobile companies conspired to restrain the development and marketing of auto exhaust control systems through collusive agreements not to compete in the research, development, manufacture, and installation of air-pollution-control equipment. Alternative engines, such as the diesel and stratified charge, were not developed during the conspiracy even though they had lower emissions and better fuel economy, and were more durable.

In 1953 the industry announced a pooling of efforts to combat the motor vehicle air pollution problem, which had been pinpointed as a major source of smog in 1951 by Dr. Arlie J. Haagen-Smit, a research scientist at the California Institute of Technology. The problem of how to control motor vehicle emissions was turned over by the industry to the Automobile Manufacturers Association (AMA), of which all the domestic automobile manufacturers were members. In reality the automobile manufacturers engaged only in lip service concerning the health and welfare of severely polluted communities like Los Angeles. Through AMA, they conspired not to compete

223

in research, development, manufacture, and installation of control devices, and collectively delayed such action to deal with air pollution.

The aggressive delaying of improvement in auto-emission-control technology by the industry was summarized by Los Angeles chief pollution-control officer S. Smith Griswold ten years after the conspiracy took root, at the annual meeting of the Air Pollution Control Association in June 1964:

> Everything that the industry has disclosed it is able to do today to control auto exhaust was possible technically ten years ago. No new principle had to be developed, no technological advance was needed, no scientific breakthrough was required . . . "almost everything Detroit has done with automobiles since World War II has been wrong from the standpoint of smog."

Mr. Griswold more recently noted:

> The greatest achievement in air pollution control proffered by General Motors to account for its years of effort is the construction of an environmental study chamber, in which they have been duplicating much of the work that has led to the conclusion that auto exhaust is the basic ingredient of photochemical smog.

The only actual progress in reducing auto emissions during the smog conspiracy came as a result of a 1959 California statute requiring that new cars sold in that state be equipped with exhaust controls one year after the state certified the effectiveness of at least two workable control devices. The auto companies claimed that such controls could not be adopted until the 1967 model year. But when California certified the control devices of four nonautomotive companies in 1964 and required the installation of those or equivalent devices on all new cars by the 1966 model year, General Motors, Ford, and Chrysler suddenly announced that they could indeed install such devices in 1966 vehicles. Their switch was clearly prompted by the risk of having to use the devices of the nonindustry certified companies.

Finally the U.S. Department of Justice brought an antitrust suit against General Motors, Ford, Chrysler, American Motors, and the Automobile Manufacturers Association, accusing the auto industry of conspiring to restrain development of effective pollution-control devices. Over the objection of many states, congressional leaders, and consumer advocates, the Nixon administration settled the case through a consent decree rather than by going to trial where the government could have obtained significant antitrust precedents in collusive trade association activity and "product fixing" as well as substantially eased the burden on those parties bringing private antitrust suits against the auto manufacturers based on the "smog conspiracy."

The consent decree reached between the government and the four major automobile manufacturers plus their trade association was entered on October 29, 1969. Although a trial may have been more effective in the battle against industry restraint of pollution-control development, the decree was nonethe-

224

less instrumental in forcing the defendant auto manufacturers to make major improvements in auto-emission-control and safety technology. The industry's contention that cooperation (that is, collusion) is the only way to improve technology has been proved false over and over again since the 1969 consent decree. In the field of emission control, the pressure of the emission standards in the 1970 Clean Air Amendments and the more competitive atmosphere of the consent decree led to significantly improved technology.

AUTOMOBILE EMISSIONS REGULATION

From both an environmental and consumers' viewpoint, auto emissions regulation can only be viewed as a rousing success. Fuel economy is up, maintenance is down, and the cost of the improved technology is repaid several times over by the reduced operating costs. At the same time, there are significant air-quality gains from the reduced emission levels. The striking gains in emissions control and fuel economy are in large part attributable to technological improvements developed under the force of the Clean Air Act.

The tremendous strides of the auto industry since the consent decree and the 1970 amendments were summed up in 1973 by Dr. John A. Hutcheson of the National Academy of Sciences in testimony before the Environmental Protection Agency on the suspension of the then 1976 statutory oxides of nitrogen emission standards. (Under the 1970 Clean Air Amendments, the National Academy of Sciences was required to make yearly reports on the progress of the auto companies in meeting the stringent statutory emission standards.) "The automotive industry, in my opinion," said Hutcheson, "has in the last three years or so learned more about the engine in the automobile they make than they ever knew before." And this knowledge appears to be growing as the pressure is kept up.

THE CLEAN AIR ACT

In order to protect the public health and welfare from the effects of air pollution and to get auto-pollution-control development rolling, Congress in 1970 enacted the Clean Air Amendments to the Clean Air Act. The amendments gave the U.S. Environmental Protection Agency responsibility for setting and enforcing standards on various types of air pollutants, but the Congress set statutory emission standards and timetables for auto emissions. The standards are expressed in terms of grams per mile for the three most dangerous auto pollutants—hydrocarbons, carbon monoxide, and nitrogen oxides. To provide the auto industry with sufficient lead time to meet these standards, Congress established the model years 1975 and 1976 as the deadline.

Despite the success of more stringent emission standards in improving automotive technology, the original statutory automobile emission standards for 1975–76 have been repeatedly delayed. They were delayed through two separate one-year extensions by the Environmental Protection Agency and one year by Congress during the height of the Arab oil embargo. When

Congress passed the Clean Air Act Amendments of 1977, it granted an additional two-year freeze of the emission standards, making a total of five years of delay but setting a schedule which is intended to be a final deadline for the auto industry.

IN-USE ENFORCEMENT

In addition to setting emission standards, the Clean Air Act gave the EPA responsibility for setting and enforcing standards for motor vehicles in use. This in-use enforcement takes the form of warranties for the emission-control systems, recalls when defects are discovered, and prohibitions against tampering with or the removal of these systems. Strong in-use enforcement is necessary because manufacturers fail to design and build their cars as well as the prototypes that are used for testing. In fact, EPA has found that up to eighty percent of the vehicles in use fail to meet emission standards where there is no in-use enforcement.

Under the Clean Air Act, every new automobile is required to have two warranties covering the emission-control system, as discussed in Chapter 6. The act gives the EPA the authority to order recalls when defects are found in the emission-control system, as discussed in Chapter 4. The act makes it illegal for manufacturers, car dealers, or independent garages to remove or tamper with emission-control systems.

CONSUMER PARTICIPATION IN AIR POLLUTION CONTROL

There are many things consumers can do to help control the auto pollution problem. These include cutting down on the overall use of the automobile and keeping the vehicle properly maintained. Take advantage of public transportation where available, form carpools to work, make fewer auto trips—where possible, walk or ride a bicycle. Keep your car properly tuned, and support local and state government programs that provide for annual vehicle inspection and maintenance to ensure that emissions reductions are being met. Use lead-free gasoline instead of leaded fuels. Lead-free fuel may cost more, but the use of nonleaded gasoline is necessary to achieve cleaner air and will result in lower operating expenses since cars using lead-free fuel require less maintenance.

226

CHAPTER 18 *Whistle Blowing*

Corporate employees are among the first to know about industrial dumping of mercury or fluoride sludge into waterways, defectively designed automobiles, or undisclosed adverse effects of prescription drugs and pesticides. They are the first to grasp the technical capabilities to prevent existing product or pollution hazards. But they are very often the last to speak out. . . .

[Yet], the willingness and ability of insiders to blow the whistle is the last line of defense ordinary citizens have against the denial of their rights and the destruction of their interests by secretive and powerful institutions. As organizations penetrate deeper and deeper into the lives of people—from pollution to poverty to income erosion to privacy invasion—more of their rights and interests are adversely affected. This fact of contemporary life has generated an ever greater moral imperative for employees to be reasonably protected in upholding such rights regardless of their employers' policies.*

Whistle blowing is the act of a person who believes that the interest of the public overrides the interest of the organization he or she serves. If that organization is involved in a corrupt, illegal, fraudulent, or harmful activity, the individual publicly "blows the whistle," speaking out against and informing everyone of the activities of that organization.

Many activities harmful to consumers and the public interest and carried on by business and governmental organizations have been uncovered and brought to light with the help of whistle blowers. For example, since the publication of *Unsafe at Any Speed* in 1965, Ralph Nader has often been aided by whistle blowers, whose information and assistance have sometimes been rendered anonymously, sometimes publicly. It was a General Motors engineer, in fact, who first called Nader's attention to the hazards of the Corvair.

HOW WHISTLE BLOWING WORKS

Many people are today healthy and alive because of the actions of conscientious and concerned individuals of both government and industry who blew the whistle on their employers. Risking job demotion or loss of employment, these disgruntled employees have stepped forward to the benefit of the general public. The beneficiaries of whistle blowing often include the owners of motor vehicles as well as innocent bystanders. Among these whistle blowers have been design engineers who were working for the auto industry and who spoke out against the company's production of unsafe vehicles. Employees of auto dealers and factory workers have also blown the whistle on callous manufacturers.

*Ralph Nader, Peter J. Petkas, and Kate Blackwell, eds., *Whistle Blowing* (1972), pp. 4, 6.

227

Whistle blowers usually hand over their "inside information" to the press or consumer groups. For example, the Center for Auto Safety frequently receives from industry "insiders" information that may lead to a recall of unsafe vehicles. Many insiders send the information anonymously to protect themselves from job loss or demotion. Some insiders are known only to the consumer group, which protects their anonymity but uses the information to benefit consumers.

In 1972 the Center for Auto Safety received revealing General Motors documents from an "insider" whose name was never made public. The documents revealed that pitman arms in 1959–60 Cadillacs were failing with great frequency. (The pitman arm is a vital steering assembly component. When it fails, total loss of steering control results.) The Center released the information to the public, petitioning the National Highway Traffic Safety Administration to order a recall of the vehicles. In 1973 NHTSA did so, declaring the vehicles defective. The government based its case in large part upon the whistle blower's information submitted by the Center. NHTSA ordered GM to notify affected owners and replace the pitman arms, but GM refused to comply.

Even though GM tied up a recall for five years through legal proceedings, the District of Columbia Court of Appeals eventually ruled that the evidence was

> uncontradicted that GM sold six times as many replacement pitman arms for 1959–1960 Cadillac models as for adjacent years, that steering pitman arm failures have occurred while these models were being driven, and that, when the steering pitman arm fails, the driver loses control of the car. . . .

The court stated that these facts demonstrate "unreasonable risk of accident" stemming from the defect—*United States* v. *General Motors* (561 F.2d 923, 924 [D.C. Cir. 1977], cert. den. 434 U.S. 1033 [1978]). The U.S. Supreme Court refused to review the decision even though GM was supported by legal briefs from Chrysler Corp., Volkswagen, and the Automobile Importers of America. GM also had to pay a fine of $400,000 for its willful refusal to recall these cars.

Whistle blowers appear in the smaller companies too. Early in 1977 the Center received an insider's report from within British Leyland Motors (BLM). The report revealed numerous specific safety defects in BLM cars and described "the games some automobile importers play with the lives and pocketbooks of consumers." After receiving the report, the Center researched its files and those of NHTSA for consumer complaints on the safety defects identified by the BLM sources. In the process, the Center identified additional defects, not referenced in the report, for a total of twenty-seven defects in four makes of BLM cars imported into the U.S.—Austin, Jaguar, MG, and Triumph.

As a result of the Center's investigation and use of the insider's report, NHTSA began a formal inquiry into the hazardous defects of British Leyland

228

cars. During 1977 and early 1978 NHTSA opened more than fifteen defects investigations involving BLM cars. The automobile manufacturer responded to some investigations with voluntary recall campaigns. A total of thirty-three separate recalls of BLM cars had been issued as of January 1980.

Because of the risks associated with whistle blowing, assisting consumer groups anonymously is a good strategy for some whistle blowers. But there are many activities that affect the public concerning which no consumer group is available to help the whistle blower release the information to the public. In these cases, the whistle blower often has no choice but to step forward individually and publicly speak out through the press. Such individuals, whether employees of the government or industry, can often expect to be fired, cast into some obscure position, or otherwise punished.

In 1978, for the first time, numerous bills were considered by Congress that would protect whistle blowers from such retribution. Efforts to protect whistle blowers also have been made by private organizations. For example, the government accountability project at the Institute of Policy Studies has provided counseling to about 200 government workers who have publicly questioned decisions of their bosses. In 1971 the Conference on Professional Responsibility was held in Washington, D.C. Some of the leading exponents of whistle blowing joined individual whistle blowers to discuss the subject. Details of the conference are available in *Whistle Blowing: The Report of the Conference on Professional Responsibility*, edited by Ralph Nader, Peter J. Petkas, and Kate Blackwell (New York: Bantam Books, 1972). Some of the whistle-blowing strategies discussed at the conference and reported in *Whistle Blowing* are:

1. Precisely identify not only the objectionable activity or practice, but also the public interest or interests that are threatened and the magnitude of the harm that will result from nondisclosure.
2. Verify the accuracy of your knowledge of the situation.
3. Identify ethical standards as well as laws, rules, and regulations that support your decision to blow the whistle.
4. Develop a plan of action: consider the personal costs and the likely response of allies and antagonists within and outside the organization.
5. Select an appropriate outside contact.

There is no tried and true formula for blowing the whistle effectively and safely. Every person is unique and every situation is different. A strategy that has proved successful in one instance may be totally inappropriate in another. It is imperative that a person considering such a bold action do so with as much forethought as can be mustered. Still, the willingness and the ability of insiders to blow the whistle are the last line of defense ordinary citizens have against the denial of their rights and the destruction of their interests by secretive and powerful institutions.

APPENDIX A —CHAPTER 18

Federal Government Addresses and Telephone Numbers

The White House
1600 Pennsylvania Ave., N.W.
Washington, D.C. 20500
(202) 456-1414
    White House Office of Consumer Affairs

Agencies

Department of Energy
1000 Independence Ave., S.W.
Washington, D.C. 20585
(202) 252-5000

Department of Transportation
National Highway Traffic Safety Administration
400 Seventh St., S.W.
Washington, D.C. 20590
TOLL-FREE HOTLINE (800) 424-9393; Washington, D.C. 426-0123
    Administrator (202) 426-1836
    Director, Office of Defects Investigation (202) 426-2850

Environmental Protection Agency
401 M St., S.W.
Washington, D.C. 20460
(202) 755-2673
    Mobile Source Enforcement Division (202) 426-2464

Federal Trade Commission
Bureau of Consumer Protection
6th and Pennsylvania Ave., N.W.
Washington, D.C. 20580
(202) 523-3727

Congressional Committees

Committee on Commerce, Science and Transportation
U.S. Senate
Washington, D.C. 20510
(202) 224-5115
    Consumer Subcommittee (202) 224-9345

Committee on Interstate and Foreign Commerce
U.S. House of Representatives
Washington, D.C. 20515
(202) 225-2927
  Subcommittee on Consumer Protection and Finance (202) 225-7790

Individual Members of Congress

Senator: The Honorable (full name)
   U.S. Senate
   Washington, D.C. 20510

Representative: The Honorable (full name)
     U.S. House of Representatives
     Washington, D.C. 20515

Call (202) 224-3121 (Capitol switchboard) and ask for your senator or representative.

APPENDIX B—CHAPTER 18

Why You Should Ask for Air Bags
When Buying a New Car

Air bags are the best protection front seat occupants can get in certain kinds of crashes. But there's a catch: air bags are not currently available in new cars. Although you cannot go into a showroom and expect to buy an air bag-equipped car, it may still be useful to try to obtain this type of restraint system. After a brief explanation of what air bags are—and why they are superior occupant protection—this Appendix will provide information and a coupon which could help you if you sustain crash injuries.

The importance of air bags is that they protect front seat occupants in the kinds of crashes, front and front angle, that account for more deaths than all other impacts combined. Like seat belts, air bags have been tested, retested and proven reliable in hundreds of actual crashes. But unlike manual belts, air bags protect people automatically, without any action by car occupants. This automatic aspect of air bags is especially attractive since less than 11 percent of drivers currently wear their manual seat belts.

Most crashes occur at low speeds and, in spite of extensive damage to vehicles, significant human damage is not usually involved. A crash has to be at least as severe as an impact of about 12 mph into a solid barrier in order for air bags to deploy. Thus, the bags do not inflate when cars go over bumps or when front bumpers come into contact with barriers at very low speeds, such as when pulling into a parking space.

When an air bag-equipped car crashes at a speed sufficient to cause the bags to deploy, sensors located in the front of the vehicle send a signal to the air bag inflator assembly. During the split second between the time the car crashes and the time the occupants crash into the vehicle's interior, bags stowed neatly out of sight in the steering wheel and instrument panel automatically inflate to cushion front seat occupants during impact. Peak inflation of air bags occurs less than a twentieth of a second after sensors signal a crash—faster than the blink of an eye.

This technology is not new. Air bag systems were invented more than 25 years ago, and they were developed extensively during the 1960's. Automobile manufacturers, suppliers of air bag hardware, and research and engineering firms have repeatedly tested air bags and found them highly reliable. More than 12,000 cars with air bags were manufactured in the early 1970's, and these vehicles have been driven over 800 million miles on public roads. As of July 1980, 242 cars with air bags had crashed with the bags deploying as intended. Many survivors of these crashes affirm the air bags saved their lives. The Department of Transportation estimates at least 9,000 lives and 65,000 injuries could be saved every year if all cars were equipped with air bags.

Although General Motors made air bags available as options on some

232

models during the early 1970's, automakers have since withheld air bag technology. They have pursued this course in spite of numerous polls showing that consumers want air bags and are willing to pay for them.

If manufacturers are withholding air bags, what good would it do to try to buy these devices? If you are ever injured in a crash, the fact that you tried to purchase air bags (feasible and reliable safety devices) could be useful in the event of litigation for injuries you or your family may have sustained as a result of the manufacturer's failure to offer you the best available restraint system. When the dealer tells you, upon inquiry, that air bags are not available, you can fill out the coupon provided on the next page send a copy of it to the Center for Auto Safety. This coupon will be on file to help you prove, after the fact of a crash, that you wanted air bags, tried to buy air bags, and through no fault or lack of effort on your part were unable to obtain an air bag-equipped car.

Another reason for sending in the coupon is that it puts auto manufacturers on notice—again—that there is a market for air bags.

Return to:
Center for Auto Safety
1223 Dupont Circle Building
Washington, D.C. 20036

On_____, 19____, I purchased a new car of the make, model and year described
below from _____located in _____,
　　　　　　　　　(dealership)　　　　　　　　　　　　　　(city)

_____ I indicated to the seller that I wished to purchase an air bag-
　　(state)
equipped car.

Vehicle Make_____Model_____Year_____
Vehicle Identification Number_____

(this number is visible through the left front windshield)

Buyer Information	*Seller Information*
_____	_____
(name)	*(salesman)*
_____	_____
(address)	*(signature)**
_____	_____
(telephone)	*(date)*
_____	
(signature)	
_____	
(date)	

*If no responsible person in the dealership will sign this or provide requested information, please indicate in the space provided below reserved for comments.

How to protect your life and save your money for about 4¢ per day

Here's your chance to fight against car fraud and for car safety

Launched by Ralph Nader and Consumer's Union and now operating independently, the Center for Auto Safety is the *only* national organization working in the public interest to eliminate the causes of auto accidents and to protect the consumer from being bilked by car manufacturers, dealers, and repair shops.

The Center for Auto Safety depends on the public for its support. Annual Consumer Membership in the Center is $15. That comes to little more than 4¢ per day—less than the price of a tank of gasoline—for an "insurance policy" that helps protect you and your family from auto accidents and helps keep you from falling victim to auto fraud.

As a Consumer Member of the Center, you will receive our newsletter, "The Lemon Times" to keep you up to date on developments in car safety and quality and discoveries in car fraud. *Your membership contribution is tax deductible.*

JOIN the **CENTER** for **AUTO SAFETY** TODAY
1223 Dupont Circle Building, N.W.
Washington, D.C. 20036
(202) 659-1126

See reverse for membership details

235

CENTER for AUTO SAFETY

Consumer Membership Form

Please enroll me as a consumer member of the Center for Auto Safety and be sure to keep me informed of your efforts with your quarterly newsletter.

☐ Enclosed is my annual membership contribution of $15

I want to give an additional contribution to help your work. The total of my check is: _____

☐ $25   ☐ $50   ☐ $100   ☐ $500   ☐ other $ _____

(please print)

Name: _____

Address: _____

Please make check or money order payable to **Center for Auto Safety** and mail to:

PT206   166

236